A History

of

CLANFIELD

in

Oxfordshire

by

Ernest Pocock

Published in Great Britain 1999
by Cornerstone Publishing, Clanfield, Oxfordshire

British Library Cataloguing-in-Publication Data

A catalogue record for this book is available
from the British Library

ISBN: 0 9537469 0 9

Every effort has been made by the publishers to check the references contained in
the late Ernest Pocock's original text. The publishers are also aware that a number
of names appear in different forms, where they may refer to the same persons. The
publishers ask that descendants of these families will understand and forgive the
obvious difficulty, in the circumstances, of being able to check the author's original
sources and intentions. Spellings of names, both of people and places, are in any
case often uncertain and inconsistent as they appear in ancient documents.

Designed and typeset by Image Makers, Clanfield, Oxon
Printed by Professional Books, Steventon, Oxon.

CONTENTS

Chapter 1   In the Beginning   1

Chapter 2   Prehistoric Peoples – Pastoral Nomads   4

Chapter 3   The Norman Invasion and the Domesday Book   15

Chapter 4   The Creation of the Parish   23

Chapter 5   Edward to Henry II   33

Chapter 6   Henry VIII   50

Chapter 7   Henry VIII's Family
            Edward VI 1547-53   62

Chapter 8   The Stuarts (1603-1688)   71

Chapter 9   Village Records from 1603-1688   83

Chapter 10 The Last of the Stuarts1660-1714
            Charles II 1660-1685   90

Chapter 11 The Age of Hanover   107

Chapter 12 Queen Victoria 1837-1901   128

Chapter 13 The 20th Century   163

Chapter 14 The Village of Memory   184

            INDEX   191

ERNEST A. POCOCK

1921–1983

Ernest Pocock was born in 1921, the 3rd generation of the family to grow up in Clanfield. He attended Burford Grammar School, where he won a scholarship to Jesus College, Oxford, in 1939. However, the declaration of war curtailed his scholastic activities, and he reverted to full-time food production on the family farm, and also saw service in the Home Guard.

In 1951 he married Joan Willmer, of Friars Court, and subsequently they had two sons and a daughter.

Outside of farming, he was a keen amateur local historian. A founder member of the Clanfield Historical Society, he submitted several contributions to the *Agricultural History Review* and his first published work on the *Mystery of White Horse Hill* appeared in 1964. Several other publications appeared over the years.

He spent a number of years researching the history of Clanfield, completing his work in the final three years of his life. He died in 1983, before he could have his book published. It is to his memory, that we publish his work now.

Thanks are due to Rosemarie Pocock, who typed the script from longhand, Ken Mumford and Rosemary Church who helped proof-read it, and Ian Welch who photocopied it. Also very grateful thanks to Ian and Carmen Smith, who typeset, designed and prepared it ready for print, to Ernest's sister, Jean Pocock, who took up the work and oversaw it nearly to publication but who passed away in 1997, and to his daughter, Rosemary, who subsequently took charge of the project and saw it through to its conclusion, and to the many others who gave the project their encouragement and support so that future generations can read about the history of his beloved village of Clanfield.

Chapter 1

In the Beginning

CLANFIELD, meaning 'cleared field', was, until the county reorganisation of the 1970s, in the south-west corner of Oxfordshire, against Berkshire and Gloucestershire. It stands one mile north of the River Thames, and the old Gloucestershire dialect can still be heard among the local people.

After the bringing-in of piped water in 1956 and the laying of a new sewerage system in 1968, the population doubled in size in just a few years through the building of a new council estate in Mill Lane.

The traditional buildings include the parish church of Saint Stephen's whose vicar, however, now has his vicarage at Bampton from where he looks after a number of other churches. The Methodist Church, formerly the old Wesleyan, stands by the side of the main street, with its modernised premises, while the old chapel has been made into a hall. It is a part of the Witney/Faringdon Circuit.

In the centre of the village is the Institute, which has seen the old 'Men Only' rule removed, so that the whole village can make good use of its facilities.

The former Plough public house has become a hotel, and the former Masons Arms is now the Clanfield Tavern.

The fields of Clanfield have been contained chiefly within the three farms of Chestlion, Friars Court and Windmill. The land of the old North Court Manor is now farmed from Bampton.

The drainage of the area has been greatly improved. Steps into the Methodist Church tell the story of floods in the 1860s and 1900s — now, thankfully, a thing of the past. The meadows no longer remain under water in the winter for weeks on end. The Thames and its main streams and tributaries have been deepened and widened so that floods from any excessive rainfall are all gone within a few days.

Knapps' was always an important local industry in the village, later run under the name of The Vale Works, which still sells and maintains agricultural machinery, now in the name of Tincknells. The Old Bakery was run as a woodworking firm, but moved to Faringdon as the result of a fire. The Old Mill at Little Clanfield is now tenanted by automobile firms, including the renovation of classic cars.

The Ram Jam Garage, so named by the first proprietor, Jack Widdowson, which began life as a barn until just after the First World War, has now been turned into cottages. The Post Office nearby still flourishes, along with its general store. Since the closure, through retirement of the proprietor, the late 'Pip' Horne, of the only other remaining village shop (next to the Clanfield Tavern in Bampton Road) the Post Office also now serves as the village newsagent.

The village school survives, although a number of village children also go to other schools in the area, particularly Buckland. The Football Club flourishes, but is no longer predominantly a village side. Neither cricket nor tennis is played any more, and the bowling green at the front of the Institute is no longer maintained.

After the Second World War, Clanfield was increasingly used by traffic as a valley crossing, so marked on the local maps, but since then a weight restriction on the newest of Radcot Bridges has stopped most (though not all) of the heavy transport coming through.

The soil around and in Clanfield is free draining and quite good. Originally there was a bed of chalk, but this was worn away and a great lake stood in its place. Over the many ages, in the bed of the lake a deep layer of clay was laid down before the water broke out at Goring and Streatley, and the area eventually drained. Then came one of the Ice Ages, bringing down a cap which melted at Black Bourton. This laid down a strip of gravel two miles wide and ten to fifteen feet deep over the top of the clay. The muck flowed on to settle between the Thames and Faringdon Hill as heavy soil. Here and there a fold of clay appears through the gravel in our parts, but not very much — only a few acres at most.

In places under the clay, water lies under pressure, and at Broadwell Mill, where the clay comes to the surface, a core of about 100 feet gave abundant supplies of water to the local farms. At Clanfield in the 1930s, a bore was put down in Church Close to get water for the Plough, but this only brought water to the surface — where was no flow, since there was not enough pressure.

When the power line from South Wales to Cowley was put through Grafton in the 1970s, foundations were dug down into the clay for the corner pylons, and great branches of oak trees, with their bark still on them, came out with the clay.

After the gravel was laid, streams ran across it, north-west to south-east, wearing into the old gravel and relaying it in low valleys, so the parish is made up of low islands and shallow valleys. The top of the islands have gravel caps, and the valleys are gravel. The best land is in between, on the sides of the islands.

★ ★ ★

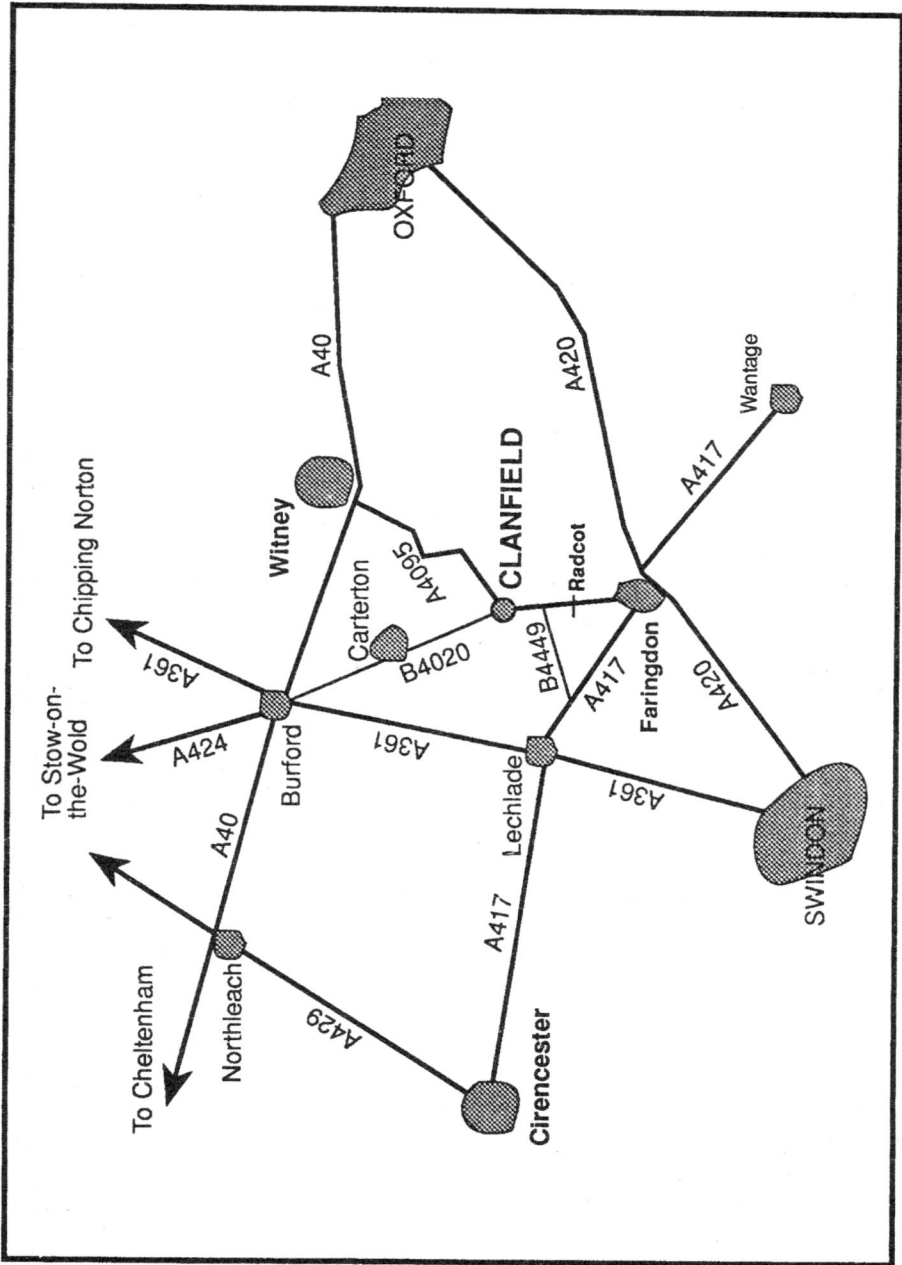

Chapter 2

Prehistoric Peoples – Pastoral Nomads

IN 1956, Mr Jack Blake was digging drainage trenches for me across 'Green Benny' when he dug up a chipped stone axe, about two feet below the surface. This is now kept in the Ashmolean Museum, Oxford. Who was the man who lost it? Did he throw it at an animal which ran off with it stuck in its side? We can only guess. A polished stone axe also came out of the Thames.

Little is really known about the early people. Hunters first roamed our land, then came groups of pastoral nomads, who built artificial caves, which we call 'long barrows', for their communal graves. That they were wanderers is seen by the way they tried to hide the entrances of these graves. If they were always close at hand there would have been no need to hide them. These people brought back the bones of their dead to bury them when they came that way again. They must have come into our land when the great forest fires of prehistory cleared vast areas in the South and Midlands.

A perfect Bronze Age axe head was found in 'The Langlies' and is now held at Friars Court. Between these two types of axe head lie countless ages and great cultural changes.

New pastoral nomadic peoples were ever coming into England, and their animals kept the 'fire-cleared' land open, and increasingly cleared the other areas. Some came from Europe, over the widening Channel, others came up the west Atlantic Coast. They travelled from Brittany due north to St. Michael's Mount for tin.

Our first records tell us of these people coming over open seas, but they must have been coming since the days when Brittany and Cornwall could almost be seen from each other.

Two interesting sites, at Chysauter in Cornwall and Skara Brae in the Orkneys, suggest that these nomadic peoples came from the south. Both of these sites are near the sea. The way that their homes were built denotes a real need for security. The homes were clustered together, joined to each other by underground passages which could each be blocked. In addition, their main entrance could be blocked if necessary. It would seem that they feared the natives. Perhaps they were fishermen amongst nomads, who feared for the safety of their sons — not that they would be killed, but kidnapped. Their homes had no roofs, nor remains of roofs. They were open to the sky.

In Clanfield, aerial photographs show much of the remains of these people. The perfect circles they produced showed something of the highly developed culture of that age. Perhaps the greatest relic is the pattern of 'ways' and 'resting places' we have now.

These travellers needed two things: a known 'way' and an artificial shelter. The 'ways' were for travelling, and the shelter was to put their animals in at night. So they marked out 'ways' of a few miles by means of a mound and raised stone from high spot to high spot, and where these crossed, a 'resting place' was built. This resting place would have covered about an acre. It was simply an earthen bank enclosure with, no doubt, a fence at the top.

The Saxons called all encampments hill forts or resting places 'Burghs'. Our land is covered with the place and field names which have the word 'burgh' as part of their name. It is interesting to note that to this day, in our area, we use the phrase "in the burrow" to mean getting out of the wind. Later generations saw fit to put the Manor House inside one of these, and we now have the expression "an Englishman's home is his castle (burgh)".

Prehistoric Peoples – Corn Growers

It is thought that in about 100 B.C. wagons came into our area from Europe, with families of farmers bringing their animals and tools. Some two or three thousand years prior to that, corn growing farmers began crossing our land. Insofar as the pastoral nomads kept our southern lands open, they were preparing the way for these corn growers. The practice of corn growing originally came from the Middle East. The stories of the first man to grow corn — Adam — are recorded in Genesis. Perhaps a small group had come at first, but later many more came. They hired the boats which the nomads had used, and crossed the Channel, taking possession of the higher cleared spots.

Security to the Nomad meant disappearing off into the woods. Security to the Corn Growers meant that they built an encampment larger than the Nomad's resting place, on an advantageous spot — not to live in, but within which they could go in times of trouble. Surrounding this, they built their homes and ploughed the land.

Other groups later followed, and a natural spread of central encampments were laid out because there was plenty of room for all. Even so, they denied the Nomads access to the land.

Gradually, these wandering peope were forced into less clear areas. Over a long period of time, as they cleared these new areas, other groups came and took possession, pushing them onwards until finally the Nomads cleared even the Thames Valley, and the Settlers then came here. The Nomads, hated by the Settlers, had to become either traders to the markets at the centres, or moved off to Wales or the north of England into the wilder regions.

In the work *Oxfordshire — Its Old Centres* which I produced in 1982, it would appear these people made their centres around us at Filkins, Radcot, Bampton, Kilkenny, Witney, Shifford and Hardwick. The centres in our area which these people made and used remain from the early Saxon period. They can be found by looking at aerial photographs.

Two of these relate to our area – Radcot and Bampton. The photographs show us many of the homes and fields of these people in our valley. 'Tarny' had three hut sites, and many rubbish pits and field boundaries dug in the gravel. 'Windmill' has two hut sites just west of the silage barn, with others in the adjacent field on the north side. 'Westfield' has hut sites on its land.

In the marshes down Gypsy Lane, in the Bampton parish, many hut sites were seen in the 1960s when the fields were ploughed a little deeper. None were overlapping, suggesting that many families were living here in a dry spell. In 1960, Mrs Dorothy Wise picked up two threshing pebbles in that area and found a threshing stone, such as these pebbles would have been used upon, against the garden wall at Chestlyons.

From the top of the combine harvester, I have seen other rings of huts, each about 17 feet across, none overlapping. That was in 'Coventry' field, on the gravel during the dry season.

In the meadows, a crossroads appears on the ordnance survey map. One would have thought that would have been much too wet in early times for a road. In Burroway a section was dug across the old Burgh. This was found to be late Iron Age, with all its walls having been burned. The burning of banks is a mystery. In Scotland some hill forts had their walls welded with fire. Why or how they burned the Burroway Bank is open to question. Possibly, the largest chunks of brick have been picked up and used as hard core. The site, and other aerial photographs, suggests that other older Burghs stood here, but as yet nothing has been found. In the ditch were found all the animal bones generally found in resting places.

The Roman and Saxon Periods

In the earliest days, British centres grouped together to form tribes, then small tribes grouped to form larger tribes. Sometimes this was done by agreement, sometimes, no doubt, by marriage, but more often than not by conquest. Double ditched encampments are the relics of tribal capitals that lost out. When the Romans came, they sealed the system and important tribal capitals became Roman cities.

To our West stands Cirencester, one of the capitals of Roman Britain. To our East stands Dorchester-on-Thames, another capital. In my work on tribal capitals I could find no others, but there is a near possibility. Near Leafield stands Lowberry, a small double banked encampment just to the north of Minster Lovell. Recently, when a bank was built across it, the foundations brought up the remains of Roman hard roads coming from the south west, and another hard road leaves from the north.

There could have been little wealth in our area. All we have is Roman/British pottery which can be picked up around the hut sites in Windmill, and a pot of coins collected by the late Mr Walter Widdowson as he worked the land in his farm at Adam's Yard. We do not know much about the Roman period in our area, but life had to go on, food had to be grown, and families had to survive with the continuing adjustments.

The Saxons

Soon after the Roman authority left Britain, peoples from the Continent above us began to pour in. Records tell us that Saxons first came to Kent as professional soldiers but then took over an area weakened by 400 years of Roman control. The counties in the East — Norfolk, Suffolk, Essex, Middlesex, Surrey, and Kent — tell of British tribal areas taken over and marked by the many Anglo-Saxons. Previous battles by Wessex forces were fought at hill forts as they came up from the South. The British were on the defensive. Here they were met at a ford – Biedcanford. The exact location of Biedcanford is not known, but it was obviously not Bedford at the backdoor — it must have been in the Thames at some unknown ford.

The first recorded date comes to us from the Saxon Chronicle which says that after coming up from the South, the West Saxons fought a battle in 571 at Biedcanford and defeated four Kingdoms, including the tribal centres at Eynsham, Benson, Aylesbury and Henley. From this basic record a few things spring to life. Previously in the record, battles had taken place at hill forts with the locals. Here, they were met at a ford. Seemingly, Benson and Eynsham replaced the 'Roman' city of Dorchester, so there had been some local government reorganisation.

In the Roman period, Dorchester and Lowberry, by Leafield, had been our tribal capitals. In the battle it was Benson, the older capital, that predated Dorchester and Eynsham. This tells us that a realignment of power after the Roman period had obviously taken place. So it would suggest that already we were part of an Anglian group of tribes reaching down to the Thames, and that by the early 500s, Witney, Shifford, Bampton, Burford, Filkins and Kilkenny were all settled, so therefore Wessex must have been a second invasion. The old capital of Benson and beyond it; Eynsham and Thame, had come back into view, and the old centre of Eynsham was made into a capital in our area. But Wessex was still not satisfied, and in 577, six years after taking over our area, they moved West and near Bath they fought and defeated the forces of the tribes contained in Bath, Gloucester and Cirencester. It was from this earliest settlement period that the folk at each centre appeared in the Folk Right, the

Folk Law and the Folk Customs. This settlement all but obliterated the British culture presumably, for they impressed themselves on the old people and ran the country through the 'Folk' courts. County names and places in the East show that the people had first settled into British tribal areas. Obviously, we were the next generation because our 'shires' are artificial. Around us the names 'Thame' or 'Churchill' from the Thames area are the only names I call to mind of British names. However, Saxon names could be just the Saxon pronunciation of the way British names sounded, in names such as Charney Brook. The question mark remains over what happened to the British families. Had they been depopulated by disease or famine? Or were they all murdered? Was the country open and ready to be settled? The name 'Tarny' — island of thorns — on land previously settled suggests this, but it takes only two decades for arable land to become scrub. However, it seems the Saxons used the British centres just as if they had taken over a going concern. So, if the British culture was weak, it lived on.

In our village the road from Bampton which came to North Court, rather than to our head manor at Chestlyon, tells us that North Court had at one time been our head manor. Near to it, on the north side, stands part of a green village, telling of insecurity when they came in. This manor, it seems, farmed all 'Westfield' in, possibly, the paddock farming method. Then, possibly at the invasion of Wessex, another group came in from Radcot centre pushing North Court Manor (called Southwick) off Westfield, leaving remnants of it at Edgerley, stretching round to Batesland and Clanfield Manor. The road from Radcot comes to Chestlyon and from Chestlyon to Bates, indicating that Chestlyon pushed out North Court, the first head manor. North Court belonged to Weald, but according to the Hundred Rolls, Chestlyon had early connections with Radcot.

From this we can gain a picture of an initial group moving in from Bampton, and then being pushed off the area by another group coming in from the South. The North Court people could have been Angles. They were here before the battle of Biedcanford. Chestlyon people could have been west Saxons coming in from the south.

Other settlements were made at Friars Court, where part of the old moated encampment still remains, and at Little Clanfield around Grafton Green, where the manor still remains opposite.

The creation of our village is very interesting. We had three geographical open fields: Barrow, Tarny and Westfield. The latter, on the old map, was called Clanfield field — which meant 'cleared field' so it would appear that this area was completely cleared long before any other area around, and the folks who lived there were called the people of the cleared field or 'Clanfield'.

Barrowfield came to us after the Domesday Book, from Bampton. Clanfield at that time, therefore, consisted of Tarny and Westfield. But the name 'Tarny' and

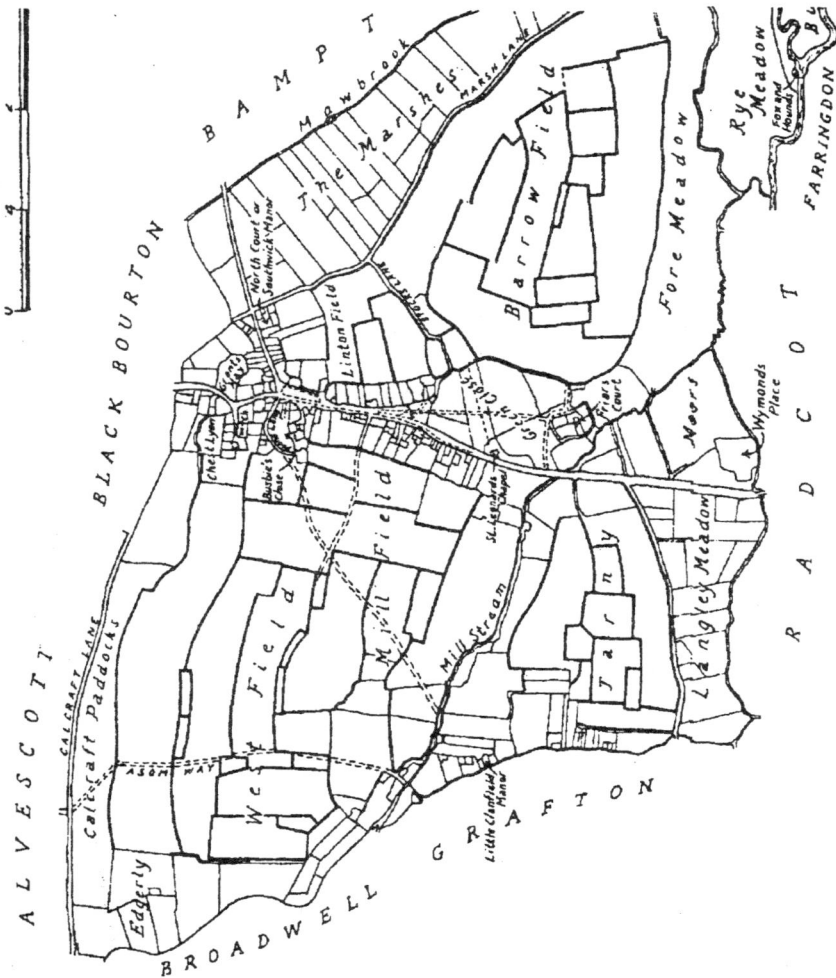

A pre-Enclosures field map built up by Ernest Pocock from his own research.
On the following pages are his maps of the individual fields. The 'Group' numbers refer to successive groups of settlers.

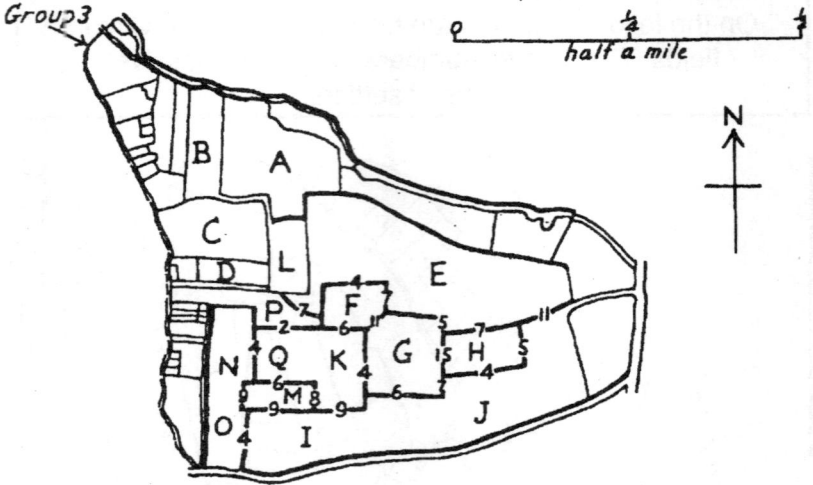

TARNY FIELD

half a mile

Furlongs with names where known

A	Hilly Ground
B	Billings
C	Buckrills
D	Belham Hays
E	Tarny Marsh
F	Tarny
G	Cripps
H	Lower Cripps Piece
I	Langly Furlong
J	Langley
K	Top of Tanny
L	–
M	Little Barrels
N	Belham
O	Grafton Green
P	Top of Tarny
Q	Tip of Tarny

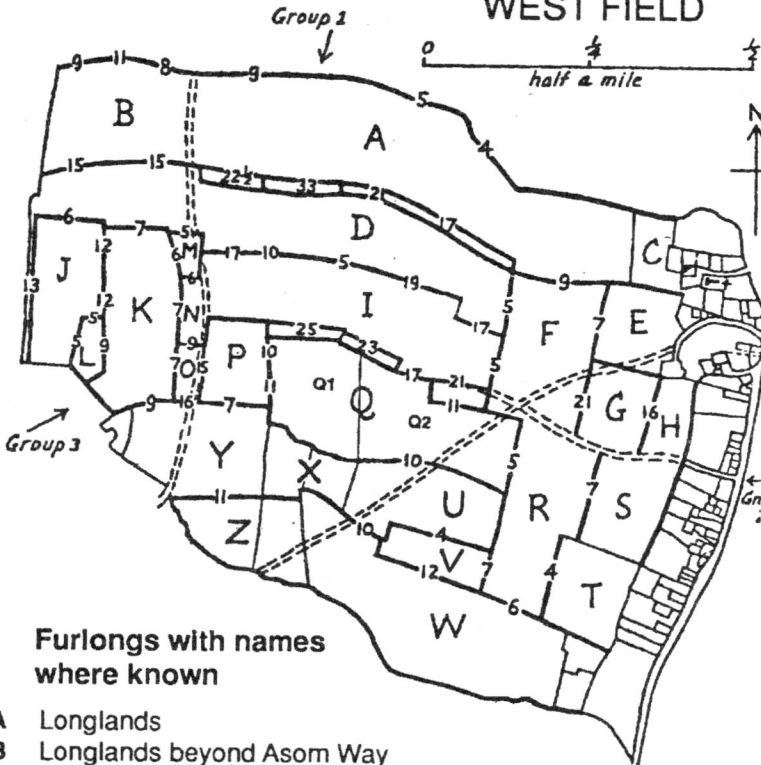

WEST FIELD

Group 1

0   ¼   ½
half a mile

N

**Furlongs with names
where known**

A Longlands
B Longlands beyond Asom Way

C Longlands behind the Church

D Redlands
E The Butts/The Sands
F Page
G The Sands
H Town Furlong
I Over Redlands
J Farther Edgerly

K Middle Edgerly
L Where ye House was

M, N, O Asom Way
P Badbury
Q Green Benny/No Man's Bush
R The Sands/Bean Land
S Town
T Home
U Gt Hillingworth
V Corn Benny
W Brook
X Green Benny
  (meadow)
Y Mill
Z Skinners

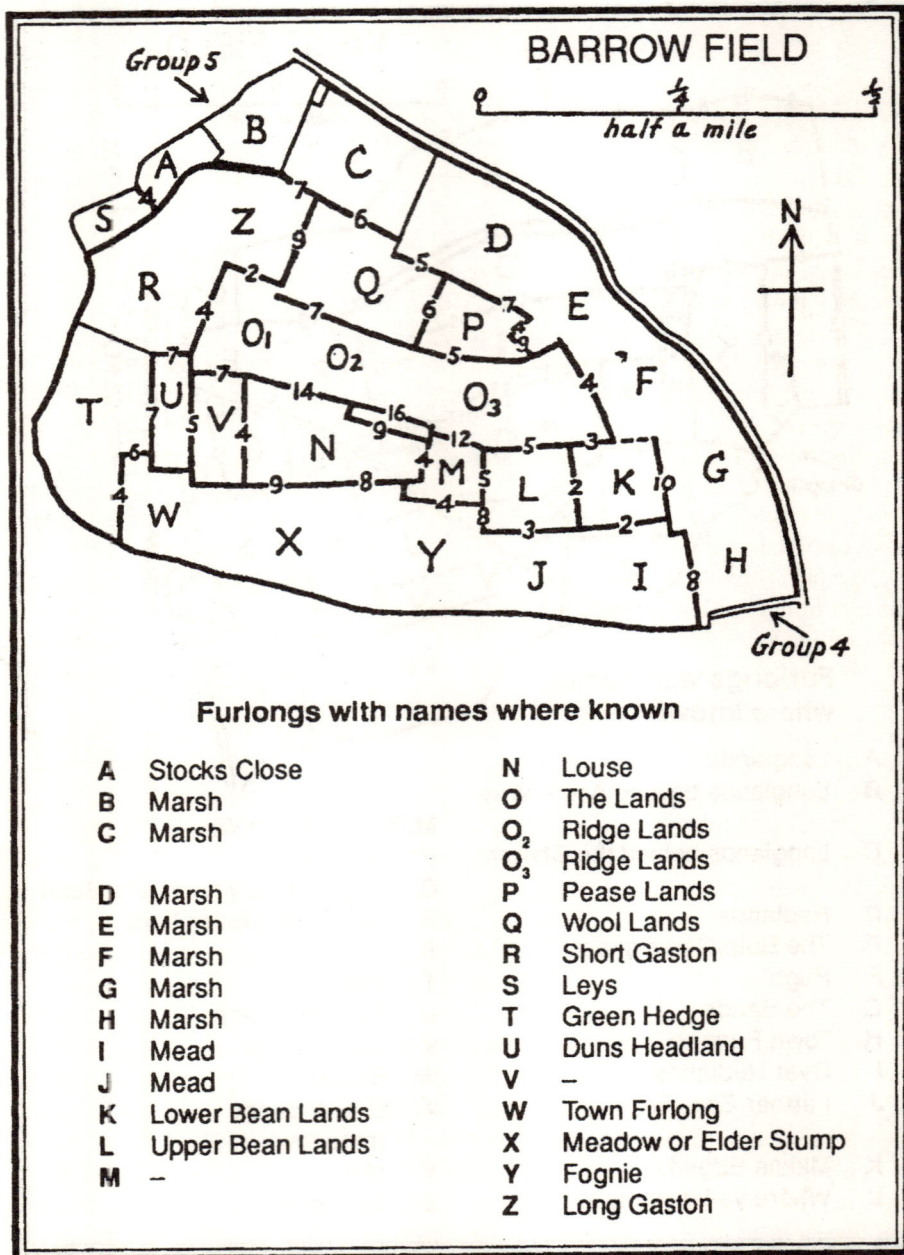

BARROW FIELD

Furlongs with names where known

A	Stocks Close
B	Marsh
C	Marsh
D	Marsh
E	Marsh
F	Marsh
G	Marsh
H	Marsh
I	Mead
J	Mead
K	Lower Bean Lands
L	Upper Bean Lands
M	–

N	Louse
O	The Lands
O_2	Ridge Lands
O_3	Ridge Lands
P	Pease Lands
Q	Wool Lands
R	Short Gaston
S	Leys
T	Green Hedge
U	Duns Headland
V	–
W	Town Furlong
X	Meadow or Elder Stump
Y	Fognie
Z	Long Gaston

'Clanfield' field suggests that the latter was cleared and in use when Tarny was still 'an island of thorns'. Eventually, however, this was added to Clanfield — so that by the time of the Domesday Book these two areas formed the arable part of our village. It would appear, therefore, that Clanfield began in Westfield.

The work we did in 1950, when we planned our open field, showed us how it all began from Calcroft Lane. By discovering that the large ridges which crossed our fields, without rhyme or reason, were the old furlong headlands, built up by the plough cleanings, enabled us not only to map out our enclosure furlongs but also, by their size, to tell the order and the direction in which they were opened up.

Then people struck out furlongs at their backdoors, and the other people of Clanfield leant over the gate and saw how much better the new method of farming was. As true farmers, they copied their neighbours and they developed a series of furlongs at the north east corner. Here Manor Farm, with its fish ponds, belonged to Southwick Manor. The first furlong was called 'Long Lands' and then, after a period, more people cleared and ploughed another area called 'Redlands' — rid or new lands. Years later, when they made the next furlong — 'Over Redlands' — named from their settlement, they were confined on the east and west.

The old settlers at North Court saw that this was a good way of farming and so in the east from Clanfield Manor and in the west from Edgerley, furlongs were marked out limiting the Chestlyon settlers. Thus their furlong plan became that of a triangle getting smaller and smaller. This was how the field developed, until all the groups had come to terms and farmed the fields as one, on a two-year rotation.

In the middle of all this, the settlers passed over the British settlement, calling the furlong 'Killingworth' or Cilla's worth', showing that a Saxon lady had been the owner, but she and the settlers had gone before the open field passed over it.

In the meantime, Tarny was being cleared by groups from Friars Court on the east and from Little Clanfield on the west. When the land had been cleared, they later joined with the Westfield so that by the time of the Domesday Book the village contained the two islands formed by the peoples around. So we see in our road patterns and open fields that there were two periods of settlers, which appears to tie up with the political structure of 571.

While Clanfield was quietly living its life, winning by hard graft a living from the soil, national events were taking place. Wessex remained in control of our area until 628 when Penda, King of Mercia, defeated them at Cirencester. Wessex and Mercia were struggling to possess the whole area. Battles were thought to have been fought at Bampton in 614 and Burford in 752. Even after the defeat of Wessex in 628, they were still in control of the Dorchester area, because in 635 the King of Wessex gave the church there to his Bishop. But by 661, Mercia owned all our land, right up to Ashdown, i.e. the Old British Ridge.

In 688, the King of Wessex brought the boundary back to the Thames and in 752 Wessex had advanced to Burford (Berry ford — hill fort, the earliest name) and fought a decisive battle there against Mercia. But in 756, when Offa came to the throne of Mercia, he threw Wessex back, defeating them at Dorchester and returning the boundary again to the British Ridge at Ashdown in Berkshire.

So, as Clanfield cleared and opened out its fields, Wessex and Mercia claimed us, depending on what was occuring between these two kingdoms. In one period we paid our taxes to Mercia and in another to Wessex. No doubt we paid up just the same, grumbled just as much and cursed the weather that affected us most of all. It may have worried the lords. Perhaps they were called to fight first for one side then for the other. However, the poor man who had to go out and get the oxen in the dark one frosty morning and plough all day, cared little whose kingdom we were part of, so long as no marauding bands came to steal the few possessions he had, or molest his wife and daughters.

It would seem that it was during the 8th century, when Mercia dominated England, possibly when the Great King Offa's reign and dominion over the rest of the tribal areas was taking place, that a great survey of England was made and much local government reorganisation was initiated. It would appear that surveyors went through the land redesigning it into units of 100 Hides. All the old settlements around the original centres were grouped into Hundred Hides which were taxation units and were based on new or selected centres.

The Hide was 'land for one family'. In Canada, when the prairie was opened up, the unit was a quarter of a square mile, 164 acres, and still 100 years later this unit prevails in sales of land. In England a similar area was used for arable, grass and scrub land. Only the arable was taxed and was the most valuable. Confusion occured because it was only this ploughed land which was taxed. This meant that the acres in the later Hides bore no relation to the full area of land for one family. So, if the land was wet or clay, the arable for economic reasons, had a small acreage, but the dry and free draining land meant a large Hide acreage.

The Tribal Hideage, a Mercian taxation account, shows us that the kingdoms were made up of multiples of Hundred Hides. Our area, which was called the Chilternsaetan, contained four thousand Hides. This constitutes Oxfordshire and Buckinghamshire. At the time of the Domesday Book Oxon had about 2,400 Hides.

Little remains from this period to tell us of what was happening except perhaps one thing...Lowberry had been our tribal capital in the British days. When the Saxons came they had moved their centre down towards the water and on the arrival of Christianity the tribal Minster was at Minster Lovell. The authority for this lies in the fact that Minster should have been in the later Bampton Hundred, but it was lifted out of that to be with Lowberry. Also, Minster received our income for land in villages like Shilton and Bampton. This affected Clanfield for years, in that we had to pay £1.3.0d a year to Minster, then Eton College, on the Bampton land which later came to us. As the King owned Bampton before 1044 this must have pre-dated his ownership. So Minster stood above Bampton as our mother or Minster Church, as a Tribal Cathedral. Our area was later called the Double Hundred of Bampton, but we do not know where the two centres were, or whether Bampton had been one of these centres.

In 825, King Egbert of Wessex defeated the Mercian King at the battle of Ellendun and he took over Mercia, making both the kingdoms one, and as a result all our battles over a tribal boundary disappeared. Soon after Wessex took over Mercia, the Danish and Viking invaders appeared and were fighting in our area, although history does not record any details about Clanfield.

At first the sea coast peoples were their victims, but soon they reached inland and eventually took over and settled much of the northern areas of our land. By 871 they had come up the Thames to Reading. Unwisely, they left the river to march to the Ashdown Hills in Berkshire where King Alfred, grandson of King Egbert, defeated them.

After many reverses, Alfred began to gain control over the Danes and then, during the latter part of the ninth century, he and his son began to build up the so-called Burghal System, which involved rebuilding selected areas to contain the Danes. He chose certain old centres on the boundary of his reconquered lands, and upon them centred all the local loyalties to local centres. So, at their command, larger numbers of men could be assembled. This may have been possible due to Offa's creation of the new Hundred areas which meant the vacating of most of the old centres.

Our nearest centre was Oxford, which was sited on a ford, and which grew in importance after Mercia and Wessex had become one kingdom. On a royal estate to the west of it were the old centres which had been built in a bend of the river. The new Burgh which Alfred built was centred on Carfax — 'The Four Ways'. Originally, 1300 Hides were allocated to Oxford, but then it was changed to 1500 Hides. This new arrangement can be seen in the Plan of Oxford. Outside each gate stood a church.

Originally, to the east, stood All Saints, but when an extension was added, St. Mary's church was then built. From that time onwards Oxford grew in importance and became a main capital. Our village, which had to provide men for Bampton to defend the area, now had to send them to Oxford, no doubt.

We do not know if the Vikings ever came to Clanfield. Most likely, the nearest they came was to Radcot, but perhaps not, as in such a narrow river they would have been in great danger. Perhaps Southrop is the nearest proof we have of their coming and settling in our area.

The problems in Oxford when, on St. Brice's Day, the Vikings were killed and, in retaliation, Oxford was sacked, were but news to us that filtered back through market gossip.

It appears that King Alfred met at Shifford. This is the probable site, because it was an ancient centre, and the old encampment can be seen on air photographs in the arable field to the west of the field in which the church stands.

Perhaps the thing that did affect us the most was the creation of the Burghal System. Under the ancient customs we, or our lord, had to fulfil the responsibility for marking the walls of our local centres — Bampton and Radcot. Each settlement also had to provide a 'soldier' for local defence. Over the years, these customs had been less severely applied. But now all these rights were lifted off the local centres and moved to the new Royal Burgh at Oxford. How Clanfield must have cursed. Our men had to be on call to go to Oxford, 18 miles away, and if there was trouble, they had to be away from their homes and fields for long stretches of time. It may have helped to maintain security, but if there was any local trouble Bampton and Radcot still had to be served for practical reasons, so the Burghal System nearly doubled our services.

The creation of Oxford as our royal centre prepared us for the day which was to come, when Oxon would be formed, and the Shire would be made out of all the 1500 Hides attached to Oxford and those north of the Thames that had been attached to Wallingford.

When Alfred died, in 901, he had called himself King of Wessex, but his son, Edward the Elder (899-925), who followed, called himself King of the Anglo-Saxons. Edward started badly, but on his death he reigned over most of the South Midlands. In every area into which he advanced, he built a Burgh to defend the area. His son, Aethelstan (925–939), had cleared most of the country by the time he died.

Peace came for three short reigns, until Ethelred the Unready came to the throne. England was prosperous and wealthy, and he employed a man called Streona to redesign the land into new local government areas called Hundreds. The problem was that a King needed to get round all his centres, and there were too many. King Alfred had done some of this but probably Streona did most, because at the time of the Domesday survey both old and new Hundred names were referred to.

In our area, an attempt had been made to create two Hundreds out of the area between the River Thames and the River Windrush. This was successfully done with the Thames, but on the Windrush the boundary had to occasionally leave the river. The old loyalties were too strong. In the west, against Gloucestershire, an artifical boundary was drawn.

In 980, however, the Danes returned. At first, Ethelred had enough money to buy them off. They came again in 1002, when King Ethelred bought them off for £24,000. He had formulated a policy of paying off the Danes with silver, in the hope that they would go away and leave England alone. This worked to a degree for a short time. However, on St. Brice's Day the English went to kill all the Danes in a massacre at Oxford. The Danes took their revenge by sacking Oxford in 1009. In 1010 they marched through Oxfordshire. In 1013 Sweyn of Denmark took Oxford. He had taken King Ethelred into exile, but when Sweyn died in 1014, Ethelred came back and threw out his successor, Canute. He then murdered the Danish Theyns at Oxford. Canute, however, later returned with a great army and threw Ethelred out.

Streona had changed sides more than once, and Canute put him in charge of the south west of the country, but he was very soon killed. Canute died in 1035.

The following year was remembered as the one in which a terrible gale ravaged England. Clanfield, no doubt, suffered badly. In 1042, after one or two 'bad' kings, Ethelred's son, Edward the Confessor, came to the throne. He was born at Islip. His mother, the widow of Ethelred, had married Canute.

A very interesting story about this Queen affected our area. In 1042 Alidin, Bishop of Winchester, gave the manor of Witney, with eight others privately owned by him, to the church of Winchester in a thank-offering to God for his proved innocence from adultery with Queen Emma, mother of Edward. She purged herself by walking over nine red hot plough shares in the Cathedral.

(Ref: Richardson, Charles, Oxfordshire Collections: Vol. 1)

It was said that Edward had promised England to his cousin, William of Normandy, as he, Edward, had no family. When Edward died in 1066, Harold, who had been running the land for him, took over. The event which followed effectively brought an end to Saxon England.

Before the Norman invasion of 1066, Saxon England was effectively governed by centres which ran the country directly under the King. The previous system of 'land for one family' had been modified, and only the senior member of the family was the landlord. Only he could go to the King's court. The rest of his family, who shared the Hide, were his tenants. He controlled and sorted out all of the problems within the Hide.

In the Saxon system, all villages were either failed centres, i.e. centres which did not become towns, or groups of farmsteads. Notionally it meant 100 lords to 100 Hides. These were divided into ten Tithings, and the ten Tithings were divided into 6 Tithes or Villes of five Hides.

In Clanfield, each villager had a confusing system of three courts or committees which each had to attend and serve. First of all there was the Manor Court, in which the landlord's authority was seen. It was from this court that a villager rented his land. The land may even have been in the next village, as the farming field and the manors did not always coincide. The second court was the Farmers' Court, and third was the Court Leet, which replaced some of the authority of the Hundred, and settled the behaviour between villages.

There was even a Saxon system of 'birth control', as no one was allowed to marry until they had a farmstead. This meant, generally speaking, that people married after their father had died. They were then older and also a lot of unmarried uncles and aunts provided a family labour force. As long as the 'Manor' operated effectively the population was 'controlled'

This system had its faults, however. The Saxon law said that for a man to be Theynworthy he had to own five Hides. This meant that there were lords who owned a whole village. When this happened the Farmers' Court did not keep them down to size and they ruled all three courts, landlords, local behaviour and farming, as if they were dictators or small kings.

Thus, the closed village began. Clanfield, however, was fortunate. It still remained an open village. All the manors were owned by separate lords. Only for a short while, as we shall see in the Domesday Book, did one lord own Clanfield. Even so, this did not last for long. The lord lived at some distance from the village, and his contact became remote. The original farms on the settlements reasserted themselves.

★ ★ ★

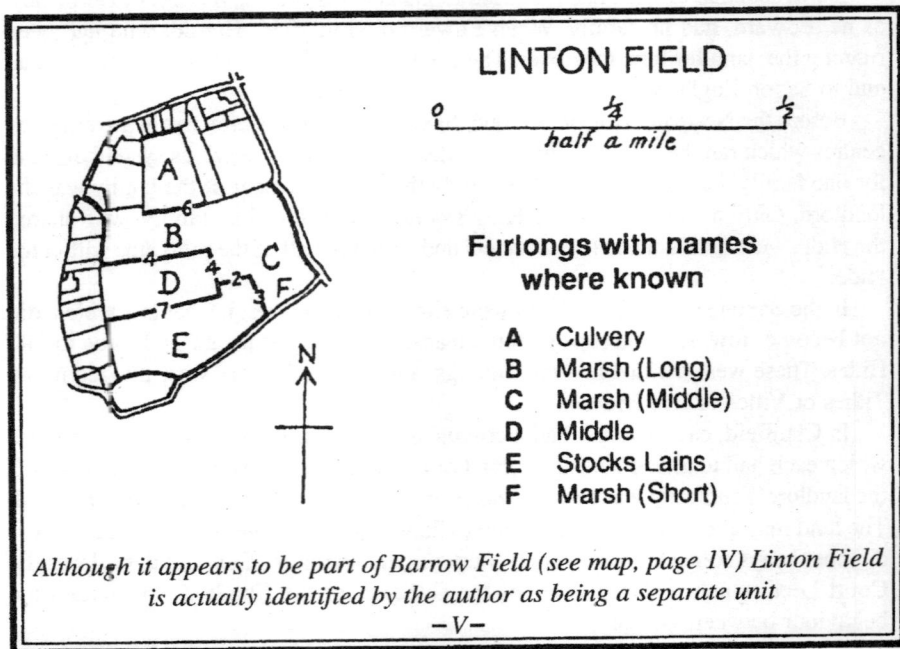

LINTON FIELD

0   ¼   ½

half a mile

Furlongs with names where known

A   Culvery
B   Marsh (Long)
C   Marsh (Middle)
D   Middle
E   Stocks Lains
F   Marsh (Short)

Although it appears to be part of Barrow Field (see map, page 1V) Linton Field is actually identified by the author as being a separate unit

–V–

Chapter 3

The Norman Invasion and the Domesday Book

IN 1066 Clanfield must have been alive with rumours about who would be the new King. News came from the Shire, through the markets, to say that the old King was dead. All expected Harold, who had been running the land, to take over, but William of Normandy, on hearing that Harold had claimed the throne, came over to England with his army as soon as the wind was favourable.

In the meantime, Harold had had to go to the north with his loyal Theyns to contain a Danish army who were too powerful for the local forces. This force was led by Harold Hardrada, King of Norway, and Tostig, Harold's brother. At Stamford Bridge, Harold of England had won when news reached him that William had landed. He made a forced march back, collecting local forces, and went to meet William, who was waiting for him. He fought against cavalry with his foot soldiers, and made no allowance for retreat in order to fight again, unlike Alfred had done. It was a long battle, lasting all day. In view of the fact that Harold and his men were tired, he did well, but pretending to retreat in confusion, William drew off some of Harold's forces until, in the end, he overwhelmed Harold's position.

William then moved towards London, via Sussex, Surrey and Hertfordshire. He burned houses on the south bank to frighten the city. He then moved west in a large circle around London and the chaos he caused could still be seen in the Domesday Book which came some twenty years later. He proceeded to block the north road so that London gave in. With limited exceptions, such as Hereward the Wake in the Fens, the country accepted him. He was anointed and crowned in Westminster Abbey on Christmas Day in 1066, after the English leaders had submitted.

Clanfield soon became aware of the Norman presence. Frenchmen appeared at the Shire and then at the Hundred meetings. There was no doubt who ruled the land, and Clanfield farmers, who in any case did not like paying taxes, liked it even less when paid to Frenchmen.

William tried to be a good and fair King but he taxed the country very heavily. King Edward had not been too demanding. William wanted up to a quarter of men's incomes. Feelings ran high and his men were attacked and disappeared. Many local revolts broke out in places such as Exeter and the north of England. In 1075, nine years after the invasion, there was a serious revolt which was quashed. Many Saxons fled from William's wrath and their estates were left without a Lord in charge. The Domesday Book shows that the Saxon nobility retained only one-eighth of the land.

William's power lay in the loyalty of the Norman Lords who had followed him to England. These he could trust. Now, he felt it was the time to repay that loyalty. Before the invasion, land ownership depended, from the days of the settlement, in being known in the local centre. Book land — land with deeds — was appearing, but it was the authority of the centre court that mattered. Kings could own estates privately, but when they owned a centre, it was really only the income that the centre produced. No Kings had owned the whole country, but William did. He had conquered it, so he could do with it as he wished. He began to share it out among his Lords, yet he did it wisely. No man was given too big an estate in one spot, so that he could challenge the King in any one area.

Among these Lords was one Roger d'Ivry, who had come over as William's butler. He was the son of Rodulph, half-brother of Richard 1st Duke of Normandy. Whilst out hunting with the Duke he killed a monstrous boar, and was given the castle of Ivry on the river l'Evre. Rodulph died three years after this — in about 1079 — and left three sons, and Roger d'Ivry, who was the eldest, inherited the castle. Roger came over with William and shared the position of butler with his brother, Hugh.

Roger died in 1084 and left a son, Roger II. Roger d'Ivry I was given 24 estates in Oxfordshire, of which he kept a third and let out the rest. In the Bampton Hundred he was given three estates, Brize Norton, Black Bourton and Clanfield. So he must have come to the Hundred Court and Clanfield for the first time as the new master.

All the previous lords had to give up their land and Roger took over. He did not, however, live here. He let this land out, together with his land at Black Bourton, to Pagen of Chedworth.

England had been run very efficiently under Streona's Hundredal system. It was like the farmer walking around the farm where all could reach him. However, to get around all the new Hundred centres, besides his estates in France, was a daunting task for any King. The older William got, the more difficult it became. Moreover, he began to realise how little he knew of his land. His Geld Tax did not bring in as much as it should have done. His own personal estates perhaps were not as well organised as he would have wished. In 1085 he had to billet a large army of French soldiers to meet a threatened Danish invasion. He had difficulty in placing them out. He realised something had to be done.

William met with his senior Lords four times a year. He had a brainwave, or some very good advice. It was decided to make the unification of the country and the concentration of government in the King's hands the prime intentions. He decided to make a survey of the whole land so he could have at hand all the facts he wanted.

At Christmas 1085, when they met at Gloucester, he gave orders for the survey to take place. A list of 16 questions was drawn up to be answered, covering details of past and present capacity of each estate in differing branches of production. It was passed to the Shire courts and then to each Hundred centre. It was here, by intent or accident, that a stroke of genius came. Landlords were to be registered or known at the Shire court. Previously, the Shire was a weakling. Landownership meant power. In one stroke he had removed from the stubborn Hundred centres much of their power, and the Shire, a court no man could control, became the power in the land. Clanfield farmers had to go to Bampton, either with the estate written down by the village clerk, or most likely, to get the clerk there to record it. It was all entered under the new Lord's name. When all the Hundred records were to hand they were taken to Oxford.

At Oxford they were put under the names of the Lord, probably in the order in which they came. When they were all assembled, men from each village, the priest, the reeve and leading man from each manor had to go and swear that all the facts were correct. The whole thing took 18 months. The finished work was given to William just before he left for France in August 1087. Immediately he realised that he had asked for too much. He really needed something he could carry about with him. So he ordered a précis to be done. When he died, as the result of an accident in 1087, most of the work had already been finished. It stopped on his death.

Later this was bound into volume one of the Domesday Book and the remainder of the unfinished part in the east was tidied up and put into volume two. As with most villages, the Domesday Book is the earliest record we possess of Clanfield. It was a brief and stylised report coming some 600 years after the Anglo-Saxons came. The entry for our village is as follows:

p29:"Pagen holds Chenefelde from Roger. 7 hides less 1 virgate of land. Land for 11 ploughs. Now in lordship 4 ploughs. 4 hides of this land are in lordship. 4 slaves there; 14 villagers with 13 smallholders have 7 ploughs. Meadow, 100 acres; pasture 6 furlongs in length and width. The value is and was £7. The land is of the King's first Holding."
(Ref: Morris J ed. Domesday Book: Oxfordshire. Phillimore, Chichester, 1978)

It is a pity that Clanfield was not mentioned in volume 2, with its fuller details. However, this does afford some information. Roger d'Ivry owned the village, that is Tarny and Westfield. Pagen was his tenant. He personally farmed four Hides. It is tempting to see the four estates of the Domesday Book matching the four estates that appear in 1242 and again in 1316, finishing up as Chestlyon, Southwick (or North Court), Hospitalers (or Friars Court) and Putts, which is now in Alvescot parish, later owned by the Abbot of Cirencester. If this were so, then four land owners were turned out by Roger d'Ivry.

The land mentioned as the land 'of the King's first holding' indicates that it was owned by the King in the first period: i.e. at Edward the Confessor's death. This tells us that Clanfield was part of the royal estate of Weald, but sold off before the Conquest. The remainder of Clanfield, two-and-three-quarter Hides, was let out to 14 small farmers and 13 smallholders. So Clanfield probably had a population of about 140 people.

In pure Saxon organisation, Clanfield should have been measured in single Hides but it was measured in odd, divided hideage farmed by many farmers and must have reflected the old British system they took over. The Saxons measured in Hides and the British measured in Virgates.

It would appear that the Lord had one plough and one slave on each farm, perhaps as a ploughman. But the villagers, having more ploughs per Hide, obviously did much of the Lord's work. The remainder of the Lord's work would have been done by the villeins who did seasonal work, and the smallholders who did his daily work between them.

The Domesday Book shows how far from the original settlement England had got in the 500 years. Clearly we and others had been in 15H (hide) estates. Clanfield's six-and- three-quarter Hides had been rearranged into four farms, but as the village was later referred to as individual Hides it would appear some Hides had been shared out, a fact common to all villages.

Old Clanfield was fully developed. Of its 1,107 acres, some 800 acres were ploughed, which required 11 ploughs to do. The remainder of the land, 100 acres of meadow and 360 acres of pasture, was obviously more of a guess. This would have been all the Langley, Green Close, Fore Meadow, Rye Meadow and the Moors.

This survey tells us that Clanfield was fully developed in Edward's time, as between then and 1086 its value had not changed. One rather tantalising part of the survey is: 'this is land of the King's holding'.

We were important, but we do not know why. Perhaps this was to do with the adjacent royal estate at Weald. But of course it was not a village with a boundary, nor yet the present village which was formed about the mid-13th century. The village at that period consisted basically of the manor farm's arable land under the two field systems of the village court, and the homes of the people that farmed it, and any grassland they had. But of course, these people could share meadows with others, as indeed must have happened on Grafton Green. And they had rights outside, as at Charney Meadow and at Nippenham. The parish boundary was yet to be drawn.

When William died our land had this wonderful record to which all men could go to claim ownership. Unfortunately for William, he was never able to use it himself. We are the greatest benefactors today.

After his death ,William's second — and favourite — son, William Rufus, inherited England. His older son, Robert, inherited Normandy. Rufus wanted to make a much better job than his father had done: he was going to rule the land by the rod. Unfortunately, nothing more was heard. He was not a good King. He was irreligious, bad tempered, and possibly homosexual. He was killed in an accident (or possibly murdered) in the New Forest when he was out hunting in August 1100.

Roger d'Ivry II, son of the Domesday Book Roger d'Ivry, took up arms against Rufus with the Barons. His estates were taken away and he died in exile. His property was later restored to his son, Geoffrey, in 1088. Early in the 12th century the direct line became extinct and then possession passed to the St. Valery family. The original Valery also came over with William the Conqueror.

After Rufus's death, Henry, William's youngest son took the throne. Henry reigned 35 years until 1135 but, of all his children, only two were legitimate and only one of these, Mathilda, outlived him. She had been educated in Germany and, knowing the prejudice against women, Henry had her brought back to England before he died to get all his leaders to swear loyalty to her — which they did in 1126, 1131 and 1133 — but on Henry's death his nephew, Stephen, claimed the throne, seized the treasury, and won the approval of the Pope, ignoring Matilda's claim to the throne by hereditary right. He was crowned on December 25th at Westminster.

Matilda was taken by surprise. She had been on good terms with Stephen — some even feel she was his mistress — but unfortunately for her, on her father's death, she was pregnant. Stephen, too, was having his problems and in 1137 was taken very ill.

Powerful Lords took advantage of this. Robert, a Baron who lived at Bampton, no doubt at Ham Court, sought to improve his own position. He began a private war, raiding the countryside. Obviously, he went outside his own Hundred, otherwise they would turn against him. As soon as the King got better he came to Bampton and, without too much trouble, captured his castle there. Matilda came over in due course. The West rose to back her up.

In 1141 Stephen was taken captive at Lincoln by Robert of Gloucester. Matilda now felt secure, but she became so arrogant that London rose against her and she had to flee back to the Continent. When she returned again, she made Oxford her centre and proceeded to fortify important sites behind it. Two of these were at Radcot and Bampton. Radcot had been the highest wharfage on the Thames and was growing in importance.

At a very early period a stone bridge seems to have been built at Radcot, before the present one. In a land transaction of 958 King Eadwig granted to his Theyns 30 Hides of land in the manor of Worth, near Faringdon.

In the description of this land it says 'first to the stone bridge and from the stone bridge eastwards along the Thames until it comes to the boundary of the people of the King's Home (Kingston Bagpuize) *(Ref: Phillips, Geoffrey. Thames Crossings: Bridges, Tunnels and Ferries; David and Charles 1981)*. Recently the footing of a fellow bridge behind the garrison was dug out in widening the back water, but no one was present to assess its age.

Bampton was becoming one of the wealthiest towns in the land. Gesta Stephamus wrote that she built fortifications 'one at Woodstock, one at the hamlet of Radcot so surrounded by water and marsh as to be inaccessible, one at the town of Cirencester, a fourth in the village of Bampton right on the church tower which had been built in olden times of wondrous form and with extraordinary skill and ingenuity...'

The garrison still remains at Radcot. It was built right across the old valley road crossing, in line with the old bridge. Until the Turnpikes built a new road at Radcot, the road from Clanfield went direct to the garrison and then detoured around the east. The present Radcot House stands with its back to the present road, for it was built facing the old road.

The Hundred Rolls of 1279 tells us that Radcot was an ancient centre. It had a gallows, market, fair and furthermore the Assize of Bread and Ale had been placed upon it in 1266. Perhaps the garrison was the original encampment of pre-history rebuilt, or perhaps it was the area between the Thames and its backwater, now the canal.

To the villagers of Clanfield the fortifications of the area must have been an important happening, and many must have walked down to Radcot to see the sappers busy digging the huge ditch, facing the bank and fortifying it with the timbers. Then the soldiers, having finished that job, marched up the grass track to Clanfield making for Bampton, and many must have followed them and watched on the following day as the carpenters were at work on the tower of the Minster church, building their fortified platform.

But the following year Stephen came with his forces to attack them. In 1142 King Stephen had recovered from his illness, "arriving unexpectedly in Cirencester with a large force of resolute soldiers".

"Finding the castle empty because the garrison had stolen away, he gave it devouring flames and after demolishing rampart and stockade to the foundations he marched his army with great determination to Bampton and Radcot. When he had taken the one by storm and the other surrendered at discretion — he valiantly went to Oxford to attack the force of the Countess of Anjou (Matilda), 26 September 1142.". It was an eventful time, as arrows and stones were flying. As he marched through Clanfield from Bampton and took Radcot, Clanfield's inhabitants must have kept their heads well down.

Stephen then marched to Oxford where, after a seige, Matilda escaped from Oxford Castle in the snow wearing a white cloak, over the frozen river, to be taken to Abingdon.

The Civil War dragged on. Phillip, one of Matilda's followers, built castles around to strengthen her position. We read again in Gesta Stephamus: "And coming to a hamlet called Faringdon in the English language, a delightful spot abounding in all sorts of supplies, he built in it a castle strongly fortified by a rampart and a stockade, and putting in a garrison that was the flower of his whole army he valourously restrained the wonted attack of the King's soldiers who had been coming out from Oxford and the castles around about to harass his own side."

The King's men, now being on the defensive, sent to the King for help. Dropping all his affairs, he came to Oxford and "with an army of vaste strength he encamped around the castle of Faringdon in the expectation of a long siege".

Stephamus goes on: "Then he instructed his mên to busy themselves with a wonderful task and not without profit, namely, surrounding themselves with a rampart and stockade that a sudden attack of the enemy might not break into their confusion, but ensconced in a sure refuge of their own, they might both provide more security for themselves and go out to meet the enemy more safely and more boldly when occasion arose and without delay setting up engines most skillfully contrived around the castle and posting an encircling ring of archers in very dense formation, he began to harass the besieged most grievously. On the one hand stones or other missiles launched from the engines were falling and battering them everywhere, on the other a most fearful hail of arrows, flying around before their eyes, was causing them extreme affliction; sometimes javelins flung from a distance, or masses of any sort flung by hand, were tormenting them, sometimes sturdy warriors, gallantly climbing the steep and lofty ramparts, met them in most bitter conflict with nothing but the palisade to keep the two sides apart."

This battle kept going for some days until those within the castle secretly, without their soldiers knowing, went to the King to know his terms and then surrender the castle to him.

If the wind had been right Clanfield's people would have heard something of this battle but, knowing what was good for them, kept well clear. It is interesting to note the reference to 'Faringdon' in the English language. Bede, in his history, often noted the fact that towns had two names in early times, presumably the British one and the Saxon one.

But help came for Matilda in the young Henry Plantaganet, her son, who was the future King. He did not do too well. First he was defeated at Cricklade, then he came to Bourton, some think Black Bourton, but possibly another Bourton, where he was defeated again. Instead of killing him, Stephen took pity on him as he liked the lad, and packed him and his men back home again, paying for their passage. Archbishop Theobald of Canterbury was instructed to draw up an agreement whereby if Matilda returned to the Continent, Stephen was to wear the crown and upon Stephen's death Matilda's son, Henry II, was to become King. Luckily for England, Stephen only lived for one more year, so ending a sad period when he really knew Matilda had the greater right to wear the crown. Henry was recognised as sole heir to Stephen's crown by the Treaty of Wallingford in 1153.

In 1145, Matilda gave up and went back home to France. Queen Eleanor, who had divorced the King of France, went to Henry to ask him if she could be his wife. It was possible that she had been the mistress of Geoffrey, Matilda's husband. Henry accepted her. He was 18 years old and she was 28. Matilda accepted Eleanor as her daughter-in-law and when Henry left to claim the English throne he left her, pregnant, with his mother. Stephen died on 25th October 1154 and Henry, at 21 years of age, was crowned on 19th December 1154.

Henry II was a sensible King. He demolished all illegal castles, no doubt the one at Bampton, and brought all the local and regional laws of the country into one common law. He was a very active King.

During his 35 year reign trade increased. Radcot grew in importance. Stone was coming from Taynton to help build the great churches of southern England. Even Old St. Paul's had Taynton stone, and it still remains in the crypt of the new St. Paul's.

The road across the Thames, swinging east and around the garrison, crossing over the rivers, by stone or by wooden bridges, now had three great new bridges built of Taynton stone, of which the southern one still remains. A drawing of the remains of the north bridge, Pidnell Bridge, was made by Mrs Davenport in 1840. It contained four arches of the same period and style as the one remaining with its three arches.

Fortunately, Baskerville writing in 1692 said: "Radcot bridge, the main stream of which boats pass through is 22 yards over and has three arches, the second bridge has two arches which lead to the weir and the third stream has a bridge over it with four arches but not for great boats to go through." But of course small boats and rafts, on which the heavy stone would be placed, did go through.

The style indicates that this bridge was built early on. The name of New Bridge existed for a bridge built further down the stream in about 1250, and in 1208 repairs had to be made to Radcot Bridge. It has been discovered in recent times that this bridge was built not on a foundation of stone, but on a raft of timber.

★ ★ ★

Chapter 4

The Creation of the Parish

DURING the whole invasion period something very important was happening in Clanfield. Until now the loyalty of the village had been determined by the Court leet and the Farmers' Court. Religion had been centred at the Minster, where the people were buried. Here lived the priests. Settlements or manors no doubt had a chapel to which the priest came to say Mass, but it was in no way a village building.

Plans were now afoot for villages to have their own burial ground. This was being encouraged by the King, who allowed Lords to pay their tithes direct to their own church and employ their own priest, if they had provided a burial ground.

Will Weatbury held Clanfield in this period. When he conveyed his manors at Clanfield and Weatbury, Buckinghamshire, to Ralph Harang in 1199 the deed says: "With Knight service or free tenure and with services within the gifts of these churches in wood and field in meadow and pasture inland and mills" *(Ref: raan Hegi. Roll 1 John No 7. 18d)*. So the deed appears to be talking about a parish and the land serving, or being served by, a church.

It would seem that before 1199 a churchyard had been given by the Lord of Chestlyon to the chapel there. So tithes had been placed upon this chapel, a priest employed, and this chapel then had the status of a village church, predominating over the other chapels within the village. So at this time and period, the grouping of manors which we have seen recorded in the Domesday Book now became a defined area. The parish boundaries had been drawn. So now a new loyalty determined the loyalty of the parish to its church. Close to Clanfield, on the east of Friars Court, lay three Hides owned by the King, but in Weald, many of whose people lived in Clanfield, it was called Barrowfield. To help Clanfield he moved these three Hides into the village field, and passed a quarter of its tithes into Clanfield so that his people could make use of the graveyard and priest.

Already, the people of the area had a chapel in Clanfield on the side of Radcot road, called St. Leonard's previously. This was later used to pick up the three quarters of the tithes on the land, which were retained by Bampton, a running sore over the years.

However, although these people's lands were put in with Clanfield, and although they paid a quarter of their tithes to the parish church, yet they remained under the manorial law of Bampton. Moreover, being of the ancient demesne — i.e. owned by the King in the Domesday period — they lived under a different law. They paid no tax, so they did not come up in the later tax records. They were exempt from the Shire Reeve control, from juries and inquests outside the manor, from the upkeep of bridges and roads, from market tolls, and could only sue or be sued in the Court of Common Pleas. This gave them privileges over the rest of Clanfield who lived under common law. Their social position was much more secure, but if they paid no taxes, it was certain they paid the King in other ways.

The new parish boundaries were drawn down the centre of the marsh on the east side of these three Hides. It is a brook called the Maw Brook, the boundary brook, or the Maw or Marsh brook or the Marl brook. In the south, the ancient meadows in Burroway and Charney were shared between Brize Norton, Alvescot, Kencot and Black Bourton, presumably divided out between these various parishes when Burroway died. These were not in Clanfield. The boundary in the south follows streams against Radcot to Grafton. Here, a community was split in two. Men had settled on either side of Grafton Green with the arable lands in Grafton field or in Tarny. The parish boundary followed the stream on the east side of the green, so those in Little Clanfield belonged to Clanfield church and the rest, in Grafton, to Langford church with Radcot, which suggests that Langford parish was there already.

The boundary on the north against Alvescot was different to that which exists now. The odd hideage of Alvescot and Clanfield in the Domesday Book shows that formerly we had been part of a 15 Hide estate which had been split into two parts. We also know that part of Ruxhill, later called Batesland and Putts, (seen in the Alvescot enclosure map as Pittslands), whilst now being in Alvescot, was originally in Clanfield. We also know that tithes were later paid from these to Clanfield church, and that we also had to pay Alvescot church 6s. So in this period when the boundaries were drawn to support our church, Batesland and Putts were in Clanfield parish, and some small portion on which the 6s tithes was paid was in Alvescot.

Indeed, as late as 1714, Batesland, being part of Southwick manor, and Putts, came under the village Court Leet which belonged to the Honor of Ewelme. We must therefore assume that in this early period the boundary between Clanfield and Alvescot lay above these two settlements on the north side. When it was moved to Calcroft Lane we do not know.

Thus, the new boundary was drawn. All within supported and belonged to the new church except, of course, that Bampton church retained a threequarter portion of the tithes on the three Hides. The Farmers' Court had to meet. The two-year rotational field divided between Tarny and West Field, was now redrawn, with Barrow Field added. This meant that not only did tenants have to have new strip, but manorial ownership no doubt followed them. So later we find, in 1685, the question was asked in Bampton about the whereabouts of the land from which the tithes on the 12 yards comes. The answer was unknown. This suggests that, by then, the 12 yards was scattered over the whole village.

In 1189 Henry II died, and was followed by his son, Richard the Crusader. He was a romantic of little use to this land, except that Hubert Walter, Archbishop of Canterbury, who ran England for him, did it well. Richard spent most of this time in France, and returned to England only twice for a brief period in 1189 and 1194. Richard (who was born at Oxford) died in 1199 and his brother John, born, as some say, at Woodstock, came to the throne. He was the favourite son of Henry II, and he spent a lot of his time in France. He separated England from Normandy, and gave independence to the towns, and he even allowed London to elect its first Mayor.

But the Barons would not accept his dominion, and at Runnymede they brought him to heel by making him seal the Great Charter called the Magna Carta on 15th June 1215. He tried to get out of it, but the shock of the loss of all his private possessions in the Wash brought on a fever, and he died on October 18th 1216.

Throughout his reign the land was plagued with inflation, from 1180 to 1220. Henry III, infant son of King John, came to the throne in 1216. Patriotic statesmen ran the land, pushing out French officials, checking Papal influence, pulling down illegal castles. Henry's one great achievement was the completion of Westminster Abbey in 1269. He was crowned at the age of 13 years, but did not rule so well as his Lords, and he allowed Papal influence to come back.

The country reacted to this. England was beginning to have a taste for freedom. The Bible, whilst still to be translated, was growing in influence. Preaching friars following St. Francis of Assisi were crossing the land and, being near Oxford, Clanfield would have been visited by some of these, preaching at the cross by the Masons Arms (now the Clanfield Tavern). They gave the common people a chance to seek out their own faith, independent of the dictatorial priest. The Mass was giving way to the preaching, and later the Bible.

Parliament was conceived, and the country was impatient for progress. Moreover, the Welsh were restive. In March 1264 the whole of the Knights Service to England was summoned to Oxford to fight off Llewellyn of Wales, and the King's enemies. Llewellyn was the ruling Prince of Wales. In Edward the First's time, Wales had been invaded by the Earls of Chester, Shrewsbury and Hereford, who took over the valleys. Llewellyn began to drive them back.

He refused to attend the coronation of Edward I and to do him homage. In 1276, Edward captured his fiancée, and later starved him out in the mountains. Llewellyn then accepted Edward, and surrendered at the Treaty of Aberconway (1277). He rebelled again, and was killed in 1282.

Locally in 1259 an unknown man had been found murdered at Wifholt. Adam, son of Richard at Radcot had been caught and put in prison at Faringdon for the crime, but he was allowed out on bail.

(Ref: Close Rolls of the Reign of Henry III AD1256-1259. London HMSO 1932)

Then again, showing the importance and use of the river in this age (1271) "Matthew de Bezill, the King's Yeoman (Lord of the manor) was granted the boat wherein Gilbert, the son of Walter the Messer, was drowned by accident in the Thames, at a place called La Jureshead at Radcot, with five-and-a-half quarters of wheat, an iron chain, a lock and 11 sacks.
(Ref: Calendar of the Patent Rolls: Henry III AD1266-1272. London HMSO 1913)

In 1274 there was trouble at Langford. After the corn had been carried in and was safely stored and guarded day and night, a stranger, John Edwards, came with a gang of 20 others by night, smashing houses, and took off the corn and other goods. The Lord Roger of Sissinghurst took the matter to court and was awarded £13.6.8d.

One of the measures Henry was to be remembered for was the Assize of Bread and Ale. Food and drink were important to the common people. He tied the price of bread and ale to the price of barley. Luckily for us, the record of this shows us that when Streona created the new Hundredal area and centred it upon a town, he did not destroy the old system. So in the Bampton Hundred Rolls of 1279 we see the Assize rested on the old centres at Bradwell/Filkins, Radcot, Standlake/Shifford, Hardwick, Burford and Witney, as well as Bampton. These had been made in 1266.

Sometime in the beginning of Henry's reign, the church at Clanfield was given to the Nuns of Elstow. This order was founded in 1078 by Judith, daughter of Adelaide, Countess of Aunale, half sister of William the Conqueror. Judith had been responsible for her husband Waltheof's death. He had first joined the Danes against William. William forgave him.

In 1074, when the English nobles tried to rise against William, they asked him to join them. He refused, but promised not to tell William about the rising. Judith later betrayed him, and told William. William imprisoned Waltheof at Winchester and after one year, beheaded him in 1075. Possibly she founded the Abbey as her penance.
(Ref: Wigram, Rev S.R. Chronicles of the Abbey of Elstow. Parker and Co. 1885)

In 1219 the Nuns of Elstow presented Robert of Hicks to the church as Rector. In 1257 Pope Alexander IV confirmed this. He wrote to the Abbess of Elstow:

The care of the office committed to us warns us that, when specially thinking about religious persons, we should bestow upon them peculiar favour and grace. Sympathising, therefore, in your necessities with paternal affection, and yielding to the prayers of our beloved brother J. Priest, Cardinal of the title of St. Laurence in Lucina we do, of our special grace, grant to you for ever the Church of Clanfield, in the Diocese of Lincoln, in which, as you assert, you have the right of patronage, to be applied, with all its rights and appertenances, to

the proper uses of yourselves and of those who shall succeed you; further
conceding to you that, on the resignation or death of the Rector of the said
Church, it shall be lawful for you to enter into possession of the same by our
authority, no consent of the Diocesan or anyone else being in any way
required, assigning a sufficient portion of the emoluments of the Church to the
Vicar, who shall for the time being serve it, to enable him to have fitting
maintenance and to bear the Episcopal, Archdiaconal and other burdens of the
said church. Notwithstanding any letters of the Apostolic See obtained through
the foresight of any persons whatsoever, or reservations, or inhibitions made or
to be made by them, or any other letters of the Apostolic See, by which a grace
of this kind could in any way be hindered or delayed." (21 August 1257)
(Ref: Wigram, Rev S.R. Chronicles of the Abbey of Elstow. Parker & Co. 1885)

It consisted in 1276 of ...

That it shall consist in all tithes arising from Curtilages and crofts in the same
parts and in the tithes arising from 2 Water Mills in the same parish and in the
annual Receipt of corn which is called Chirchesseth and in all the Hay arising
from a meadow which is called the Moot and also in Mortuaries and in the
Tithes of Lamb Wool Calves and Milk and all other obventions belonging to the
Alterage by what name soever distinguished and also in 3 qrs. of wheat and 3
qrs of Tramesii (supposed to be a species of corn under the name summer corn
- See Aineworths Dictionary) at the feasts of all Saints to be received every
year from the said nuns at Clanfield, and all the residue of the said Church
under what name soever comprehended out of charity and as far as a Diocesan
may or can do. We grant and permit them to have and convert to pious, and
their own uses according to the concession of the aforementioned Pope,
nevertheless so that the said nuns shall pay the pensions said to be annually
due viz. 23/- to the Prior of minster and 6/- to the Rector of the Church of
Alvescot (Aifletiscot) as they are bound to do and from henceforth fully desist
from the demand and exaction of an annual pension of one mark which the said
Nuns have heretobefore been accustomed to receive from the Church of
Clanfield and all other ordinary Burdens, as well as repairs of the Chancel and
construction of the same as need shall require as also with respect to Books
and other ornaments of the Church aforesaid, and other things which were
accustomed to be done by the Rector. The said nuns shall do and bear except
the procurations and synodals to the Archdeacon and with respect to the
procuration to the Archdeacon we have ordained this rule to be observed, that
when the Archdeacon of the place for the time being ought to be furnished with
Procurations of Meat and Drink in the Parsonage House he shall be supplied
with the provisions by the Nuns and the Vicar shall contribute in money the

customary sum towards the expense, but the residue of the Expense shall be paid and borne by the Nuns. And if it shall happen that the Archdeacon of the place shall be entertained then the Vicar shall pay to him in money the Customary Procuration.

And the said Nuns in acknowledgement of his right shall pay him 3/- besides the due Procuration prescribed to be paid every year. All extraordinary Burdens of the said Church shall be borne by the said Nuns and the said Vicar in proportion to their respective rates of proportion of the profits of the said Church. And the Vicar shall pay the Synodals and serve the Church by himself and other proper Ministers and the Nuns shall build and provide for him a competent house upon the lands of the Church or other place free from all Secular service before the feasts of St. Michael next ensuing. Also we will that if the said Nuns shall presume to contradict or in any carticle oppose this our ordination that then the grant and acceptance thereof shall be void and of no effect."

So Elstow took over Clanfield's church and kept the rectory. So when the next clerk was appointed in 1276, Richard de Hallingworth, he was a Vicar.

In 1220 the Carricute Tax was charged on all teams of oxen ploughing in midsummer. Clanfield had nine teams and paid 18s.

In 1242 the tenants in chief or main tenants were recorded. In Clanfield there were James Savage $1/2$ Knights Fee held off Ralph Harang of St. Vallery, that was Chestlyon. Alistair Cheney $1/4$ Knights Fee held off Ralph Harang of St Vallery, that was Northcourt and then Phillip de Clanfield $1/2$ (or $1/4$) Knights Fee also held off Ralph Harang of St Vallery and Will Babel $1/3$ Knights Fee held off Ralph Harang of St Vallery. These last two were Putts and Friars Court.

Henry died in 1272 and was followed by Edward I who reigned for 35 years. The work that Edward was most remembered for was the Hundred Rolls, another record of the country, like the Domesday Book, but with much more detail. Clanfield was one of the lucky villages, our record remains.

This was the age of the Crusades. Henry had arranged one in 1270, which was to be paid for by a levy of one twentieth of every man's estate. This raised £30,000. It nearly fell through, but Henry's son, Edward, decided to lead it. William de Valance of Bampton went with him. He relieved Acre, took Nazareth, was nearly killed by the poisoned dagger of the Emir of Jaffa, who pretended to be attracted by Christianity, and was planning further campaigns when news reached him of his father's death. He was in no hurry to return, and after two years came back and was crowned in 1274.

He was a good King. Law and Parliament developed. Villeins began to obtain their freedom, the wool and cloth trade grew. In 1290 he sent 16,160 Jews back to the Continent — they had come over with William — which was a very popular move with Parliament and the clergy.

Clanfield had changed in many ways between the Domesday period and the Hundred Rolls period. The overlord Roger d'Ivry's title had passed to the St. Vallery family, to the Westbury family, to the Harang family and then to the Earl of Cornwall, and played very little role in the history of our village thereafter. The four Hides, or farms, which d'Ivry had left to Pagan to run seem to appear now as Chestlyons, Friars Court, Southwick (which we now know as North Court) and Putts.

Chestlyons, the head settlement, came to Richard Savage in 1242 and 1275 to his nephew Richard Chasterlon, who gave the farm its modern name of Chestlyons. Richard died in 1279 and left it to his son, Hugh, who became a Knight of the Shire.

Southwick (North Court), the original settlement, was sold by Walter Westbury to Ralph de Chesney, whose family held land at Ducklington in the Domesday Book. De Chesney gave the farm to his sister, Alice, on her marriage to Lord Warin of Plays. When her husband died she gave it to the Priory of Southwick on condition that her husband could be buried there.

This Priory had been established in 1133 at Porchester by Will de Ponte d'Arches, Sheriffe of the Royal castles at Porchester and Winchester. In 1145 it was moved on to a single Hide they owned at Southwick. It was an order that had problems and a bad name in its early days. The problems all seem to have been centred on Brother Andrew, the Prior. He liked the good life. Archbishop Picken had to temporarily remove him, rationing him to three loaves a day and two gallons of beer. He was to sleep in the Dorter and eat with the other canons. If he ate out he was to only have bread and water. Later the Archbishop ordered that the door between his quarters and the garden was to be walled and he was confined to the cloisters until he produced a proper accounts book.

This manor, as we have noted, was not in Clanfield, but part of it was in the adjoining parish of Alvescot, being Rookshill, later called Batesland.

Gift in free alms, by Alice de Chesneto – for her salvation and for the souls of Sir Ralph de Chesneto, her brother, of Warin (Guarin) de Plaiz, her lord, who is buried at Southwick, and of her lord Robert de Eston, and all her lords, kinsfolk and friends – to Southwick Priory, of 3 virgates in Clanfield (Clenefeld), with all appurtenances, and the meadow called Inmede, from the hide which her brother Ralph gave as provision for her, with 25 acres from the demesne (dominium) on Rocheshulle, and with all men, tenants and their households. The priory will be quit of all service and secular exaction, saving royal service, for which, when it is required, the whole hide is assessed at 1/4 knight's fee. Witnesses: Robert Amari; Ralph Amari, his brother; and many others.

(Ref: Hanna, KA ed. The Cartuleries of Southwick Priory Part 2: III 289. Hampshire Record Office for Hampshire County Council 1989. Printed by Hobbs, Southampton 1805/89)

Another part of Clanfield belonged to the Knights Hospitalers. This order was a nursing order, formed about eight years after the first Crusaders liberated Jerusalem in 1100 from the Saracens. It caught the imagination of the age and in the Bampton Hundred it had been given a meadow at Radcot, Quenham Meadow in Grafton, ploughland in Weald, 1½ yards in Brize Norton, 6 yards at Westwell, besides an estate at Clanfield.

It would seem that the Knights Hospitalers had been given some land early on and in about 1150 an order was established in Clanfield. In the early days of religious orders, Monks and Nuns worked in the fields. But when a new order was established in 1180 at Buckland in Somerset, Agnes of Clanfield was sent there. Presumably she was the only one at Clanfield. Orders needed three of each sex. She may have been too attractive to leave or such a prude that they were glad to see her go. Gifts of land were made to the Hospitalers and after 1242, according to the Hundred Rolls, they had been given a gift of one Hide and four acres by Phillip Batayle. In 1242 this land was reported in the Book of fees as ⅓ of a Knight's fee by Heredes William Baynel. (There seems to be some confusion between the Hundred Rolls and the Book of Fees between Phillip of Kranfield, presumably Batayle, and Baynel and presumably the ownership of Friars Court and Putts).

The last one, Putts or Pitts lands, is now in the Alvescot parish and was given by Baynel to the Abbey or Cirencester. This remained attached to Chestlyons for many years, although it was outside the village in later years, but it paid tithes to the church.

A third estate appears in the Hundred Rolls in the possession of Osney. This is now called little Clanfield Manor. This was made up of various gifts recorded in the Osney Deed. "Matilda Buckerel gave 16 acres of arable land in Clanfield and Nicholas Niceturned gave 10 acres in 1240." Of these gifts Nippenham, which is now in Bourton Parish, was said to have been in Clanfield.

Osney Priory, to which these gifts were given, started on Osney Island in 1129 by the wife of Robert d'Oily Junior. Robert had married a woman who had been a mistress of Henry I, in his youth, and who had given Clapham Manor as a dower. In 1154, Osney Priory was raised to an Abbey.

It ran a bank for the town of Oxford, but paid no interest on the monies deposited with it as that would have been usury and usury was a sin. However, they so managed to place it out in one way or another that its capital appreciated, and they naturally became one of the wealthiest houses in Oxfordshire.

An interesting note was put in at the end of the Osney Deeds in a later hand. The Deeds were compiled in 1280. Richard Chasterlon died in 1279, but another Richard appeared from about 1316–1350.

"In CLANFEDE there are 8 hides of land, of which hide contains 4 virgates. Three of these hides are of the ancient Demesne of Bampton, (viz. MONKEYSHYDE, NISTERNON and WESTERNE) and five hides are of the common law and of the Honor of St. Valery: of these the first if called PREFERTHENDELS, and is in the hands of RICHARD CHASTLION and his tenants. The second FREYNESHUYDE does not pertain to RICHARD. The third is called RICHMANNEYES HYDE; it likewise does not belong to RICHARD. The Fourth is called PERSONEYESHYDE, and it is doubtful of whom it is held, whether of RICHARD or of other lords. The fifth is called SMYTHESHYDE one year, and another year MILNERSACRE, and the whole is held of RICHARD."

The village of Clanfield in 1279 can be visualised. There were people living around Barrowfield, some in Burroway, on the Lower Green and Friars Court. The six free tenants which Robert de Stock left his son were in Stocks Lane. They went from Lower Green to Stocks Lane Close, where his house must have been. His private estate had six cottages paying 6d rent. There were a further six cottages, totalling 18.

The Hospitalers had six serfs tied to the manor, paying various rents from 3s4d to 9slld. They farmed theirs themselves as free tenants. Southwick had two free tenants, six villeins. Chestlyon had 12 free tenants, and in Green Benny six serfs, 13 cottages.

So, in old Clanfield we had about six families at Friars Court, eight families at Southwick and about 39 families at Chestlyons. So we see that already by 1279 most houses were around the church. The total population of the village would have been about 71 houses — say 320 people, less those, of course, who were living in Bates Lane and Rookshill, which became Alvescot.

In 1275 King Edward came through the village. He had stayed at Radcot, and whilst there wrote the Close and Patent Rolls. This must have been a great day for Clanfield. No doubt many were called to serve at Radcot, perhaps some had to pay, but the sight of the mighty entourage wending its way slowly through the green lanes to and through Clanfield must have been something for all to remember.

On January 30th 1277 a John Payne of Clanfield was imprisoned at Oxford for the death of William Savage. This was mentioned in the Close Rolls. James Savage, who had been here in 1275, had no heir, leaving Chestlion to Richard, but later on in the village records the Savage family, gents, were still here in 1589, when one of them married Jane Blagrove, of the Mill at Black Bourton.

(1279) Richard le Fretwell held Norton Brun of the Earl of Cornwall for ³/₄ of a Knight's fee which is of the conquest and does suit to the Earl of Cornwall, with a horse fully equipped for 40 days, when ever he attends the king in an expedition, and the said Richard does suit of court at North Oseney for 3 Weeks in 3 weeks. 11 free tenants hold of him, who did suit at court to the Earl of Cornwall, at Clanfield, and 4 bondsmen.
(Ref: Richardson, Charles. Oxfordshire Collections: Vol 1)

In 1291 another Crusade was planned, and to finance this a levy was made on all the livings. Clanfield came under the Witney Deanery. The money was not to be paid to the King until he actually went on the Crusade on June 24th 1293. But Pope Nicholas IV died in April 1292, so the King seized the money.
(Ref: Denton, Jeffrey H. Robert Winchelsey and the Crown: 1294-1313. Cambridge University Press 1980)

The list of finance raised was as follows:

Langford	60.00.00	
Witney	40.00.08	
Bampton	46.13.04	
Clanfield	40.00.00	the three portions
Burford	30.00.00	
Standlake	15.06.08	
The More*	14.13.04	
Ducklington	10.13.04 }	
Norton (Brize)	10.00.00	
Taynton	8.13.04	
Shilton	7.06.07	
Clanfield	6.13.04	
Prior of Minster	1.03.00	
Rector of Alvescot	0.06.08	plus in the Clanfield portion
Astall	6.13.04	
Westwell	6.13.00	
Bourton	5.06.08	
Kelmscot	5.06.00	
Minster	4.13.06	
Alvescot	4.13.04	
Cokethorpe	2.00.00	

* *The More is north of the 'Rose Revived' public house at Newbridge. It has long since gone. Minster's £1.3s. in Clanfield came from Bampton originally and was placed on Barrowfield.*

Chapter 5

Edward to Henry II

ONLY fragments of news come to us from our village at this time. In 1307 King Edward died, and was followed by his son Edward II, who inherited the family weakness of homosexuality and who made as his friend Piers Gaveston, a Frenchman, and one of the leading men of the land.

In 1307 Piers held a great tournament which was a 'marvellous' affair full of colour and competitions with the King as star guest. The King created him Baron Wallingford. He later raised Piers to the office of the Earl of Cornwall, head of the St. Valery lands, of which Clanfield was a part. This caused a lot of bad feeling and the barons tried to get rid of him. The King agreed to move him, but went back on his word. Piers' activities, however, began to embarrass the King, so that in the end the King took him into captivity at Scarborough.

Aymer de Valance, Earl of Pembroke, who was living at Bampton and one of the most important barons in the land, was given the job of bringing him captive to London. On reaching Deddington Castle in Oxfordshire, Aymer for some reason decided he must visit his wife at Bampton. He put Piers in the Rectory House. Whilst he was gone, the barons descended on Deddington and took Piers out and killed him. He was beheaded on Blacklow Heath, Warwickshire. *(Ref: Crossley A, ed. The Victoria History of the Counties of England: Oxford vol. XI. Oxford University Press 1983)*

Piers' body was taken to Oxford and buried in the Church of Blackfriars. After three years the King took the body to Kings Langley in Hertfordshire, and buried it with considerable pomp.

William de Valance was a son of Isabel, widow of King John, and Hugh de Bruce. She was a god daughter of Louis V and had been engaged to Hugh before John took her as his wife. She remained loyal to Hugh, and after John's death, she married Hugh. So William was half brother of Henry III. He lived at Hereford Castle, but fought in the Holy land.

On his return he was banished by the barons. He returned and fought a battle at Northampton, but fled in defeat to France via Lewes. He returned again to fight, and his possessions were restored to him. He was killed in France in 1296 leaving three sons. John died in his youth, William was killed by the Welsh, and only Aymer remained. (He took part in the disastrous battle of Bannockburn.)

The King, at times, treated Aymer very badly but he ate humble pie on all occasions, and so Aymer maintained the royal patronage. He built up estates in Scotland,

and was allowed to crenellate Ham Court in 1312, and so this became the official building of Bampton Castle. In 1312 it was Aymer, Earl of Pembroke, who requested from the King five years' Pontage on Radcot Bridge, to be collected by Robert de Putre and Robert de Karr, the stewards of Radcot and Faringdon.

The following year saw the chase of the age. The Reeve of Cuxham was taking an ox from Abingdon market to Cuxham. It escaped at Dorchester and was chased for two days, finally to be caught at Filkins, having travelled 25 miles. *(Ref: Harvey PDA. A Medieval Oxfordshire Village: Cuxham - 1240 to 1400. Oxford University Press, 1965)*

This story reveals that the countryside was all open land, that there were just a few bushes and trees and closes around the villages, but beyond the land and meadows was a vast open prairie. Yet the fact that it was all open made people feel much safer than those who lived amongst the woods, which were full of outlaws and vagabonds.

England now had a population of some five million people and was going through a very bad spell. For some reason the weather went haywire, and from 1300 to the end of Edward's reign there were great extremes. Because of this the food prices jumped and animal plagues broke out. In 1315–17 the plague affected sheep, and in 1319 it affected oxen.

In the summer of 1316 there was continuous rain for 100 days in Europe. England had her share. The harvest was a failure. The winter that followed was as severe as any we have known. In 1317 it was a little better, but there was starvation and the people had eaten some of their seed corn. The harvests of 1317-1318 were also failures, and famine abounded. The good years since 1220 were coming to an end.

The population began to decrease, land was left empty. On top of this there was political disorder in the land, as the King and the barons were at enmity. Lesser barons plundered the land.

The King now had another male friend, Hugh Despenser. The people had had enough. The barons asked the King to abdicate in favour of his son. This he did in 1326, and in 1327 he was eventually murdered at Berkeley Castle near Bristol.

Edward III reigned for 50 years. He was crowned, aged 15, married at 16 and had had a son by the time he was $17\frac{1}{2}$ years of age, when his wife was still only 15. He was a good King, but it took him 20 years to bring peace and security within his kingdom. Then trouble came.

The big tragedy of Edward's reign was the Bubonic Plague. People began to suffer from glandular swellings, caused by the poison, killing them some four to seven days after they were taken ill. It had come overland from China, taking eight years. We had been free of plague since 1000 AD. It must have attacked the towns first, and even Parliament was frightened to meet in London,

We have no facts about how the plague affected Clanfield, but even the King lost a daughter, and the Archbishop of Canterbury and half the York clergy died. At Witney, before the plague, the bishop had in one year 5 Heriots, the tax each person's estate had to find upon his death. In the year of the plague it was 57. Out of the 77 small farmers on the bishop's estate 57 had died — seven out of ten. The food was just not gathered in. *(Ref W.O. 1908)*

At Buckland in 1347, the corn sales dropped from £33.14s 2d to £8.7s.1d.

At Eynsham, Tilgarsley was depopulated.

(Ref: Crossley A., ed. The Victoria History of the Counties of England: Oxford vol. XI. Oxford University Press 1983)

The well known children's game of Ring-a-ring-o-roses apparently comes from this tragedy. The plague was the 'rosy ring rash' which appeared in the early days of the illness. 'Posies' warded off the plague or relieved the smell. Sneezing was the final symptom before the victim dropped down dead.

Somewhere at this time in our history the settlement of Benny, along Calcroft Lane, as well as the settlement around Chestlyon, disappeared. It could have been a slow and gradual death, as settlements move, but it could also have been as a result of the Plague.

After about seven years new plagues seem to have appeared. In 1361–1362 it was one which chiefly killed the children. Another followed in 1369. The population had now ceased to grow. Labour became a scarce commodity. But this was also the age of invention. The butter churn was developed, and the scythe held by both hands replaced the sickle held in one. Water power was being used more often, and near us the Oxford colleges expanded on cheap land, as so many had died in the towns.

The King, getting the feel of his own power, stood up against the Pope. Towns began to grow again, and travel improved. Gough drew his famous map of England in 1360. Perhaps the greatest force was that let loose by Wycliffe at Oxford. He was a master at Balliol College. He translated the Bible, and from his teachings there followed a spiritual revival. The faith of the people had been shattered by the plagues. Now a new faith appeared. Its followers were called Lollards, which means 'mumblers', and it would appear that they were possibly charismatics — "people who spoke in other tongues" *(Ref: The Bible, New International Version, Acts 2)*. The Mass was now giving way to the Bible and its preaching.

It was a pity that Edward reigned so long — his son, the Black Prince, died one year before he did. So, when in 1377 he died, it was his grandson, a youth of 10 years, who followed him.

One troublesome event is recorded in Clanfield at this time. Richard, son of Gilbert Talbot, a descendant of Aymer de Valance through his sister, complained to the

King's court that he had been assaulted by Richard and William Chestlions, brothers, and others, who had carried away his goods and assaulted and imprisoned his servants. This interesting note, of course, reminds us that part of Clanfield was in the Bampton manor and that the Talbots were a Bampton family, and the other part, the old part of Clanfield was under the Chestlyon group. Here were two brothers who were actually living in Clanfield — they were not just the owners, but were living here.

In 1328 Clanfield appeared in a taxational list. It was interesting that in the Domesday Book we had been eleventh in the Bampton Hundred, now we were fifth, paying £7.0s.10d out of the £151.17s 9d that was raised. In our village, 44 people were taxed, ranging from 19s.10d down to 7d. The Prior of St. John paid the most, 19s.10d, Peter Balden paid 7s.8d, John Elliott paid 7s.3d, Richard Chestlion paid 7s, Robert Dillon paid 5s., Ralph Bridgewell paid 5s., and so on.

In 1341 we had to pay up again. St. Peter's was being built in Rome, and this time our village had to find £8.4s.0d. We were now eleventh again in the Bampton Hundred.

In 1347 Radcot Bridge again had to be repaired. Pontage for five years was again given to Robert Stephens and Henry d'Woodcut. The importance of the river and of Radcot is shown in the year 1351, when an order went out that the Thames had to be cleared of all gorces, mills, stanks, stakes and kiddles from London to Radcot Bridge near Oxford.
(Ref: Calendar of the Patent Rolls: Edward III AD1350-1354. London HMSO 1907)

A list was made of the value of the Exeters' manor at Bampton. This was the deanery on the east side of the Shill Brook. It is a most interesting document, and part of our village came under this manor which was associated with St Leonard's Church.

An extent of the Manor of Bampton made there on the first day next after the feaste of St. Frideswide the Virgin, in the first year of the reign of King Edward, the son of King Edward II, 1327, before Clement de Hampton, Steward of the Lord Thos. de Stapledon, Canon of the Church of the Blessed Peter in Exeter, who say that there is one court within the Barton containing four acres of land built on with houses as follows:-
"There is one gate with a certain upper chamber built over the same dilapidated, — one Granary to the said gate adjoining covered with stone. There is one ancient Hall covered with thatch. There are two upper chambers, one of which is for the Lord, and the other for the clerks both with chimnies and closets covered with stone. There is one Buttery with a Larder, one kitchen

with a bakehouse and one dairy covered with stone, and one house covered with thatch to dry the malt of the Lord. And there are in the same place two Granary's covered with thatch one of which is for the corn of the Lord whose length is 156ft. breadth 30ft. and the other Granary for the Tithe corn whose length is 109ft. breadth 28ft. There is also one ox stall covered with thatch whose length is 136ft. breadth 20ft. There is also one stable for the Lord's horses covered with thatch whose length is 53ft. breadth 23ft. There is also one house for the beasts of the plough of the Lords whose length is 32ft. breadth 19ft. And the easements of the same court of the Houses and Buildings aforesaid is worth by the year 20s. and there is a certain garden of 8 acres with the fruit and herbage value one year with another half a marc. There are in the garden two wine presses value by the year and there is one Dovehouse worth by the year half a marc.

"There is also of ancient tenure eight yards of land liable to Tax in the lands of the Tenants of which Will Rolff hold one yard paying therefore yearly and every year rent of Assize 3s.9d at three annual terms by equal proportions." To wit.

"And a customary Aid per Annum of 20d. at the Feast of St. Faith the Virgin, and shall plow for one day to winter seed with half a plow and a days work is worth 2d. Also the same with spring seed and shall plow for fallow once with half a plow having first put his beasts of the plow the same for the following with the oxen of the Lord in the pasture for the time assigned for that purpose, and when the tenants of the Lord shall join their carts he shall join his cart with his companions and there shall plow till the warning of one day at the least and a days work is worth 2d. And if the Lord shall warn him after the Feast of St. John about the Feast of All Saints in the place of the said pastures he shall have one bundle of straw and shall harrow at the Winter seed thrice and at the Spring seed thrice and a days work is worth one-and-a-half pence, and shall carry wood with his cart and his companions so that they two make one cart for three days at the will of the Lord at any time and the work for half a cart for the day is worth 2d., and shall have a small spear which is called a Bule and shall plow for three days and a days work is worth 1/2 and shall mow the aforesaid meadow for three days and ought to have of the Lord for his meat 2d.

"And the first day that he begins to mow he shall have with him the men of Aston and Chimney of the Lord for all of them 4d and if those of Chimney come by themselves they shall have 2d. and those of Bampton and Aston 2d. and the number of mowers shall be 27 and the Bailiff shall give notice and warn them four days and they ought to have for the work aforesaid half a quarter of wheat of the Granary of the Lord whether better or worse, and four cheeses of the

dairy whether better or worse and 8d. for one meal of all of them and one
bundle of Potherbs and one dish full of oatmeal and one dish full of salt and
they shall not say what the dish ought to hold and one bundle of straw or wood
to make their pottage and in the evening then shall have of the grass as much
as he can lift with the staff of his scythe and the days work of the said Will.
Rolff, beyond Reprises to him for the share belonging to him is worth 1½d.
and shall make hay and make hayricks in the meadow then for three days and
the work of one day is worth Id and shall mow thrice in Autumn with all his family
except his wife and shepherd for two days at his own cost and the third day at
the cost of the Lord for one meal if for the whole day they shall have worked,
and if they have not worked unless to the 9th hour they shall live at their own
proper cost which same work cannot be rated on account of the uncertainty of
the persons, because it may happen he may have an hundred of his family
besides the before named persons. All are bound to attend which if they shall
not do so the Lord of them at the next court shall greviously amerce.

  And he ought from the feast of Peter and Paul even to the feast of St. Faith the
Virgin mow for one hour or carry the corn or hay dung of the Lord with one
man one cart and one horse during the time aforesaid except the Days of the
Sabbath and Feasts at his own Charge. Nor on Sabbath days although the Lord
shall be willing to hold court to the same during lthe time aforesaid according
to the custom of the namor he shall not be bound come. And if he shall carry
corn for the whole day to the end he shall have one Garb then. And if he shall
carry hay for the whole day shall have hay enough in the meadow for his horse
and shall carry nothing late for the Lord. And it is at the will of the Lord to
have these services or at the Feast of St. Faith the Virgin 15 days. And they
shall say that he ought to work in the meadow and in plowing before the Feast
of Peter and Paul and not afterwards unless in allowance of other work. And
shall carry for three days with one horse the corn then for the distance of so
many miles that he may be able to his own house late to return, but if it shall go
further it shall be at the cost of the Lord. And the amount of the carriage shall
be three Dishes of Wheat and Beans and half a quarter of Barley and the work
of a day beyond Reprises is worth 1d.

  And he shall thresh corn for half a day when the Lord shall have occasion to
the 9th hour. And if he shall thresh till Evening the Lord shall give to him One
Meal. And the work of a day above reprises an halfpenny. And shall tread
Busas that is make turf for one day to the 9th hour and shall be given 2d. And
as often as he makes Malt shall give to the Lord two Flaggons of Beer or 2d.
And this is at the will of the Lord and nevertheless one for an assize Broken
and shall give to the Lord for an Heriot the best beast of whatsoever sex or
kind it shall be. And if his wife after his decease shall live for one year and one

day next after his death the Lord shall have the heriot in manner aforesaid otherwise not and shall be Bailiff when to that office by the Court he shall be chosen.

This was the typical work of one man's rental:

Hugh Boyd holds one Messuage and four acres of land near the Chappel of St. Leonard paying per annum 6s.8d and shall have the herbage of the said Chappel and the tithes of the meadow of Simon la Palmer in Weald in Borewere and shall maintain the said Chapel in covering. All the tenements and cottage at Aston, Chimney, in Clanfield are bound to give the Lord as often as the Malt 1d and its worth per annum by estimate 2s.

"Shall also take at WEYLDE the Tythe Corn of all the Land which Francis de Clanfelle holds in the village of WEYLDE and tythes if pidgeons and also tythe of one Croft in which the Dovecote stands and shall take also in the same village the tythes of half a yard of land of corn and hay which John Soulys holds and of all the land and meadow which Simon Hurt, Richard Torchard, Richard Joy, Will Stych, Will Codon, Simon le Palmer hold except 15 acres which belong to Simon le Palmer and of ¹/₂ yard, land which John Child and Ralph Strong hold and ¹/₂ yard land which Thom. Edwaker holds.

And so it goes on.

Also at Clanfelle shall have of the court of the Abbess of Elstowe 6d.

Also shall have of the Rector of ALVESCOTE 2 bush. of Wheat and of the Lady Emma de la Penne in the same town ¹/₂ acre of Wheat and shall mow it. In the same manner the Rector of EDYNGTON holds at HORTON shall have of the Lord of the same village ¹/₂ acre of Wheat and ¹/₂ acre of Oats and of the Court of the Abbot of Osney in the same village have an acre of Wheat and 18 garbs of wheat and 18 garbs of Barley or Malt corn and shall demand it at the door of the granary of the Abbot. Shall also take of the tythe of 2a and ¹/₂a of the land of Will Rolff and 2a of the land of John SMELT and 1a in the Vale and ¹/₂a on LEWINOFIELD of the land of John Walter and of 1a of land of Walter Elliot and ¹/₂a of land which was of Hugh Folk in the Vale and the whole Tythe corn of all the land of the same tenants being in their Crofts.

Also shall take a moiety of the Oblations of everything at the altar of the parish Church of Bampton except Money of which they will take the third part and shall take the half of the Oblations of the Chappel of St. Andrews de Bene. There is also one Chappel at Clanfelle on the land of the Farmers in Honour of St. Leonard of which the Vicar of Clanfelle shall have a fourth part of the oblation and of the rest the farmers shall take a moiety.

1245 — The Chapel of St. Leonard of Rottol was in a bad state, it had recently been rebuilt by Leonard who held one of the portions."

When Richard II (1377–1399) came to the throne, England was really alive. His grandfather had reigned too long and his father had spent too much time overseas. The people wanted more freedom and power. They did not like the sale of pardons from Rome.

The great spiritual movement of Wyclif (sic), the original translator of the Bible from Latin into English, had repercussions. John Wyclif was a Yorkshireman who defied the Pope's authority. He began as a reformer in the last years of Edward III. At first the Friars, who believed in poverty, were for him, but as more and more attacked the Pope's views of transubstantiation they left him. He retired to the rectory of Lutterworth, where he wrote many tracts. He produced the first full English version of the Bible. At Oxford the Monks and Friars were against him, although clergy and scholars were for him. The Archbishop of Canterbury expelled Wyclif from Oxford, so he went more for the faith of the working man and not intellectualism, which was very popular.

People were, as a result of Wyclif's influence, prepared to do something about the sale of pardons and the lack of freedom. Political agitators moved through the land. At Bampton, Witney and Eynsham there were riots, possibly on the market days, caused by serfdom, low wages and the cost (heaviness) of taxation.

A labourer's wages had been fixed by law for thirty odd years. Since the reign of his father, Edward III, the Statute of Labourers (1350) was imposed, and another statute of 1372 ordered labourers who left home for higher wages to be branded with a letter 'F' for false.

All of this came to a head in the Peasants' Revolt. Instead of more freedom, the country had been saddled with a very heavy Poll Tax averaging 1s. a head over 15 years, going from £1 down to 4d. to help pay for the French wars. Less people paid than in 1377, so the King sent further men round to check up on it and this caused the revolt. In 1381 the people marched to London, led by Wat Tyler. His demands were
1. That all men be free from bondage, no serfdom.
2. That all should be free to buy and sell anywhere.
3. Pardons for all insurrections, treasons, etc.
4. No more than 4d. acre for acreage held in bondage.

This was not a Lollards rising, but of the common people who wanted to bring in the 'Great Society'. The Chief Justice was in circuit when the revolt broke out. A mob chased him in the fens. He almost escaped to his boat, running from his pursuers, but a woman standing near the water recognised him and pushed the boat out into the water. The mob caught him on the bank and killed him.

Manor rolls were burned. Men sought their freedom from their Lord. A contingent went from Oxford to join in, When the peasants came to London they were kept out on the south side, and hunger began to make some of the men go home. The King spoke to the leaders from a boat, but nothing came of it. At last they were allowed over the bridge into the City, where the citizens entertained them. In the north the rebels were also allowed into the City. For three days they, including the contingent from Oxford, had possession of London City. It is noted that John O'Gaunt's property was destroyed, but he was in Scotland.

The King met the rebels outside the walls and gave them all they wished. Men returned home with their Charters of Liberty. However, whilst the King was out the rebels entered the Tower. The rebels still held London. The King agreed to meet them again at Smithfield. Wat Tyler, who approached the King, was killed, but the young King rode into the peasants, stilled them and led them away. A very brave act. London was saved. The King then went back on all his promises of freedom from serfdom. When his subjects showed their charters of liberation he said "Serfs you are and serfs you will remain." The peasants were very badly treated; no mercy was given them by the King.

In 1387 the King was in trouble with his Lords. It was a time in which the Barons, mostly the King's relations, were in revolt against him. The King was in a difficult position, because in an age of private armies, the Barons together could muster more men than he could. So the King had sent his favourite lord, Robert de Vere (Duke of Ireland, 9th Earl of Oxford) into the Midlands and the Welsh borders to raise troops to bring into London. The Barons knew they had, at all costs, to stop these troops from getting through, or they would lose their cause.

The island between the streams of Radcot was chosen for an ambush. The Duke of Gloucester, uncle to the King, was sent into the Midlands with a large number of troops to block every road back to London and force de Vere south. Lord Arundel was to block the road from Burford to Witney and Newbridge. Lord Derby, the future Henry IV, was to block Radcot bridge, where this army was to be trapped.

The story appears to be this:

It was December 20th and a foggy day which made it impossible to see very far. De Vere with 5,000 troops, having spent the night at Stow on the Wold, and being told by his scouts that all roads to London were blocked, moved south to Burford. As he rested there for a meal, news reached him that his advance party had had a brush with Arundel's troops on the Witney road. He then decided the best thing to do was to take the nearest road into Berkshire and so get round these forces. He made for Radcot where there was a bridge which would allow him to get his baggage over the river, and so reach Faringdon for the night. But as he marched south, in a great hurry, he made a fatal mistake — he never sent scouts back to check his rearguard.

Little did he know that at a prudent distance he was being followed by all the forces that had blocked his way east. On reaching Radcot he found, to his dismay, that the road was blocked by the force under Lord Derby, who had pulled part of the bridge out so that he could not get his baggage over. He conferred with his officers. The men were tired and hungry, they had been marching all day and were looking forward to warm quarters at Faringdon. It had been a dry autumn; the river was low. He decided to rush the bridge and the old ford.

The colours were raised, the troops were drawn up ready for the attack. Sir Thomas Molyneux, Constable of Chester Castle, was at their head, whilst de Vere, no doubt, was discreetly behind making sure there were no deserters. Suddenly, to Molyneaux's horror, he saw a great host of troops coming out of the mist down the Clanfield causeway. He quickly summed up the situation as it applied to himself, and, galloping over the bridges out of the island, disappeared in the gathering gloom across the meadows towards London. He tried to rush through the ford on his horse, missed it, got into deep water and was easily dragged off and killed as he floundered out on the other side.

The troops, with their leader gone, were in no mood for a fight. They immediately surrendered to Gloucester who, taking away their weapons and equipment, allowed them all to go off back to their homes.

Meanwhile, de Vere had galloped off to the next bridge at Newbridge but as this too was defended with archers, perhaps in case he had got past Arundel, he galloped on to ford the river by Bablockhythe. A tired and dejected man must have knocked at someone's door very late that night. Eventually he was able to escape to France.

(Ref: Salzman, LF ed. The Victoria History of the Counties of England: Oxfordshire vol. I. Oxford University Press 1939)

The Barons, who could now tell the King what to do, soon became unpopular, because the next year they voted themselves £20,000 presumably to pay for this campaign. However, in 1389 Richard, now 22, regained control and 10 years of peace followed. He set up a fund of 4,000 marks to pay for the wounded and dispersed of Radcot Bridge. By 1398 all claims wer said to have been settled.

But in 1398 there was trouble again. In our area bands of armed men met at Bampton, and "they chose captains and leaders and on Palm Sunday paraded the villages proclaiming as they went: 'Aryseth, aryseth all men and goth with us: who so will not he schal be ded' — and wounding and ill-treating those who would not join them. It was interesting to note that the chief malcontents came from Bampton, Witney and Eynsham, that Western District of Oxon which all through the history of Oxon had shown a restless and independent spirit." **(Ref: Page W, ed. The Victoria History of the Counties of England: Oxfordshire vol. II. A Constable, 1907)**

In 1399 Richard tried to recoup his position by a general pardon except "to all those who in company with the lords assembled together at 'Haryngey and Rodcotbrigge' contrary to their allegiance, but that their pardon be wholly received to his own person". He did not trust the others and wanted to handle that one personally. **(Ref: *Calendar of the Close Rolls: Richard II, AD 1396-1399. London HMSO, 1927*)**

Richard's reign came to an end in 1399 when Henry landed at Ravenspur to claim his inheritance. Richard submitted to Henry and abdicated.

In Clanfield, life went on... Perhaps, having a strong baron at Bampton, the village was somewhat protected. The march of the two armies through Clanfield in 1387 must have been very frightening. Perhaps the most frightening was the plundering that must have followed as the soldiers made their way back to Wales. They were not really soldiers, they were levies who were going to be soldiers.

Tired and hungry, they had to sleep rough somewhere, and many a home in Clanfield and in the villages on the path had to suffer, with food and birds stolen. No single house could resist a group of men, and women would have been fair game. No doubt in Clanfield, as in other villages, much Welsh blood was introduced.

During the reign of Henry IV we hear of several things which were happening in Clanfield.

In 1391, John Symonds and John Fisher of Radcot were again given the pontage for two years to repair the bridge there.

The Friars Court Rolls have survived dating from 1394. From these we can see that "Muschet and Steven Smith shall show the agreement of their tenament. Richard Cross, John Watter, William Pursey, John Alchurch, Robert Carter, Simon Webb, John Dokaland, John Geremer, John Holle, Stephen Camp, John Athote are in debt, Will Carter, John Rocce, John Muschet and Stephen Smith hold land by copy of Court Roll".

In 1396, at Chestlyon, Elizabeth, granddaughter of Hugh Chasterton, having married Will Garmon, now owned the estate. The owner of Chestlyon was now no longer a Chestlion by name. The Chestlion family had lasted for 120 years.

An interesting snippet comes out that John Silvin Eacheater, Oxon, Berkshire, ordered to remove the King's hand and meddle no further with the manor of Grafton and messuage and croft in Clanfield called Wyman's Place. This is the first time this reference comes to a settlement that we find on the side of Radcot road, which we will refer to later.

Henry, who had stood with his army behind Radcot bridge in 1387, now took over the land. When he was crowned his head was so full of lice that it had to be shaved and to stay bald for many months. In The History of Bampton p121, it said: "In this year (1400) ... the men of Wantage, Faringdon, Bampton and no doubt Shifford which belonged to to Henry's family rose in favour of Henry and defeated partizans of King Richard at Cirencester."

Richard had been put in prison at Pontefract, but his friends tried to get him crowned again. They stormed Windsor Castle at Christmas to capture Henry, but he had been forewarned and escaped to London with his family. He sent a force to capture Richard's friends at Cirencester and butchered them there. Richard soon died in prison in rather questionable circumstances. However, his friends kept trying to oust Henry and from 1401-1408 Wales was in revolt. Henry developed epileptic fits and died in 1413, aged 46 years.

It was an age of spiritual life and conflict. Great cathedrals were being built, yet people, led by the Lollards, were questioning the authority of the church.

In 1401, at Smithfield, London, Will Sawtre was the first Lollard to be burned for a 'heretical view of the nature of bread in the Mass'.

In 1409 John Bably, a taylor of Evesham, was burned for refusing to believe in transubstantiation, the actual changing of the Bread and Wine at the Mass into the body and blood of Jesus.

It was also an age of writers, fighters and sailors. Our ships were reaching the Baltic and the Mediterranean. Yet still every man carried on his person a short sword.

In Clanfield, in 1408, John Abraham had been illegally taken prisoner by Constance la Dispenser, Robert Rous and others from Bampton, and he was awarded £300 damages. *(Ref: Calendar of the Close Rolls, Henry IV AD 1409-1413, London HMSO 1932)*

Henry's son, Henry V, followed him to the throne. Already, during his father's illness, he had been running the country. He was a very handsome, athletic type, a man of 26 years of age. He was loyal to the Church.

A great friend of his father's, John Oldcastle, a loyal warrior and a Lollard, was handed over by him to the church in 1414, in an attempt to stop Lollardism. This was a very sad affair. John believed that the teachings of the Church regarding the Mass, i.e. that no natural bread remained after the consecration, were wrong, and that they were a corruption of the scriptures. Confession was not a necessity for salvation but contrition was.

When he was asked what honour he would pay to the crucifix he said he would wipe it and keep it clean. When asked of his attitude to the Pope he called him 'Anti-Christ'. He was declared a heretic and handed over to the secular justice to be burned.

The Lollards rose to go to London. They came in groups. The King captured them group after group, hanged 37 and sent the rest back home. In this confusion John Oldcastle had escaped, but after three years he was caught in the Welsh mountains at Cae'r Barwn near Welshpool, in December 1417. Henry's brother, John Duke of Bedford, had him tried and hung as a traitor and roasted alive as a heretic.

Henry had married Catherine of Valois, daughter of King Charles of France, in 1419 — a very lively girl. He became very ill and had to be carried on a litter. He died on 1st August 1422. His widow enjoyed herself very much at court and finally married Owen Tudor, a Welsh clerk, after three years. She had three children by him.

In this age the long bow had come from Wales and a man could fire six arrows a minute for 300 yards, compared with the crossbows which could fire one or two arrows a minute.

When Henry V died his son, Henry VI, inherited the throne. He was just nine months old. His maternal grandfather, Charles VI of France, died just one month later, and Henry was proclaimed King of France, too. When he was nine years old his forces burned Joan of Arc in France. He took over the throne in 1437, married the passionate and lovely Margaret of Anjou in 1445. During this time he completed his new educational foundations — Eton and King's College Cambridge. He began to go mad in 1453 when he was reduced to speechlessness, and from then on had bouts of madness. Meanwhile the land lay ungoverned. Piracy was rampant in the 1440s and 1450s.

In 1455 open civil war began, a court quarrel between Lancaster and York.

In 1460 there was a very wet summer. In that year, 2,000 men of York landed at Sandwich, defeated the King's forces at Northampton and took him prisoner in his tent after the battle. He was put in the Bishop's Palace in London. Edward IV, the Yorkist leader, was made King.

Henry's wife made various attempts to get him back onto the throne. He escaped, but was caught once again, wandering helplessly in Lancashire in 1465. In 1471 he was put in the Tower, and after various attempts by his wife to free him, was killed by Edward.

Henry was a very religious man, and in 1480 was seen as a Saint. When he founded Eton and King's College a yearly sum of £1s.4d. which Clanfield had to pay to the Minster Lovell Priory from the Bampton part of our parish, was transferred, so Clanfield has a share in Eton College, although, as far as is known no-one in the village ever went there.

In 1451 Thomas Chalkley, late of Clanfield, was in trouble for not appearing before the Justices of the Bench to answer William Warbilton Esq. and Marjorie, his wife, regarding a debt of £100.

Edward IV came to the throne in 1461. After the turbulent years of Henry VI, he brought stability, He was 19 years of age when he came to the throne, 6ft 3ins and very good looking — very popular with the ladies. Peace reigned and trade increased greatly. He visited Oxford in 1481, late September. He was at Woodstock, and went to Oxford to see the nearly completed Magdalen College. Just after sunset he was welcomed by a great crowd with torches, and he stopped at Magdalen for three or four nights.

His life became a battle with Warwick, who tried to run the country over his head.

Edward married Elizabeth Woodville in 1464, a widow with two boys. Warwick captured the King, who then escaped to France. Edward eventually defeated Warwick in a battle at Barnet. So ended to Battle of the Roses.

Edward spent the remaining 12 years of his reign building up the land, and died in 1483, possibly of typhoid. His eldest son, Edward V, was 12. The Barons tried to make him King. He reigned from April 9th to June 26th and was then deposed by King Edward IV's brother, Richard III, who had been helping rule the land. Edward V and his young brother were put in the Tower and disappeared.

Richard was 31 years of age. In 1483 he crushed a revolt led by the Duke of Buckingham, who was attempting to put Henry Tudor on the throne. In 1484 Richard lost his only son and then his wife. He lost the will to live. He met Henry Tudor on Bosworth Field in 1485, and should have won with his larger forces. However, the Earl of Northumbria would not commit his forces for the King and stood back, blocking his retreat. Richard rode into the battle seemingly to die.

Henry VII, born before his mother was 14 years old, was the grandson of Henry V. He came to the throne in 1485. Just two years later an attempt was made to remove him. Lambert Simnel, the son of an Oxford organ grinder, was made out to be Warwick's son, Edward VI. Henry produced the real one from the Tower. After a battle, Henry captured the lad, but instead of killing him, gave him the job of turning his spit. Later he became a falconer, and died a natural death.

In 1487 Henry had married Elizabeth, heiress of the house of York. Their son, Arthur, married Catherine of Aragon, but as both were under 15 years old they were not allowed to sleep together. He died five months later of consumption. The Queen died the next year in childbirth. The King died six years later, possibly from consumption.

Henry was a great King and Statesman. He built the first castle to have a library.

This was a great maritime age. America had been discovered by unknown sailors who talked about the Isle of Brazil, lying to the west of Ireland. In July 1480 the ships "George" and "Trinity" had been sent from Bristol to find it, but they did not sail far enough. Our sailors had previously been fishing for cod near Iceland. They met with trouble, so they sailed west for new fishing areas. These they found by 1490, around Nova Scotia.

In 1492 Columbus was trying to organise an expedition to find the land mass. Henry failed to back him. Spain did, and received the honour when he discovered America. So Henry backed John Cabot, who officially discovered Newfoundland in 1497, and his son, Sebastian, found Hudson Bay the following year.

Meanwhile, in the Netherlands, Erasmus was preaching against the establishment and made bitter attacks against the worship of images and relics, and the worldliness of the clergy.

In Germany, Luther was challenging the power of the Pope.

In England, Cranmer was making a name for himself, and printing began in London in 1470. But when Henry died in 1509 a new door was about to open in England that was to affect every parish in the land.

In the meantime, in Clanfield, at Chestlyon, the Gernan family gave way to Ralph Lathan, a London Goldsmith. The last Will Gernan had died and he had left it to his aunts, Joan and Elizabeth. Elizabeth married Sir Thomas Hill, and it eventually came to her daughter, Elizabeth, who had married Ralph Lathan. Ralph was in disgrace with Henry VIII, but he was pardoned in 1509, when Henry came to the throne. Like many who financed Henry, he became very wealthy, and in 1509 he was given the job to be 'during pleasure' searcher in the Port of London, with moiety in the Court of Forfeitures. Ralph bought many estates in the land, but he only kept Clanfield for seven years.

At Fryam, or Friar's Court, there was an interesting Court Roll of 1499/1500. It came under Quennington Commandery. Brother John Bothe was the commander there. It was as follows:

Thomas Osmond held Clanfield and Radcot as 6 virgates of land and pays 66s.8d per year. He is a tenant at will (this meant that either party could end the tenancy whenever they wanted). *He is to find a priest for the chapel as others have done before. John Umfrey senior holds 1/4 virgate, and Notte and Bellham hayes Closes, 2 acres each and 20 acres of arable paying 20s. per year. He also holds a toft (house site) and close of 1 1/2 acres lying in Losmede formerly held by John Reynolds 20d. a year.*

John Benson holds a close and messuage, 1/4 virgate and 5r formerly held by Will Aylif at 7s. a year. Dominus Robert Mulchet, Chaplain has a mess. and V of free land formerly held by Richard Mulchet at 3s. a year and also 2 tappers worth 13d. to place before the statue of St. John in the chapel at Clanfield. Aldeln Whytes has a mess. called Brus, 1 acre close and 1/4 virgate and 1 acre formerly held by Will Aylif at 6/- per year. Will Besell holds close called Wymans 12d. per annum. Henry Janyor holds a close next to the parish church formerly held by his father Will at 12d. per year. John Vafrey holds a mess. and close of 1 virgate and 1 1/2 acres with 1/2 a farendal lying in the meadow called Whydan 25s. and 4d. a year.

In this document we see that the tenant had to provide a priest for the chapel as others had done, and that in the chapel was a statue of St John. We do not know where in Friars Court the chapel was, but in recent years a portion of tracery, possibly from out of the chapel window, was dredged up out of the moat. The estate is put at 6 virgates or 1 1/2 hides. We remember in the 100 Rolls that they held 1 hectares and 4 acres in Old Clanfield and in Weald or New Clanfield, one ploughland with 10 acres at Radcot. We also note that Church Close, in which the Plough Hotel now stands, was once part of Friars Court Manor.

At Southwick a series of courts were held from 1476–1508. In July 1476 they had a problem over a Ville called Sullebury. The villein by birth, Richard Cottman, and his issue Thomas, had both died with no known issue. There were two free tenants attending the court, William Warbulton and John Attmore. Five people were named: William Wedger, Richard Yapman, James Pyper, John Wheeler and Will King. The last four had to repair their tenements before the next court. Yapman is a name that survived in Clanfield until the 1970s as Yateman. It means 'the man in charge of the gate'.

On October 19th 1496 Philip King, John Wheeler and Henry Wetherhamhad allowed their tenements to fall into disrepair, and had to repair them before the next court or pay 13s.4d, 6s.8d and 10s. respectively.

William King, a copyholder, had died. The Lord took a Heriot, the tax paid on death, of one cow or its value, 6s.8d. His son, Phillip, asked to become a tenant.

William Pyper and John King took a tenement called 'The Marsh'. This would be somewhere in association with Marsh Lane, either the meadow or the Clanfield end.

On 25th October 1502 some of the above were in trouble again. John Wheeler, Henry Wotherham and Will Pyper let their roofs become ruined, and they were ordered to repair them by the next court or pay 40s. Obviously they needed rethatching.

On 15th October 1503 "John and Matilda Chambers, man and wife take a mess. with lands and gardens adj. of 1½ V. They hold it for their lives at 22s.10½ a year. They shall maintain and repair the mess. at their own expense. They shall pay 20s. as 'entrance money'.

On 17th October 1506: "John and Will King, villeins, live at Broughton and Lechlade without permission. Rich Draper took corn by horse and cart from his Lord. John Wheeler and John Bucket took trees, corn and barley. John Bucket unlawfully entered Trapdoro house. Eadrigg Legg failed to pay a fine. All are held at mercy (guilty) and pay 6s.8d."

On 14th October 1508: "John Wheeler holding a mess., and 1¾V (Virgates) has encroached on land by the rectory. The Bailiff shall take away his land as already there is a writ against him in Westminster of trespass against his Lord. John King is living in Clanfield in a tenancy of Rich Draper on another manor. Will King is living at Broughton. Robert King at Lechlade. All are villeins land without licence."

Other small titbits of information come to us.

In 1467 Will Janver, late of Clanfield, husbandman, for not appearing to answer Will Gernan on a debt of 4 marks.

In 1461 a Chantry Roll says there were 57 'Houselyng' people and that there were lands of 11d in value to fund a lamp in the church and 5/- a year to fund an 'Obit', no incumbent or ornaments. *(Ref: **Richardson, Charles. Oxford Collections: vol. 1**)*

'Houselyng people' were communicants. 'An Obit' was a service in commemoration of a dead person. The parish was served by an outside curate and there were no sacred images.

Two early wills survive from this time, John Pope Clerk, one of the Bampton vicars, died in 1499. He left 3s 4d to help repair Clanfield church, and 20 of the best elms in Cote and Yelford to the Abbess of Elstow to repair Clanfield Rectory, also 6s 8d to do up the road between Clanfield and Radcot — a very thoughtful man. It was possible that he may have been our curate at one time.

Dame Emote Farmer died in 1501 at Witney and left to her son, Richard, "all my land lying in Clanfield, Beney and Westweld". By her first marriage she was a Wenman, a family who soon enter our story.

★ ★ ★

Chapter 6

Henry VIII

SO MUCH begins to happen here, that surely this King must have a chapter on his own. Henry was the second son of Henry VII. The first son, Arthur, died of consumption just after he had married at 15 years of age. Henry VIII came to the throne at 17, and was crowned at 18. He married his brother's widow, Katherine of Aragon, who claimed to be a virgin. They had one daughter, five stillbirths and many miscarriages.

Henry was impatient, he badly wanted a son, and tried to get a divorce. Cardinal Wolsey would not help, so Thomas Cranmer obtained his position by helping Henry to get it. Luther made Henry's break possible with Rome. Luther's reformation almost annihilated the prestige of Rome as a religious centre for some years.

In 1527, the Holy See had been sacked by the armies of Charles V, Emperor of Germany and the King of Spain. Lutherans accepted the Lollards. Ann Boleyn, Henry's new girlfriend, played hard to get, but by January 1533 had to get married, and a divorce was rushed through. He married her on 28th May, but the child was a daughter. In his search for a son, thought so necessary for the realm, Henry passed through other marriages. Only Jane Seymour, who died in childbirth, provided him with a son, Edward, who would follow him upon his death in 1547.

We have a series of interesting Rolls from Friars Court for 1511–1520. It was the Clanfield, Grafton, Bourton, Westwell court, with a view of Frankpledge. Frankpledge was of 10th century origin in London and Kent, whereby people had to group themselves in tens, each member to be responsible for the rest of the ten or tything. Later on all had to belong.

To take a view of Frankpledge meant to hold court. Several Lords of the manor could hold it, and then people had no need to go to the Hundred Court. The Roll for Friars Court said: "Each court has at first Essoins nil, (meaning it is fully attended). Property is accounted for." In October 1511 they say that "John Clark, to whom was transferred at the last court the house of Joan, widow of Will Humphry, holds the house in ruinous condition and he will be fined 10s. at the next court if it is not repaired. Henry Janver's house is also in a ruinous condition and he will be fined 5s. at the next court if if it is not repaired." (Neither did anything, it would seem, for they were fined 10s. and 5s. respectively at the next court.)

In November 1512 Janvers still had not repaired his house, and he was to be fined again. In the court of April 1513, Janvers had repaired it, but, no doubt as he had been such a nuisance, they decided that he would have to do some more to his house or be fined 3s.4d by October 1513. At the same court his widow is responsible for those repairs, or would be fined 40d. She was in trouble for selling bread under weight, so no doubt they were bakers. (She had also been fined 2d for the same offence in May 1512).

Ditches came under the jurisdiction of the court. In May 1512, John Lococke had a ditch next to the road called St Leonard's in a bad state of repair. John Clark also had a ditch in a close as far as Charny that needed repairs. The rivulet called the Millke, or brook, as far as Charny, needed repairs. In 1512, John Clark was fined 5/-for not repairing his ditch. In April 1513 he had still done nothing. But no more is heard of him, so he must have repaired it in the end.

Bridges also came under the court. In November 1513 "the jurors present that Ashen Bridge be repaired under fine of 5s." In November 1518, the bridge near the land of John Turfrey needed repairs and had to be done by the following Christmas or he be fined 4s. In November 1519 they ordered that no one should break the bridge made by John Clark on his land, under penalty of 20d.

There must have been some trouble here. The Court Rolls goes on: "they present that John Turfrey has blocked the cart way into the field of John Clark. He is to unblock it or be fined 2s. They present that John Clark and John Clark Jun. and Thos. Lathar and all other tenants of this manor are not to make destruction to each other or be fined 40d."

Road repairs came up on November 1512, when the whole village (Friars Court end, presumably) had not sufficiently repaired the causeway lying near the chapel of St Leonard's.

In May 1512, the butts within the house needed repairs. In November 1512 there was a fine of 5s. for not repairing the butts sufficiently. By April 1513, nothing had been done and if the 'Butte and sagittandum' (shooting butts) has not been repaired they would be fined 6s.8d. Other weapons had begun to replace bows. The pinfold also needed repairs or they would be fined 10d.

Neither of these had been repaired by the October court in 1513. The vill (sic) was fined 5s. for the former and would be fined another 6s.8d if nothing was done and Jakeman, presumably the man responsible for the pinfold, was fined 40d on the latter.

Boundaries were very important. In November 1518, Will Pawling had destroyed the boundary marks in his close between the Butts and the land of the Prior of St. John to the hurt of Thomas Lathar. It was to be put back by Christmas, or he would be fined 6s.8d.

Animals were the court's concern. In November 1512, John Wenman of Chestlion had put 6 beasts in the church close belonging to Henry Janver. He had to take them out. In April 1514, he again allowed his cattle to stray onto the manor and was fined 20d.

In April 1513, John Clark had a white sheep, a year old, off the Prior of Exeter since the Feast of St. Mark. The Prior was allowed to have it back for 12d. In October 1513 another white sheep, about two years old, lay in the hands of the farmer of the Demesne. It could be redeemed for 12d. In November 1518, Will Pawling had allowed several of his cows to stray into the customary close held by Janver, at the east end of the church. He was fined 20d.

Behaviour also came under the court. In May 1512 Elizabeth, wife of Aldelm Whiting, had a cloak of Will Andrew, valued at 16d. She had to return it and pay a fine of 6d. She also took five 'anadas' of goods of John Carter valued at l0d. She was to return them and pay 6d. John Chambers was fined l0d. Aldelm Whiting was fined l0d.

Richard Greford and Matilda Chambed were fined 10d for fishing by night in the common pond of Clanfield and taking fish worth 4d. Will Hicks was fined 4d for selling bread under weight in November 1512. In April 1513, Will Baker of Faringdon was also fined 2d. Will Hicks was again fined 2d. John Duret of Faringdon was fined 2d.

In November 1519, there had been a fight between John Wenman and Will Pawling with Thomas Lathar. John and Will were fined 12d each. Will had apparently cut some of the growing corn of Thomas Lathar. For this he was also fined 20d. John had molested animals in the common field and he was fined 40d.

There was a lot of trouble in Clanfield at that time. In November 1520, there was more trouble. Will Pawling had tried to take the close of Janvers at the east of the church, of which Thomas Lathar was the tenant. Will had to pay a fine of 40d. John Wenman was also in trouble again. He had dumped rubbish in the common pasture. This had to be removed and his ditch, called Belbam Heyridge, had to be cleared under penalty of a 20d fine.

It was very important that men obeyed the farmers court. In April 1513 Richard Beytham (tenant of Robert Reynold), John Clerkesen, Aldelm Whiting were all fined for cutting the corn too soon before common permission had been granted. They were fined 2d

Relationships between the different manors also came up. It was agreed in April 1513 that the court of Friars and of Richard Wenman's (Chestlyon) should meet in the church of Clanfield (the nave) on the feast of St. Philip and St. James and 'take view of all Mete and Brinde' in the lordship (boundaries and stones) and that the said Mete be put in the right place at pain of a 6d fine.

Land, too, was transferred. Birnis, a mess. (messuage), close, part of a close of a quarter virgate and half an acre, formerly let to Will Alif at 6s. a year, was now let to Aldels Whiting and his wife. In October 1518, Robert Wakefield and his wife, Agnes, heiress of John Lamboard, asked for 1 virgate freeland, once in the tenancy of Robert Muachet, the Chaplain, at a rent of 4s. per year.

Will Bezell, when he died, had a close of freeland called Wymans, lying between the house at Clanfield and Radcot towns end and the Moor close. This now had to go to John Fettiplace, his heir of full age, at 12d a year. In November 1518, Henry Janver and Agnes, his wife, gave up a close down by the cemetery of Clanfield church at 12d per year to Thomas Lathar.

Southwick has a court roll surviving for 1521 and 1528. These are not from the Court Leet, but just manor rolls. In the former, John King, son of Will King, was still in trouble for living outside the manor. He came to the court, and was summoned at 50 years of age. Also, Henry and Will Cotmore, sons of John Cotmore deceased, were living at Brize Norton without licence. They had to appear at the next court.

In the latter roll, Will Carter took over 1 mess. and a quarter virgate formerly held by Henry Weder, to hold it during his life and that of his two sons, John and Thomas. Also, Thomas Fettiplace had taken over the estate of his late father, John, called Jaccatis, at 40d. per year.

Henry VIII lived in an age when the power of Rome was being challenged. In England, the Lollards were continually challenging it. In the Netherlands it was Erasmus, and in Germany it was Luther. Henry realised that he, in England, could gain at least financially by breaking with Rome. He fell out with Cardinal Wolsey, the son of an Ipswich cattle dealer. He had crossed Rome by getting his divorce and, in 1533, he and Archbishop Crammer were excommunicated. So he got Parliament to stop sending monies to Rome.

The breach with Rome was finalised when he got Parliament to make him the Supreme Head of the Church of England. He then proceeded to regularise preaching in the churches, and in 1536 he produced the Ten Articles of the Church of England, influenced by Luther's teaching. Priests were ordered to recite to their congregations the Articles of Faith, the Commandments and the Lord's Prayer.

The images in the churches were despoiled by Thomas Cromwell. At the same time he kept the Lollards in their place.

John Longland, Bishop of Lincoln, set out to eradicate heresy from his diocese. In Henry's reign there was considerable persecution of the Lollards. He had no patience with them. In John Fox's 'Acts and Monuments' are listed, among all the others, those people in this area who were reported to the authorities. One John Pope of West Hendred was the government agent in this area, and he went through reporting on people in 1520.

In the Burford area, one had bought a Bible, others were meeting to talk about the bible and their faith, some had spoken out against pilgrimage and the Mass. Among those was John Clark of Clanfield. He had been heard to say "all the world was as well hallowed as the church and churchyard, and that it was as good to be buried in a field as in the church or churchyard."

The people who were reported, under pain of being burned at the stake, were under the orders of John Langland, Bishop of Lincoln, who had "everyone to go upon a market day thrice about the market of Burford and then to stand up on the highest steps of the cross there, for a quarter of an hour (there were faggots to remind them of the burning of martyrs). Everyone also had to bear a faggot of wood before the procession on a certain Sunday at Burford from the Quire door going out to the Quire going in, all the High Mass kneeling with the same before the High Altar.

Also everyone was to fast bread and ale only every Friday and on Corpus Christi on bread and water only during their lives. They also had to say, every Sunday, Our Lady's Psalter once through.

None of them was to hide their mark of the cross (branded) in the cheek, neither with cap, hood, etc., nor to allow their beard to grow past 14 days, nor to hunt together except in the open at market, fair, church, inn or alehouse where others may see their humiliation."

Perhaps time stopped the penance in the end, but did John for the rest of his life carry the hideous scar on his cheek? No doubt, he would have eventually grown a beard to cover it.

(Ref: History of Burford R.J. Rook, p.97)

In 1536 Erasmus died, as well as Tyndale, the bible translator who had finished his translation, and was strangled and burnt as a heretic in Brussels. Revolts broke out in the north. Henry hated Tyndale, but his bible, completed by his friend John Rogers, was made available to all in 1537 by Thomas Cromwell. (This was the year in which Henry's mother died, a victim of 16th century medicine, and his son, Edward was also born.)

In 1538 Henry ordered that a printed bible of the largest volume, the Coverdale version, be put in every church and be paid for by the parson of the parish — a very costly and precious thing. He ordered that a register of every birth, death and marriage be kept in every parish, but unfortunately most of the earlier records are gone.

Henry loved money. Thomas Cromwell was good at getting it for him. The religious houses, now being past their original intention, except for providing food for beggars, had great wealth. Henry cast envious eyes on their possessions, now left undefended by his break with Rome.

In 1534 he ordered a list of the value of all the properties to be made. This was called the Valer Ecclesiasticus. Then Henry's minister set about dissolving the religious houses. In 1536, all houses under £200 were dissolved. In 1538-40 all the rest were dissolved. It was done very carefully and very humanely. Heads were pensioned off, priests were given livings. In all about 5,000 monks, 16,000 friars and 2,000 nuns were sent out into the world.

In 1540 the mighty order of the Knights Hospitalers was dissolved. John Leyland rode around England in this period trying to record and save all the libraries that were at risk, and then through his studies went mad!

Many people made fortunes out of this great upheaval. The prosperity of the period is reflected in the fact that many people could pay cash for these estates, but as far as Henry was concerned, he soon squandered it.

In 1539 the nuns of Elstow were dissolved. In 1530 they had been amongst four religious houses disciplined by Bishop Langland. They wore shoes and clothes which were too pretty. Their headgear was too high and needed bringing down over the face. *(Ref: Wigram, Rev SR: Chronicles of the Abbey of Elstow, Parker and Co. 1885)*

When the deeds of August 26th 1539 gave all to the Crown, there were 24 nuns pensioned off. The Abbess was given £50 a year, the Prioress £4 per year, the former Prioress and Sexton were given £3.6s.8d. a year, nuns £2.13s.4d. per year. Half was paid at Michaelmas and half at Ladyday. In the *Valer Ecclesiasticus*, the Elstow estate in Clanfield was valued in the following ways:

Vicarage

Abbey of Elstow proprietor of Rectory. Hugh Thomas was the vicar. Vicarage valued at tithe and profits — £8. Procurations and synodals to the Archdeacon and Bishop of Lincoln 10s.7^3/4d. Same to the Bishop for indemnity 3s. These were paid annually to a priest to serve the cure by ancient custom, but not allowed on expenses (£4).

Total: 13s.7^3/4d. Clear: £7.6s.4^1/4d. One tenth paid annually to the Crown – 14s.7^1/4d.

Rent of one mess. and certain arable lands and meadow owned by or payable to Bishop of Lincoln 10s.

Rectory of Clanfield £5.6s.8d.

Expenses: Eton College (pension to Eton college of rents of Abbey of Elstow for tithes in Bampton) 23s., sometimes 24s.

Archdeacon of Exeter for procuration (looking after Clanfield's affairs) and

synodals (cost of paying for a synod) 12s.6^3/4d. Vicar of Clanfield 3 qrs of wheat, 3 qrs of barley for pension £1.10s.

When the rectory was sold to John Edmonds it was described as: "County of Bedford, Parcels remaining formerly of monastery of Cheistowe. The Rectory of Clanfield in the county of Oxon.The farm of the whole rectory there together with all great Tithes, woods, and underwoods, fruits from House, garden, crofts, meadows, pastures, together with all parts and emoluments of the same rectory, except the advowsom of the parish church."

"This is in the tenure of John Edmonds of Kencot, having been demised to him by an indenture of 20th February in the 20th year of Henry 1528–29, for him to hold from the Feast of Nativity of John the Baptist next coming after the above date for a term of 10 years, paying this in equal portions of Christmas day and Feasts of St. John the Baptist. To the Lord King.

To the Vicar of the church of Clanfield for time being three-quarters of the fruits of tithes and three-quarters of ORDEI (3 qr wheat, 3 qr barley/hay) *[See Valer Ecclesiasticus]*.

To Eton money of value of 23s.

To Rector of Alvescot 6s.8d per annum for time the indenture lasts.

Total 106s.8d.

Examined by Will Cavendish Audit."

[Note to say that John Edmonds is now of Deddington, county of Oxon. John Edmonds also bought Friars Court.]

The Parsonage of Clanfield 106s.5d.

The clear value of the premises is £17.14s.9d of which one tenth is 35s.5d. There remains clear £15.19s.4d of which rates at 20 years purchase amounteth to the sum of £319.6s.8d.

Add thereto for woods 66s.8d. The whole £322.13s.4d to be paid in form following, i.e. in hand £161.6s.8d and within three months £161.6s.8d. Mem: The King must discharge him of all encumbrances except leases and rent of woods. Signed Rich Will. Whorwood, Thos, Malow, gents. Edward North, John Williams, 1543."

In another reference Edmonds had the advowsom as well.

In the *Valor Ecclesiasticus*, the Clanfield estate of the Hospitallers of Quenington was valued as follows:

Rent of both free tenants	15s.4d
Rent of Customary tenant	£8.0s.11d
Farm of manor by long lease	66s.8d
Total	£11.7s.7d

Expenses rent paid to the Earl of Shrewsbury	66s.8d
Rent paid to Mr Fettiplace	13$\frac{1}{2}$d
Total	67s.9$\frac{1}{2}$d
Net	£7.19s.9$\frac{1}{2}$d

(Ref: Valor Ecclesiasticus: Temp Henry VIII, vol. II, 1814)

Friars Court was sold to John Edmonds, late of Kencot, now Deddington, who was tenant of Clanfield Rectory. The record says:

"Parcels of land and Possessions formerly of the Prior of St. John of Jerusa-

lem in England Manor of Clanfield in the County of Oxfordshire. A parcel of
the former Commandry of Quenington, Gloucestershire.
  Rents and Issue from divers free Tenements there on oath 19s.5d.
  Rents of customary Tenants annually £7.18s.8d.

  The farm of Capital Mansion of the said Manor in the County of Oxon with all
  lands etc. belonging, without woods and underwoods as Richard Clark holds it
  by Ind. under seal of Convent of former St. John in England, rent 66s.8d.

Profits of court	*7d*
Common fines etc. annually	*3s.4d*
Total	*£12.8s.1d*

  Examined by Will. Bygg, aud.
  (Note: The King's Majesty hath no more lands, ten. of Clanfield, save these
  parcels by me Will Bygg.) The rest had all been taken."
  (Ref: Valor Ecclesiasticus: Temp Henry VIII, vol. II, 1814)

A further description was found of the lands granted to John Edmonds in 1535 by
Henry VIII:

  "The Manor of Clanfield parcell of the possession of the late Priory of St.
  John's Jerusalem in England. Thereby growing about the situation of the said
  Manor and of three tenaments pertaining to the same and in the land thereto
  belonging 200 polling Elyms and ashes of 80 and 100 years, growing up to
  timber, plough bote, and carte bote, which he bath byn accustomed to have
  there and for tymber to repair the said three tenaments and to maynetayne the
  hedge and fence about the said lands and 100 resydent value at 8d. the tree,
  which in the total £3.6s.8d by me Will Cowper (Cobby)."

Richard Clark died in Clanfield in 1571 and in his will he stated: 'To Solomon my
eldest son £4.0s.0d at 20 years of age and the great pot that came from Fryam Court
and a cupboard that came from FryamCourt and also six sheep." As he had four
children under 20 years of age it would seem that his father was tenant at Friars Court
at the dissolution.

Friars Court was further described, when it was passed within the family in June
1548, as 12 Mess 300 land 160a Meadow, 100a Pasture, 200a common pasture, 20a
woods, 100s. rent. Free fishing in the Thames in Clanfield, Welde, Burton, Grafton
and the Rectory and advowsom of the Vic. of Clanfield.

Southwick was not declared in detail in the *Valer Ecclesiasticus*, but put in one
large amount. Southwick surrendered on 7th April 1538. The Prior was Will Norton

and he was given the very large pension of £66.13s.4d per annum. There were 12 canons, all of whom received pensions of Wrothesley. The Priory went to John White, 'a mean, fawning servant' who grumbled about it when he pulled the church down and made the property into his home. He paid £251.13s.4d. *(Ref: Doubleday, H Arthur and Page, William ed. The Victoria History of the Counties of England: Hampshire and the Isle of Wight vol. II. Westminster, 1903)*

In the Minister's accounts for 1540–2 the King granted R. Ingram by letter patent the Southwick holding in Clanfield.

Richard Ingram of Wolford, Warwickshire had to pay a rent of 5s.7d. He paid £218.4s.2d for Southwick and two other manors at Northaston and Aldeborne in Wiltshire. *(Ref: Letters and Papers, Foreign and Domestic: Henry VIII, vol. 15. London HMSO 1896. Kraus Reprint Ltd 1965)* Ingram soon sold Clanfield, however, in 1542 to Will Reynolds. It was called the manor of Clanveld, Oxon, with appurtenances in Clanveld and Alscott, Oxon'. *(Ref: Letters and Papers, Foreign and Domestic: Henry VIII, vol. 17: 137, 2. London HMSO 1900. Kraus Reprint Ltd. 1965)*

The lands owned by Osney were also passed over in two parts. In 1542, the Osney land in Clanfield was given to Christ Church College, Oxford. A later reference is made to a part of Clanfield Manor under Christ Church being leased with Burton Rectory to Will. Dryng and son, in the tenement of Wm. Pallyng. *(Ref: Letters and Papers, Foreign and Domestic: Henry VIII, vol. 21 part 2. London HMSO 1910. Kraus Reprint Ltd. 1965)* It is listed as "land in Clanfield granted to the Cathedral of Oxford two tofts with two closes lying in the township and fields of Clanfield in the tenure of Will. Pallyng and rent per annum of 10s".
(Ref: PRO E315/827, N° 47).

A second estate was listed as Pallyngs estate, is latterly called Belham Hays Billy's in Fox Meadow.
(Ref: 1610 CH, Ch. 812).

Henry's bankruptcy forced the sale of the monasteries' land, so he did not become an absolute monarch as he could have become, or he could have given some for education and charity as he had first meant to. It was the gentry or rising yeomen who did best out of the sale.

Another account which comes to us from this period was the Muster Rolls, which were drawn up in 1542 of archers and billmen. Clanfield had nine men to bear arms. The lists for our area were as follows:-

Bampton Hundred:

Wytney parish	70	*Browghton*	2
Bampton Delan	3	*Brightenden*	11
Bampton Halymote	20	*Astall*	13
Bampton Doyly	2	*Kentcott*	2
Hadden	2	*Burton*	12
Lewe	4	*Chimney*	6
Bresingnorton	10	*Helforde*	5
Burforde borough with parishes	88	*Fylkyns*	3
Upton and Signett	3	*Stanlake*	20
Aulscott	7	*Cockethrup*	3
Bradwell	14	*Kelmecot*	5
Canfield	9	*Astoon*	15
Brighthampton	2	*Westwell (harness only)*	12
Duckelington	12		
Shifford	6		

(Brightendon lies between Standlake and Brighthampton.)

(Ref: Letters and Papers, Foreign and Domestic: Henry VIII vol. 17. London HMSO 1900. Kraus Reprint Ltd. 1965)

During this period Chestlyon, which had been owned by Ralph Latham the goldsmith and Elizabeth (Hill) his wife, was sold to Richard and Anne Wenman of Carswell, Witney, a local clothier and wood stapler. Richard died in 1533 and left it to his son, Thomas. Thomas became a knight and died leaving it to his oldest son, Richard of Thase, who let his younger brother, Thomas, hold it for him. When Richard died his son, Thomas, tried to get possession from his uncle Thomas, but it seems that Uncle Thomas held on to it. **(Ref: C. Pro. Ser 11. 193/29)** When Uncle Thomas died he left it to his two sons, Richard and John.

It was during Henry's reign that the first wills began to appear in Clanfield. In 1546 Clanfield was transferred from the Diocese of Lincoln to Oxford. Perhaps the wills survived because Oxford was a new broom and better organised. Will Pawling (Pallying), tenant of the Osney land, died in 1552. He left it to his son, Andrew. He left 40s. and 3 yards of land belonging to Osney after the death of 'me and my wife'. He left 2d. to the 'mother' church of Oxford and 4d. to the poor man's chest.

It may have been that an appeal had recently been made for the mother church and also to help provide relief for the poor after the dissolution of the monasteries. William's other son, John, married a widow, one of the Turner family who bought Southwick, and her son, Drew, was later to hold that manor.

When Thomas Barlow died in 1547 he left 2d. to the mother church of Oxford, 12d. to the church of Clanfield and 'one of my coats' to Andrew Taylor. The rest of his estate he left to his wife and daughter, Joan.

Edward Martin died on 6th October 1546, a small farmer. He left 2d. to the mother church of Oxford, 2d. to the church altar of Clanfield. To his son, John, he left an ox bullock, to Christian, his daughter he left a heifer, and to Margaret, his maid, he left a chylor sheep. To Thomas he left his house and to Thomas and Toby (his sons) he left "half of my crop each to pay half and do half for two years space. Also to them half my household and also two mares of dun colour. To Thomas, my cousin, and to my wife her part, to have them whilst she is a widow."

The Oxford church mentioned in these wills was the cathedral, and I think the chylor sheep mentioned means a white sheep.

In the years 1542–46, Henry raised £430,000 in subsidies from the owners of land, both spiritual and temporal. They had to pay over three years, half the first year and a quarter each of the next two. The Clanfield list of payments was as follows:-

8s.4d	John Reynolds	£20.00
3s.8d	Will Pye	£11.00
3s.8d	Will Pawling	£11.00
10d	Thos. Whitehorn	£5.00
10d	Edw. Marston	£5.00
18d	Rich. Palzeke	£9.00
10d	Nicholas	£5.00
10d	Will. Pallynge ye younger	£5.00
4d	Simon Virarey	45s
12d	John Clark	£6.00
4d	Alex Reynolds	£4.00
3d	James Edney	£3.00
4d	John Luckock	£4.00
3d	John Rogers	£3.00
1d	Henrie Rogers	20s
2d	Andrew Pawling	40s
1d	Thomas Laffer	20
10d	John Pyp	£5.00
1d	Will. Carter	20s
2d	Robert Merett	40s
2d	Thomas Salow	40s

1d	*Will. Andrew*	*20s*
2d	*John Cotta (Colett)*	*40s*
1d	*John Martin*	*20s*
1d	*Ellen Martin*	*20s*
1d	*Allys Collett*	*20s*
1d	*John Hadde*	*20s*
1d	*Robert Edherly*	*20s*

From this list we see that Will. Pawling, Thos. Barlow, Richard Yateman, are among those whose wills have been quoted. The most wealthy was John Reynolds who owned Southwick Manor. For some reason the Wenmans of Chestlyons are not mentioned — neither are the Edmonds, because Friars Court had not been made over by then.

★ ★ ★

Chapter 7

Henry VIII's Family

Edward VI 1547–53

WHEN Henry died, his son Edward, a lad of nine, came to the throne. The land was run by his uncle, the Duke of Somerset, who became the Regent. Somerset lasted as Regent for only two years, a very hectic two years in which, as an ardent Protestant, he tried to move too fast in his fight against 'superstition and idolatry'.

Henry's officials had not finished confiscating all ecclesiastical properties. In the churches all paintings and sculptures of the old faith that were left were removed. Services were to be held in English. Priests were allowed to marry, and were now called Ministers. Mass was forbidden. Ridley led a move to get rid of the stone altars and replace them with the 'Table of the Lord'. He and others had realised that this was an appendage from the Jewish Temple, and was not the 'Table of the Lord' around which Jesus and His disciples sat in a Jerusalem home.

This was the age of Latimer, a great preacher, philosopher and story teller, who could raise a mob with his light-hearted approach.

We do not know how much Clanfield was affected by all these changes. In 1461 the Roll said we had no ornaments, and our stone altar had disappeared. If our services had been in Latin it must have been a tremendous change for English to be used, though I expect many grumbled.

But one thing certainly did affect us. With the disappearance of the religious houses, the free meals for the beggars and poor also went. In 1540 the clergy were asked to make an appeal from the pulpits that people be asked to leave money for the poor in their wills. This was later organised in the hands of the churchwarden and two others, later called the overseers to the poor, and a poor box was put in each church.

The wills of Clanfield reveal such a change. In 1546 Edward Martin had left 2d. to the church altar in Clanfield. But in 1549, when William Carter died, he left 4d. to the poor man's chest. William Carter Snr. left the same in 1550, Joan Carter left the same in 1553 and William Pawling left 4d. in 1552. Nicholas Samuel left 2d.

The Duke of Somerset, however, was moving too fast for the ordinary people. He brought about his own downfall when he tried to stop enclosure by law. This might have helped the ordinary people, but the men of power still wanted enclosure. So in October 1549 he was replaced by John Dudley, the Earl of Warwick, and was executed in 1551.

Warwick tried to get the king more involved in the running of the land, with some success, but the King's time was running out. A plague of sweating sickness went through the land in 1551 (as had also happened in 1508, 1517, and 1524). In 1553 Edward died of consumption. Before he died he had altered the law of succession, and Lady Jane Grey, daughter-in-law of the Duke of Northumberland, became Queen. But the people objected that it was a plot to exclude both of Henry's daughters — Mary and Elizabeth. Many wanted to go back to the old faith, and so Mary, daughter of Katherine of Aragon, was proclaimed Queen.

Edward died a Protestant, but now a great change was to come over the land. For five years England was filled with terror as Mary sought to bring the old faith back by force. All Catholics were freed from prison, all Protestant leaders were encouraged to flee overseas. Those who, like Cranmer and Ridley, refused were imprisoned. In 1554 England was officially brought back to Rome. From 1555–1558 some 282 heretics, of which one third were clergy and a fifth were women, were burnt. At Oxford, in Broad Street where the cross stands in the road, Ridley and Latimer were burnt. Cranmer recanted. As it was raining so hard he was allowed to speak in St. Mary's Church in the High. But regaining his courage, he attacked the faith instead, and was stopped, taken out and burnt. Priests were ordered to leave their wives or they would get no pension. But just as Somerset went too far, so did Mary. The public would not stand seeing so many leaders burnt, and they began to see them as martyrs. Mary's record was appalling. Every week there were, on average, two people burnt.

John Foxe wrote a book of Lollard martyrs up to the time of Henry VIII. He had been born in a wealthy home in Boston, Lincs. His father had died while he was young, and his stepfather was a rigid Romanist. He came to Oxford, and during his second year at Magdalen, the trio Pearson, Teatwood and Filner were burnt in the green meadow at Windsor by the Thames.

He became a Protestant at Oxford, and resigned in 1545 to save being expelled and went to live at Coventry. He fled the country, to France, as soon as Mary became Queen. After her death he came back to London, ill and destitute, in October 1559. His list of all martyrs was eventually updated to the death of Elizabeth, and his *Acts and Munaments* was published in 1563. He died in 1587. The list stood as follows:

Henry VII burnt 10, Henry VIII burnt 81, Edward VI burnt 2 before he abolished burning, Mary burnt 283, Elizabeth burnt 2.

However, sad as this was, it pales into insignificance compared with the Inquisition which slaughtered all Protestants in Spain and Italy, the consequence of which, economically, these countries still pay for today, no doubt — for they killed their best and most go-ahead stock.

Mary is remembered for one practical thing. She placed the repair of all roads on the roll of the parish, and all had to give the equivalent of four days of eight hours work per year.

Mary died a sad woman who could not have her own way. She married Philip of Spain in 1554, which was not very popular. She thought she was pregnant, but instead had a fatal disease. Her husband left her after one year and went back to Spain. She died seeing England recoiling from Rome in 1558.

Elizabeth, Mary's half-sister, came to the throne to reign for 25 years. She was much wiser than her sister and made no strong religious conviction that would offend any part of her people. Her first act which gave confidence was when she called in all the debased coinage of her father. Unfortunately, it was later devalued by the increase of gold and silver that came from raiding the Spanish possessions.

She gradually allowed the Protestants to regain their position in the country, and so in 1570 she found herself excommunicated by Pope Pius V. The reaction she had to face was twofold. Catholics, now seen as rebels, sought to bring back Mary of Scotland to be Queen. The second one was more of a problem. A school of priests, the Jesuit Mission, was set up on the Continent to be deliberately sent into England to 'bring her back to the faith'. England, however, saw this as a political move, and did not want to be tied to Rome economically as well as spiritually. The Catholics who left Oxford set up a seminary abroad as a centre of Catholic beauty. Scores of young English attached to the old religion went there and then came back to England.

To try and combat this, all those who had sons abroad were to bring them back and swear loyalty. Jesuits and priests would be punished. Priests were seen as rebels. Priests were searched for up and down the land. The priest's rooms hidden away in the large surviving houses of our land are relics of that age.

The act of the Pope and the deliberate incursion of the priests into our land meant that the Catholics, who would have been granted freedom under Elizabeth, became persecuted and from 1585 any Catholic priest in our land could be prosecuted. But this was a brief period compared with the persecution of the Lollards, and small scale compared with the burnings by Mary.

To encourage the faith, Elizabeth ordered a new Prayer Book and people were fined 12d if they did not attend the church. The Catholics, at first, were allowed to have their own Mass. The extreme Protestants, now called the Puritans, never however had the backing of Elizabeth.

Her other great problem, of course, was Spain. This land was exploiting the discovery of America. All the wealth of gold and silver built up by the ancient peoples was now being shipped back to Spain. Elizabeth's buccaneers were seizing the gold. In 1588 Spain sent an Armada of 37 large ships and 93 transporters against England. We had less than about 40 large ships all told and about 150 small private ones. Nine of their larger ships were sunk, and only half eventually got back to Spain. The surviving crews died soon afterwards of disease. England lost one ship.

A second Armada followed in 1596, but a storm destroyed 30 ships. A third Armada followed in 1597 but again they were driven back by bad weather. A fourth came in 1600, but again failed to reach England. Such was the determination of the Spanish. The wars and skirmishes with Spain lasted until Elizabeth's death in 1603.

The people of Elizabeth's reign had many social divisions: gentle folk and simple folk, owners and workers. A labour force now existed which could be employed. In between owners and labourers were the Yeomen — small farmers and tenant farmers.

The poor were a problem. Persistent vagabonds had been either branded with a 'V' or had an inch iron put through their ears, but this had now stopped. Instead, they were stripped to the waist and thrashed, then sent off home. They were a big nuisance, perhaps worsened by the enclosure system.

Elizabeth tried to stop enclosure. She placed a poor rate on all properties and she encouraged people to organise a seven year apprenticeship. In 1601 she made a Poor Law stating 'convenient houses and dwellings are to be erected on ways to common land at the charge of the parish for infirm or impotent people and for those whose work is provided in the parish'. No records exist of a poor house for our village, but tradition says that at one time it was part of the gables of a tudor house.

In fact, the following quote from the diary of the Duke of Stettin's Journey in 1602 shows just how far England was ahead of other nations in their attitudes to the poor and their welfare: "Much pleasanter to go about for one is not molested or accosted by beggars who are elsewhere so frequently met within places of this kind (The Royal Exchange). For in all England they do not suffer any beggars except they be few in number and outside the gates. Every parish cares for its poor. Strangers from distant places are sent from one parish to another, their wants being cared for till at last they reach their home".

During the latter part of her reign the weather was very bad and harvests became disastrous. Oxfordshire did not suffer at first like the rest of the country, but from 1580 it began to feel the effects. In 1586 and 1594–7 corn became very scarce. The price rose from 20/- a quarter (4½ Hundredweight) to 52s.4½d. In 1587 a Government survey was made of all the corn stocks in the country and orders were given to take surpluses to markets in Oxford, Woodstock, Witney, Banbury, Deddington and Chipping Norton. The reply from the Bampton Hundred to this request was "the corn faileth out to be veri skantt" — a very poor crop.

Again in 1596-7 wet summers and bad harvests led to famine. An armed rising was arranged to meet at Enslow Bridge (where the Rock of Gibraltar pub is now) to murder the enclosing landlords and to march to London. Support was hoped to come from Witney, 'a town full of poor people', but it was nipped in the bud. *(Ref: Page W. ed. The Victoria History of the Counties of England: Oxfordshire vol II. A Constable, 1907)*

In spite of these setbacks Elizabeth's reign was remembered as a good one. Will Harrison's description of England in Elizabeth's time was of old men, a large number of chimneys being built, wooden platters and spoons replaced by silver and pewter. Bolsters on beds replaced the logs, sheets were used and proper staircases instead of ladders. *(Ref: Fellows, Arnold. The Wayfarer's Companion: England's History in her Buildings and Countryside. Oxford University Press, 1937)*

Trade had increased, towns were rebuilt, manor houses were rebuilt. Bricks, coal, glass and furniture trades were developing. Villeinage and serfdom were now a thing of the past. In 1603 Elizabeth died, and like all of Henry VIII's children, with no issue. For many years after she died the bells were rung on 17th November to celebrate her reign.

During the three reigns of Henry's family Clanfield had been changing much.

Chestlyons

The Wenman family of Carswell, Witney, had taken over the Manor in 1512 from the London goldsmith, Charles Latham, and the family had possession all through those reigns. Richard, a Yeoman clothier and wool stapler of Carswell, had bought it with his wife (Ann Bush). He had died in 1533 and was buried in the north aisle of Witney church.

The estate came to his son and heir, Thomas, who married Ursula Twilford, who lived at Carswell. He was a merchant of the Staple of Calais and was later knighted. Chestlyon, as we remember, was held by the Wenman family. Uncle Thomas held it in spite of a court action by his nephew to reclaim it as part of his late father's estate. When Uncle Thomas died, his own sons, Richard and John, were not of age. It seems that he left the estate in trust to Humphrey Fitzherbert, whose son, John, had married Uncle Thomas's sister, Anna Wenman, then the aunt of the two boys. As soon as the boys came of age they sold their estate. However, Richard retained Potters on the Lower Green.

In the Leys subs of 1581 we note that not only did Humphrey Fitzherbert hold goods valued at £6.10s, that is Chestlyon, for the two sons of Thomas but also another John Wenman held £3.5s (half the above). Richard sold his part of Chestlyons to his uncle, John Fitzherbert, in 1595 who sold it the following year to Leonard Wilmott, and John sold the rest in 1597 to Wilmott, so by 1597 Leonard Wilmott was the owner of Chestlyons. Both sons had decided to sell on becoming 21 years of age.

Some time during that period a large medieval hall was pulled down. Only the vestibule or gatehouse survives, and a double 'Elizabethan period' home built with the old portion remaining in the north east corner. Inside remains a Gothic arch. No doubt, a relic of this pulling down is the south window in the barn opposite the church.

A portion of Friars Court Rolls from 1513 states that "it is ordered that the homage of the court and of the court of Richard Wayman should meet in the church of Clanfield on the Feast of Phillip and St. James and there take view of the full 'mete

*The junction, showing the old Mason's Arms (now the Clanfield Tavern)
and (right) the old Primitive Methodist chapel, now a private house*

A modern view of Radcot Bridge, looking upstream towards Lechlade

A watercolour painting of the thatched stable at Windmill Farm

and bound' in the two lordships and say at the next court the said 'mete' has been put in the right places at pain of 6d". Mete and bound probably means stones and boundaries. This is interesting, as we see the parish church was used, as of course it was, for village business in the nave.

Friars Court

In 1548, the Patent Rolls records that the estate passed within the Edmonds family as 12 messuages, 300 acres of land, 160 acres of meadow, 100 acres of pasture, communal pasture, 20 acres of woods, rent 100s. —free fishing in the Thames in Clanfield, Weald, Bourton and Grafton. Bourton had a share meadow in Charney.

In 1558 John Edmonds died, and the estate passed to his three daughters, Agnes, Mary and Elizabeth.

Southwick

As far as Southwick was concerned Richard Ingram had sold it to William Reynolds in 1542. William had died in 1545 and it went to his son, Richard, who was 11 years old. In 1557 Richard, now of age, sold it to Adam Turner as 5 messuages, 2 cottages, 200 acres of land, 40 acres of meadow, 60 acres of pasture, 6 acres of wood, 100 acres of heath and 3s.7d. rent, communal pasture in Clanfield and Alvescot.
(Ref. Pat Rolls February 1556)

Adam Turner and Agnes, his wife, parcelled out the Southwick manor amongst the family in 1576. To Thomas, his son, he gave Batesland, which was the new name for the Rookshill estate, with Bushey Close, Clanfield. To Robert, his son, he gave Edgerly farm. The manor of Southwick he gave, no doubt, to his oldest son, Drew, who died intestate in Clanfield in 1573, or most likely to Drew's own eldest son, also called Drew, who died in 1602 in possession of the Manor. Widow Turner, who was a Keyill of Southrop, married John Pawling, husbandman, who had a previous family and with her had four more children before he died in 1583. When Drew junior died in 1602, he gave it to his son, Thomas. It must have been Drew's family who rebuilt the manor house before the front portion was later added in the 18th century.

In Clanfield itself this was the age of building. The original part of The Plough Hotel must have been built in about 1660 as a gentleman's residence. It was part of Friars Court manor.

The yeoman's farmhouses were appearing. At about this time a furlong between the Clanfield street and the stream that originally went down to the west of it was taken out of the village field and the strips were developed. This furlong was owned by Friars Court.

A painting of the thatched stable at Windmill Farm shows that it is probably one of the earliest houses built (see page VII). The age of the houses can be seen by the fact that they had rubble quoins and each end sloped in some 6" 9", the idea being that if it fell, it fell inwards.

The wills of Clanfield show evidence of the coming of Mary to the throne and the renewed importance of the altar. In Edward's reign, money was left to the poor man's box. In Mary's reign, Richard Yateman left the high altar 2d. in 1556. John Clark died in 1557 and left to the high altar 4d. for tithes forgotten. He must have had a guilty conscience. Christine Pawling died in 1558 and left the high altar 4d., and the rood light 2d. Evidently Clanfield still had its rood light, even if the income for it from the land had been taken away.

In Elizabeth's reign Richard Taylor left 1d. to the poor box in 1583. He also left 4d. towards the church repairs and 2d. to the church. The value of this estate in his inventory was £13.8s.4d and his house was two up and two down. Andrew Clark left a peck of corn to the poor and 6s.8d to the Clanfield church. This was in 1596. His estate was valued at £65 and again his house was two up and two down. Mary Taylor left 2s.6d to the poor in 1580 and 1s. to Clanfield church. John Clark left a cash debt of 71s.11d and a credit of 12s. Richard Clark left debts of 91s. in 1571. John Pawling, who farmed Osney land at Little Clanfield, left nearly £100 in 1583. Robert Turner had debts of £6.13s.9d and his estate was valued at £23.4s.10d in 1592.

Drew Turner, however, who died at North Court in 1601, had debts of £49 and an estate valued at £53.14s.0d. His house had eight rooms and a cellar, and he had glass in the chamber over the hall. All his money was in his property.

John Wicks died in 1589 leaving an estate of £21.0s.10d. His estate was the land and buildings from Mill Farm to the (former) garage. Andrew Clark, husbandman, had a house of two rooms, 6 store cattle worth £9, two teams of oxen, 4 heifers and a calf, 60 sheep, 3 horses, 29 pigs, 13 pounds of barley, 8 pounds of wheat, 4 pounds of pulses (peas), hay and straw worth £4, and in all the value came to £95.7s.6d. John Sperrinke, a wealthy yeoman, died in 1601. He left 2d. to the church of Oxford, 6s.8d to the poor of Clanfield and 12d for repairing the church bells.

At Radcot Chris Kempater died in 1589. He left 3s.4d for repairs to Clanfield church. To every poor householder in Clanfield he left half a bushel of wheat and half a bushel of malt. He had on lease the parsonage of Clanfield, of which he left half to his wife who died in 1604. One of his overseers was "my master Thomas Fettiplace" who was lord of the Radcot manor.

Clearly, of all the inventories on record John Pawling of Osney land and Andrew Clark were the wealthiest.

One will is of great interest. William Clark died in 1580. He left half an acre of barley in Barrowfield against Stocks Lane and half an acre of wheat in Tarny. From this information we can see that by that time the village was practising a three-year rotation system.

The Ley Subsidy Rolls came up in Elizabeth's reign, but only a few from Clanfield

Chestlion Farm

The Plough Hotel

A modern photograph of Northcourt

Friars Court (taken in 1904)

were mentioned on it. Somehow many missed it, others were, perhaps, recorded in other villages. They were as follows:

Clanfield and Grafton, Elizabeth I. *(Ref: MS Film 15 No. 320, 1558)*

Robert Dawes in goods 6s
John Pawling in goods 5s
Alice Clark, widow, in goods 5s
Richard Clark in goods 5s
Alex Reynolds in goods 7s
Thomas Whitehorn in goods 5s
John Cokke in goods 8s
Richard Clark of Grafton in goods 6s

19th Year Elizabeth I. *(Ref: MS Film 38 E179/162: 19 Elizabeth I Co Oxon)*

Thomas Pawling in goods £5.5s
Walter Savage, gentleman, in land £5.6s.8d
Christopher Kempster in land £4.4s
Richard Ardeyn in land £4.4s
Thomas Sperrinke in goods £4.4s
Thomas Bennet in goods £3.3s
Andrew Clarke in goods £3.3s
Robert Dayer in goods £3.3s

23rd Year Elizabeth I. *(Ref: MS Film 15/320: 23 Elizabeth 1*

Humphrey Fitzherbert, gent, in goods £6.10s
Walter Savage, gent, in lands £5.13.8d
John Witman, gent, in goods £3.5s
John Pawling in goods £5.8s.8d
Christopher Kempster in goods £4.6s.8d
John Sperrinke in goods £4.5s
John Arnold in goods £3.5s
Andrew Clarke in goods £3.5s
John Bennett in goods £3.5s

(Ref: Oxon Court Rolls and Lay Subsidy Rolls)

Elizabeth was granted four Subsidy Rolls. The last one was still being collected in 1605, after she had died.

According to the Patent Roll of 1572 Thomas Farmer of Hurles Park, Salop, Esq., sold to John Seymour of Cote, gent, a messuage and close called Lewtis, with one yard and common trees, in occupation of John Sperrinke of Clanfield, husbandman, at 13s.4d rent for 21 years. By 1575 this land had been sold to John Hogeson who sold it to John Arnold als Gillam with two further yards. This was part of Chestlyon manor. John Wenman later bought it and Will Sperrinke bought it from him. This name is now lost. This is most interesting, as it is the first note we have of the common trees. These would be the withies down the village street.

(Ref: Calendar of the Patent Rolls, Elizabeth 1 vol VII, 1575-1578, vol VI 1572-1575)

★ ★ ★

Chapter 8

The Stuarts (1603–1688)

AFTER Elizabeth's death in March 1603 the people were seeking a Protestant ruler, and asked James VI of Scotland, aged 36, to become James I of England. Rejoicing at his crowning was stopped by the plague, which killed 30,000 people.

Like Elizabeth, James tried to steer a course between the extremes of Puritanism and Catholicism. He did bend to the wishes of the Puritans, however, for an improved version of the Bible, and the King James edition was the version that resulted, based on Tyndale's Bible.

However, many Puritans would not accept his authority. Three hundred lost their livings and many left on the Mayflower to go to America. The Catholics, taking advantage of their liberty, stayed away from church — so new fines were imposed.

In September 1603 James, with all his entourage, came through Clanfield going from Wadley to Burford. *(Ref: Witney Gazette, Saturday April 15, 1911)* This must have been a quite memorable occasion for the village.

In 1605 there was a gunpowder plot, and it can be seen that in trying to please all, King James not only turned the Puritans against himself but also the Catholics. After that, on November 5th, a special service of Thanksgiving was read in the church. Bells were rung and bonfires burned.

To this day in Clanfield and elsewhere we still celebrate, but only with bonfires and fireworks. (This was really an older custom which was based on fires at the time of Hallowe'en to strengthen the declining sun).

James had financial problems because gold and silver were devalued. He was at loggerheads with Parliament, but the common people loved him. He had family problems. His wife became a Catholic and his oldest son, Henry, died in 1612. He made duelling illegal. He died in 1625, whilst the land was at war with Spain.

Charles I, his son, followed. Again, plagues as bad as in the time of James played a part in Charles' crowning. He attempted to be impartial, but he really leaned towards Catholicism. Archbishop Laud, who also leant towards Catholicism, was given a free hand. He silenced puritan writers and clergy. He made people kneel at Communion. He put the heavy table back from the church into the position of the altar. He put rails between the nave and the chancel.

He made people bow to the altar when entering the church, a practice which many Anglicans still continue. He enforced attendance at worship and tried to make the whole church building used for worship only, trying to remove all secular activity from the nave — something which became accepted some 200 years later. Puritans were again encouraged to leave the land, and some 60,000 did.

Charles became at odds with Parliament. They wanted more power. He believed in divine right and full control of the army. For 11 years he reigned without Parliament. In 1640 he was forced to summon Parliament again to get more money.

The feeling against Catholicism can be seen in the reference of the Rector of Ducklington's diary which states that early in 1640 the soldiers at Faringdon killed their captain, because he was thought to be a Catholic. They pillaged and stole in the surrounding countryside. Did Clanfield suffer?

(Ref: Goadby J, compiled by. 1288 and All That - A history of Standlake village, 1978)

In these uncertain times Parliament, perhaps in order to find out how strong Catholicism was in the country, drew up a Protestation, a declaration of loyalty to the Protestant faith, King and Parliament, which everyone was asked to sign.

Part of this Protestation for Oxon is lost, but parts of the Bampton Hundred survive. It tells us of all the males over 18, and gives us a comparison of the population in the Bampton Hundred.

The Parliamentary Commission sat at Woodstock from 14th February 1641. This was before the change in the calendar, as in modern reckoning it would have been 1642. Clanfield signed its declaration — at least the Vicar wrote down all the names. None refused. We had no Papists. This list was taken to Woodstock on 23rd February by Phatnell Denton, Clerk (the Vicar), Solomon Clark, Constable, John White and Thomas Blagrove, Church Wardens, John Chapman and Robert Turner, Overseers.

Phatnell Denton was to die two years later, in April 1644. The White family appear later in our village history. The Blagroves were seen later to be the millers at Little Clanfield.

The declaration said: "We do certify that according to your direction we have given the Protestation with the names of those that have taken it, not any one refusing it in witness whereunto we have set our hands this day and year above written."

Following this declaration there was a list of 95 names:

Protestation Returns 23rd February, 1641

Clanfield: none refused to sign.

Francis More	John Pearson	Solomon Crass
Leonard Smith (Chestlyon)	Thomas Pinnock	John Tull
Walter Bennett	Francis Pinnock	William Pauling
Richard May	William Wood	Roland Franklin

John Sperrinke
Anthony Pauling
John Tailor
Anthony Stevens
Syman Pauling
John Veatman
Solomon Yeatman
Thomas Stevens
John Stevens
Adam Turner
Henry Moore
Henry Adams
Thomas Adams
Robert Turner
Nicholas Veatman Snr.
Nicholas Yeatman Jnr.
Richard Yeatman
Richard Laffin
Alex. May
John May
John Laffer
Robert Laffer
John Booth
Thomas Booth
John Whithorne
Roger Crass

Simon Dier
John Goodenough
William May
Alex May
John Pauling
William Stevens
William Clarke
William Blagrove
Thomas Winchcome
Richard Winchcome
Solomon Carpenter
Adam Heyes
Richard Goff
Simon Pauling
Thomas Curtis
Solomon Clarke
Ralph Simons
Richard Clarke
Thomas Lucket
John Bucket
William Ponter
John Arnold
John House
Edward Duber
Thomas Duber

Nicholas Carpenter
Thomas Carpenter
Richard Veysey
John Sheaperd
Thomas Coles
Thomas Lake
John Waine
William Waine
Richard Pencot
Simon Cinch
Nicholas Hules
William Hobbs
John Gun
Solomon Arnold
James Hill
John Linsey
Richard Francis
John Harris
Thomas Temple
William Yeaton
Robert Lauder
John Arnold
Thomas Barnes
Richard Hamand
Francis Whithorne

Witness

Phatnell Denton *Vicar*
John More
Thomas Blagrove (His sign)
Joseph White (His sign) *Church Wardens*
Solomon Clarke *Constable*
Jo. Chapman & Robert Turner *Overseers*

Clanfield must now have been a village of some 200-250 people.

The following is a list of the estimated comparisons of populations within the Bampton Hundred.

	1642	1931
Witney	1250	5050
Burford	932	907
Standlake	325	534
Broadwell	192	
Filkins	282	397
Holwell		65
Aston }		
Cote }	280 }	
Chimney	35 }	
Brighthampton	43 }	555
Shifford	70	39
Bampton	255 }	
Weald	250 }	1167
Clanfield	237	477
Brize Norton	215	516
Ducklington	190 }	
Yelford	}	
Hardwick	215 }	606
Asthall	188	285
Black Bourton	160	200 (Only 2 in 1901)
Alvescot	142	278
Broughton Pogges	95	47
Lew	85	97
Grafton & Radcot	90	77
Kelmscot	80	144
Langford (Berks)		267

So in a period which saw the doubling of the population from 1642–1931, the population of Witney had gone ahead fourfold, Burford has stagnated, and Filkins dominated the Broadwell group in spite of the fact that Broadwell was the head. Shifford, Broughton Pogges, Lew, Radcot and Grafton, Westwell and Chimney were shrinking communities. In 1642, Weald had an equal population with Bampton, but its former glory fell, as in later years Bampton grew at the expense of Weald. Clanfield's population only doubled.

As part of his claim to run the country, Charles raised the flag at Nottingham in 1642. Parliament took up the challenge and the Civil War began. The Church and the

Catholics supported the King. The reformers and Puritans backed Parliament. Geographically, the north and the west, the fringes, supported the King, and the south and east, the progressive part of the country, supported Parliament. The Fleet was loyal to Parliament. In the south the King made Oxford his centre. Prince Rupert held Abingdon with an advance party.

In 1644, Parliamentarians took Abingdon. Royalists tried to retake it in 1645 but failed. On New Year's Eve in 1642 there was an engagement at Burford. A royalist ammunition convoy stopped in the town. Sir John Byron, who was in charge, was rather caught out. He had reconnoitred towards Cirencester, but not, apparently, towards Witney.

He was going north to Stow, and had possibly come through Clanfield. He had come through Burford on the Friday and was resting on the Saturday. At 7.00 pm he began to feel that he ought to move, and as he was about to do so, Parliamentarian forces attacked down Witney Street in the dark. Byron got his convoy over the bridge for safety, and then went back in the dark to drive off the Parliamentarian forces. They retreated to the White Hart Inn. Byron was wounded in the face by a halberd, a long-handled spiked battle axe. He retired to get more men. As he again approached them, one of his men was shot and killed. In the darkness the Parliamentarians were disappearing out of the back of the inn, leaving six of the men there dead.
(Ref: Gretton MS. Burford Past and Present. G Packer and Son Ltd, 1920)

Soldiers were stationed at Witney and during the year two soldiers' wives and one baby died. During the skirmishes in the area two soldiers were killed at Witney in March, one in June, one in August, one in September and four in October (a much larger skirmish) and one in November.

Early in February of 1642, fighting was taking place around Broadwell.

Two soldiers billeted there were killed on the 6th and 17th of February. In May, the fighting was around Bampton and one soldier garrisoned there, Charles Lee, was killed.

In August of that year the King, going from London to Bristol, dined at Faringdon. In September, whilst trying to stop the Earl of Essex from getting to London, he came from Northleach and stayed the night at the home of Lady Ashcomb, Shield House, Alvescot. This site is now under the west end of the aerodrome runway. The following day, with all his men, he marched through Clanfield to Faringdon, a great and fearful sight for our villagers.

As Parliament was seemingly getting nowhere in the war they called in the Scots to help them, which they did — at a price — during January 1643. Further skirmishes took place in our area. On February 2nd a soldier was killed at Brize Norton. At Burford a French Lieutenant (Andrew Royer) was killed. In March, an Irish soldier was killed there. A Filkins man, Will Callis, was, no doubt, going to Burford when he was caught in a fight and was badly shot. He was taken to a surgeon in Burford, but died in his arms and was buried on July 4th.

Abingdon fell to Parliament in May 1644, and the King came through Faringdon on his way back to Oxford in November of that year, and decided to make Faringdon, and its great house, his headquarters locally. Apparently, he called at Buckland Vicarage for the night. Perhaps the company with him was small, as he was now fleeing from Worcester. The Vicar looked after him and apparently gave him breakfast the following morning. He was a stern Catholic. A stone tablet records this in Latin (but it was not put in until 1876), and a mulberry tree was planted there to record his visit. *(Ref: Wright ASN. The History of Buckland, Holywell Press Ltd, 1966)*

Faringdon was badly provisioned so the new Governor, Colonel George Lisle, set about diverting all local animals to Faringdon market rather than Abingdon, a fact about which Abingdon complained to Parliament.

On June 8th 1644, the army of the Earl of Essex (Parliamentarian) passed through Clanfield, going from Burford to Faringdon. This fact was found in the diary of a soldier. *(Ref: Camden Series)*

In November 1644, Royalist troops rested at Clanfield. Richard Symonds, a captain, made a note in his diary of what he saw in our church. He wrote: "An altar tombe covered with marble, a brass inlaid sans shield, north aisle chancel". 'Here lyeth Leonard Wilmot Gent, who died at his house at Clanfield 25th June 1608, aetat 59.' A flat stone adjoining. 'Here lieth the body of James Jyde Gent, 24th March 1610'. In the chancel a flat stone 'John Rogers of Clanfield ob. 20th May 1635'."
(Ref: Camden Series)

Again, in the following year, skirmishing took place in our area. On February 20th a soldier of Sir Marmaduke was buried at Burford and a soldier was buried in Witney on 28th February, perhaps the victims of the same skirmish between Burford and Witney.

The following account of the Civil War locally can be seen in '*Faringdon in the Civil War*, C.H. Hartmann:

> "On April 15th Cromwell met and defeated a strong body of Royalist cavalry
> under the young Earl of Northampton at Islip Bridge, north of Oxford. He took
> some 200 prisoners and four colours, including the Queen's own standard 'being
> a crown in the midst, incircled with divers Flower-de-Luces wrought in gold,
> with a golden cross on the top.' The routed troops were pursued to Bletchington
> House where they took refuge.
> "Cromwell took the garrison of 200 men. He decided that Bletchington was
> not worth holding and did not remain there long, but set off in a south-westerly
> direction towards Witney. On April 26th he heard that there was a body of

Royalist horse before him, and sent Colonel John Fiennes forward to attack it. Fiennes encountered it somewhere near Faringdon and put it to flight, taking 40 prisoners, a large number of horses and three colours, with the loss of only ten of his own men. This Royalist Cavalry seems to have been part of a force sent from Faringdon to strengthen Woodstock against Cromwell and forestall an attack by him.

"Their task accomplished, they were now returning to garrison. The 300 foot soldiers in this party were under the command of Sir Richard Vaughan, and on April 27th Cromwell received information that they were not above three hours' march in front of him. He immediately sent his 'forlorn' in pursuit of them. (The 'forlorn' were picked troops, usually volunteers to whom the most dangerous tasks were allotted).

"The Royalists were overtaken by Cromwell's 'forlorn' in the fields on the outskirts of Bampton in the Bush. A skirmish ensued in which most of the casualties on the Parliamentarian side appear to have been horses. The Royalists were able to get into the town before Cromwell came up with his main body.

"They had put up a barricade and occupied a strongly-built house before his arrival at eleven o'clock that evening. They slighted his summons to surrender, and resisted all attempts to storm their barricade during the night with 'some good resolution', in Cromwell's own words, that they could not be forced from it.

"He was obliged to wait till morning, when he sent a drum to them calling them once more to surrender. Their answer was that they would not do so unless they might march out on honourable terms. Cromwell sternly replied that they must submit all to mercy. This they angrily rejected. He insisted and made preparations to storm the house. But first he sent them word "to desire them to deliver out the Gent and his family" — presumably the owners of the house. They must, he repeated, expect severity if they put him to a storm. They agreed to his demand, and after some further parleying, decided that the odds against them were too great and that they must, after all, yield to mercy.

"The bullet holes can still be seen on top of the Deanery House basement door, the soldiers apparently having fired from the top of the church. A side ground level window has shot marks.

"Cromwell came through Clanfield with his horse on April 28th, 1645, and passed over the Radcot Bridge for Faringdon where it is thought he made camp on The Folly. He now held the town, and sent off to Abingdon for foot soldiers to support his cavalry. About 500-600 came.

"At three o'clock in the morning on April 30th the assault on Faringdon House was begun. Supported by Cromwell and his troopers, the foot advanced with ladders and attempted to scale the walls. But when Captain Canon, who reared the first scaling-ladder and was himself the first to ascend it, was taken prisoner by the defenders with an ensign and eight troopers who followed him, this method of attack was promptly given up. After 14 men had been killed and several more of the besieging troops had been wounded, Cromwell decided that the attempt was too costly and abandoned it."

From: Pocock, EA. Radcot and its Bridge, 1966:

"Four days (May 4th) later, whilst he was in conference at Newbury, he learnt from prisoners that a body of Royalist cavalry was in the area preparing to attack his headquarters at Faringdon. Immediately he returned to Faringdon and, finding it all quiet, sent a small number of cavalry under Major Bethel to see if all was well with the men he had left on guard at Radcot Bridge. The moon was beginning to rise as Bethel and his men cantered down the road. It was two days past full, and had risen that evening about 7p.m. Bethel was greatly relieved to find everything all right and there was no sign of any enemy.

"Just to make sure, he decided to trot on up the road towards Clanfield in the moonlight to see if anybody was about. What he did not know was that already the Royalist cavalry were spying out the bridge. Having passed through Lechlade, they had come along the meadows road (now lost) and had sent some on foot to see if the bridge was guarded. These heard Bethel come down the road from Faringdon, and counted his number as he rode by them. There were 23, which was five more than they were.

"Quickly they fetched their fellow soldiers who, with loaded muskets, quietly lined up along the ditch facing the moon. Soon they returned. Bethel they allowed to pass. The remainder were like sitting ducks silhouetted against the moon. At that range there were none wounded, all 18 were killed. Bethel and the remaining four being thrown from their horses, were captured. The bridge was easily taken. Radcot House from now on was garrisoned by Royalist troops.

"Further skirmishing was taking place all around us. Gaunt House near Standlake, held by the Royalists, came under attack. Twelve Royalist soldiers from there, out gathering or stealing supplies, were captured on May 30th. Royalists were ill paid and had, usually, to live off the land. They would often plunder the goods of their unwilling hosts without paying a penny. "On May 31st, Sir Thomas Fairfax decided to attack. On June 5th one soldier was buried at Ducklington. On July 2nd two unknown soldiers killed in a skirmish near Radcot were buried at Clanfield, and again an unknown soldier was buried *here on July 14th. Parliamentarians attacked Radcot, two were killed and one died later, no doubt, from his wounds."*

The Royalists of our area were a problem to the Parliamentarians.

"Meanwhile, the Royalists were sending out men into Wiltshire foraging for food as they had such large numbers to feed in their garrisons. To stop this, the Roundheads put some troops at Lechlade and asked for Gloucester cavalry to be at hand. On November 22nd Captain Aytwood set off from Radcot with 30 horses to drive them out, but found them much tougher than he thought. He succeeded in getting himself shot in the thigh, and had to retire, threatening to return with larger numbers. He immediately sent word to Faringdon.

"They sent off a party of 100 foot soldiers and 150 cavalry who were to charge into Lechlade after dark. When they arrived there at seven o'clock the nearly full moon was high in the sky and the Roundheads, having been forewarned by Aytwood, were waiting for them. As the Royalists entered they were met by a withering fire from 60 musketeers hidden behind a wall. Six of the Royalists were killed, and it took an hour and twenty minutes to extricate themselves with their wounded. Being fearful to cross St. John's Bridge nearby, lest they should be ambushed again, they made off along the meadow road to Radcot.

"About half an hour after they had got away, the Roundheads' cavalry appeared on the scene and, taking some foot soldiers with them, set off in pursuit. The Royalists, slowed down by their wounded, were overtaken just as they were getting to the Manor House at Radcot.

"Confusion and panic must have reigned as 150 horses and nearly 100 foot soldiers, with the wounded, tried to get through the Manor gate to safety. Major Duett, who was in charge of the Royalists, must have personally led the fighting rearguard, for he, with 20 others, was killed, 30 or more were taken prisoner and 26 horses and 60 firearms captured. One wondered how many of the killed were the wounded men trampled to death beneath the frightened horses. The Roundheads were free to take all they could find in the moonlight outside the walls. A few years ago Mrs. Lumsden, then the owner of Radcot House, whilst tidying up the bank outside her west wall, came upon various bits of armour. Relics, perhaps, of this gruesome occasion."
(Ref: Pocock EA. Radcot and Its Bridge, 1966)

On April 27th 1646, the King, realising all was lost, left Oxford, secretly crossed May Bridge in disguise, with two attendants to give himself up to the Scots. On May 3rd Fairfax laid seige to Oxford. He then sent out troops to block up and take all other garrisons.

Colonel Sanderson was sent to Radcot on May 11th, but seemed frightened to do anything about the garrison in the House until a fortnight later when reinforcements, under Colonel Cook, arrived.

"When it became apparent that Colonel Palmer and his men inside Radcot House had no intention of surrendering, the Roundheads decided to take it by storm. The fighting in and around the house became so fierce and so close that in the end the Roundheads were throwing grenades into the house itself, one actually falling right through the damaged floor into the cellar below. Colonel Palmer now knew the situation was hopeless.

"After some six weeks of siege, food was short and now much of what was left was spoilt by the grenade. He decided to surrender. One hundred men paraded from the house and laid down their guns on the ground on the grass outside, whilst the Roundheads kept them covered. But such was the discipline of the Roundheads that although six of their number lay dead all the Royalists were allowed to go off to their various homes. The war for Radcot was over."

Sir Robert Pye, the son of the owner, was sent to take Faringdon House. No serious attempt was made to take or damage his own family's home. Its negotiations for surrender were made at the same time as that of Oxford.

Article XXIV of the agreement was as follows:

That the garrison of Farringdon shall be rendered to his excellency Sir Thomas Fairfax and the governor, gentlemen, soldiers and all other of what quality soever with those garrisons, shall enjoy the benefit of those articles in every particular which may concern them they rendering the garrison accordingly as Oxford.

The capitulation was to be on June 24th and about 10 o'clock in the morning of that day the garrison of Faringdon marched out under arms with bag and baggage, and with all honours of war, leaving only their ordnance ammunition and stores of spare arms behind them. Faringdon had the distinction of being one of the last places to hold out for the King.

Faringdon suffered sorely. Two years later, in September 1648, there was a draft order in the Lord's Journal for a collection to be made for the assistance of the inhabitants of Faringdon and Westbrook in repairing the ruin caused to the habitations, goods and church, which were demolished and burnt by the enemy's garrison; the damage was assessed at £56,697.4s.0.

Clanfield would now sleep in peace. No more Royalists foraging and stealing, no more fighting. Life could go back to normal.

Charles, however, who thought he was secure with the Scots, found that he was handed back. He did escape in 1647 and fled to the Isle of Wight. The Scots now came to his aid. Cromwell defeated them in a three-day battle near to Preston. The army took over the running of the country.

The King was captured, brought to trial and executed on June 3rd 1649. His eldest son, Charles, was made King of Scotland, and in 1651 he brought his Scottish army into England, but Cromwell defeated them at Worcester. He escaped, then we have the story of the oak tree. He reached the south coast and went to France.

Cromwell's army, so well trained and zealous in battle, became disenchanted after the war. Boredom, wages not being fully paid, fear of being sent to Ireland out of the way, and political agitators amongst them, were the causes of the rebellion that broke out. One large group from Salisbury came to Newbridge, found that the river was blocked, amd moved west to cross the river and to proceed to Burford. It may be that they crossed over the Burroway ford, and years ago I remember the old men saying how, in that area, rifles were dug out of a mound there. This has always been a mystery to me.

These men, about a thousand of them, came to and settled around Burford in the villages and were resting, feeling secure on Sunday May 13th 1649 when those at Burford were suddenly attacked by Parliamentarians pouring in from both directions, west and east. Quickly, they were overpowered, many escaping to surrounding villages. The prisoners were put in the nave of Burford church for three days.This was still seen as a community hall.

On trial, four were condemned. The soldiers paraded on the church roof and watched whilst three were shot. The bullet marks can still be seen on the church wall. The fourth was reprieved and was said by some to be a spy, who was condemned to give him his cover.

Cromwell and Fairfax, with about 2,000 men or dragoons who most likely had ridden with the soldiers through Clanfield that night, rested for a while at Burford and then went to Christ Church, Oxford for dinner the following day.

Peace again reigned.

England, however, hated extremes and was always ready to turn against it. Cromwell was walking an unknown path of government. He won power for Parliament, but found he could not trust them with it. Like all quick revolutions the latter is no better than the former. True revolution can only come slowly, yet Cromwell was a great ruler. He made England respected overseas. However, he died on September 3rd 1658, worn out and desperately ill.

Cromwell's son, 'Tumbledown Richard', was no match for the generals. The land was in chaos. General Monk came from Scotland to create order.

A new Parliament was called in 1660. The Puritans had lost, but they were now accepted and not suppressed. The King may have been sent for, but he came as a servant of Parliament and the country.

After the war many of the cavalry horses that had been acquired by the army were sold. These were bought and used by the farmers for ploughing instead of using oxen.

★ ★ ★

Chapter 9

Village Records from 1603-1688

Friars Court

This manor was in the hands of the family of the three daughters, but in the Protestant Rolls of 1641, Francis More heads the list.

Southwick

Drew Turner had died in 1602, leaving it to his son, Thomas. In 1633, Thomas died and had sold it to John and William Castle who took possession after the death of Thomas' wife. At that time Southwick stood as five messuages, 60 acres of land, 20 acres of meadow, 30 acres of pasture, 3 acres of wood, 30 acres of firs and heath. Rent 3s.7d. There was some communal pasture in Clanfield and Alvescot. The value of all this was £120.

Chestlyons

In 1608 Leonard Wilmot died. He was a very wealthy man, one of the rising yeoman families that came up after the Dissolution. His family came from the Baldons area of south Oxfordshire; some were living at Henley, and some in Witney. In fact, he left his estate to his brother, William, who lived in Henley. Leonard's widow occupied Southwick until her death, and then it went to William's grandson, Leonard Smith. Leonard Wilmot left £10 in his will to be given to the poor at his funeral in 3d. and 4d. doles; £7 was also given for the buying of a new bell at Clanfield "at such a time as the inhabitants have by mutual agreement bought and had it delivered".

Between the making of his will in March 1607 and his Codicil in 1608 he must have inherited a considerable sum, for he was able to leave a further £350. Wilmot is mostly remembered by the fact that he left a perpetual charity of "£20 out of 'his farm and chief manor house at Chaslings in Clanfield where he has dwelt, and out of six yard lands in Clanfield and out of several parcels by estimate 63 acres lately purchased off John Wenman'. To the relief of the poor he left Burford £4, Witney £4, Barcot £2, Clifton £1, Nuneham Courtenay £1, Bampton £2, Clanfield £3, Marsh Baldon £1, Toot Baldon £2. Leonard's tomb was in fact recorded by Richard Symonds, the Royalist officer, in 1644.

The tenant of Southwick was allowed 5s. expenses each year for paying the charity in later years. Clanfield paid out the £3 on Good Friday of about 13d. per house. The Charity Commission of about 1800 said this was wrong, and that the money should have been paid to such persons as did not receive Poor Relief.

In 1614 Leonard's widow, Catherine, died. In the meantime she had remarried a Mr. Hyce, who seems to have been living at Wyck Farm in the village. Catherine left a long and detailed will of all her gifts to the family and friends. She had no children. She left her lease in Busby's to her father, Thomas Prince. She left a gold angel to her sister's mother-in-law. She left her last wedding ring to her brother-in-law, Mr William Hyde. She left Leonard Wilmot's signet ring to her brother-in-law, William Wilmot, and her first wedding ring to his wife. To every cottager of Clanfield she left 2d. She left various sums from £5 to 6s.8d to seven men servants and three girls. She left a 22s. piece of gold to the vicar, Thomas Twiss, and to his wife "my silk russet kirtle and stomacher".

In 1618 William Taylor the elder, husbandman, died. He left his estate to his widow, Marguerita, and her son, William, 'Desiring them to live together lovingly and in the fear of God'.

In 1619 Bartholomew Turner, yeoman, died. He probably lived in Burroway. He left to John Turner of Clanfield, baker, "my mar, my pitch net and my coffer with the books there". To Christopher Holmes, the Vicar, and William Pimnock, tailor, of Clanfield, "My best flue net". In his inventory, valued at £20.8s.4d, his boat and nets were valued at £1.

In 1620 Christopher Holmes, the Vicar, died intestate. On his deathbed at Highworth he was visited on July 5th 1620 by Robert Langton, Highworth clerk (vicar) and others. His wife, Margaret Holmes was present. Mr Langton asked him: "Mr Holmes, here is your loving wife, how do you mean to disperse of your goods? Are you willing your wife should have them towards the aid of your children?" Whereupon, Mr Holmes said he would give 10s. to Christopher Holmes, his eldest son. All the rest of his goods whatsoever he did give to his loving wife, to Thomas, his second eldest son, and Ann, his daughter, to be divided between them.

In his inventory he was worth £29.17s.0d. The vicarage had a study, parlour, hall and milkhouse, no kitchen, two bedrooms, one of which was for the children. Mr Holmes died at Highworth shortly after he had gone there. Thomas Twiss, whom he replaced as Vicar, was one of the witnesses of his inventory and he was then of Buscot.

In 1622 Marie Rogers died. She was one of the daughters of John Edmunds, who received a third of Friars Court. She lived in a large house of three downstairs rooms, a cottage adjacent, and four other rooms and a court. Upstairs there were six bedrooms and attics. In her kitchen, she had window leads and in her court one pump. Her estate was worth £53.8s.6d. In her will she left to the parish of Clanfield 6s.8d, a sum of £4 to the poor of Bampton, £4 to the poor of Witney, and 24s. to Clanfield on the day of her funeral. She left £3 to the vicar, Phatmell Denton, but she had been in the custom of giving 40s. a year to the poor of Clanfield, 20s. at Whitsuntide and 20s. at Christmas. She left £20 to her daughter, Julia, on the condition that she continued this custom.

Isaac Meysey of Radcot, fisherman, died in February 1626. He left 6s.8d to the parish church at Clanfield. He had a business of which he could lease one year's profit to his five younger children in turn. He leased the house below the bridge. He left an estate of £42.11s.0d and lived in a house of six downstairs rooms and four bedrooms. This must have been the Wharfage at Radcot.

William Burri, husbandman, died in 1627 and left 4d. to the church of Clanfield. His estate was valued at £38.6s.4d and he was in partnership with Robert Shilton and Ann Shilton, his wife. Shilton died in 1639. Will's widow died in 1635, and also left 4d. to the church and asked to be buried "as near as may be to my husband". Their youngest daughter, Frances, who had looked after her parents, married Robert Reynolds, of London, soon after her father's death.

Adam Laffter died in 1628 and left 12d. to the church of Clanfield. He was a carpenter. His estate was valued at £60.10s.2d. His tools were valued at £1.10s.0d. He was also a small farmer, having 5¼ acres of corn plus his fallow. His house was a hall and stairs with a good chamber over it and another at the head of the stairs. He also had a cock loft over his milk house, and a work house adjacent.

William Sperrinck died in 1633, a very wealthy man, having been left his estate by his father in 1601. He left 12d. to the church, 4d. to the mother church in Oxford, a peck of corn to each poor householder in Clanfield. He owned a messuage, 3 closes and 1 virgate bought from Drogo Clark and a messuage called Lewtis, 2 closes and one virgate bought from John Wenman, and Barrowhays, a messuage yard and one acre adjoining, all part of Chestlyon Manor. He left an estate valued at £184.1s.0d. In it was a sword and a dagger valued at 5s., his books worth 13s.4d, three linen wheels, and apples. His house consisted of six rooms downstairs, three bedrooms, 2 attics or cock lofts. There seems to have been some feeling between his wife and son, and he said he hoped they could settle things amicably.

Lewtis, we remember, was sold by the Farmer family to John Seymour in 1572, and in 1575 it was bought by John Arnold (alias Gillam). It was in the occupation of John Sperrinck, so John Wenman had bought it and sold it to William Sperrinck. Barrowhays was later said to be by the village pound. Will lived at Barrowhays or Lewtis. The value of both of these was 20s. per annum.

In 1633 Richard Cooper died, a yeoman. He left the remaining years of his lease of the property to Ellen Pettifer, who seems to have looked after him in his old age. To another lady, Elizabeth Matthew, he left a 41 year lease on a house he owned, and some timbers and stones at the back of the bakehouse to extend it. He left his daughter, Mary Barfield, the ownership of the baker's house and in one quarter of which Thomas Curtis, the baker, lived; to his daughter, Elizabeth Atkins, the house and quarter where John Coles (als Taylor) lived, and timber to hedge against Bourton Marsh, with stable, hay barns and timber boards in the barn to help build John Coles' house. He probably lived at 'The Bull'. Coopers Close adjoined the farm against the main road, and there was a large baker's oven in The Bull house.

In 1636 the first of the Adams family appeared — Robert, who was a carpenter and farmer. His inventory was valued at £37 and his carpenter's tools were valued at 10s. His house had three down and three up, plus attics.

The first will and inventory of the Stevens family appeared at this time too. Edward Stevens left an estate valued at £15 to his wife, and son, Thomas, in 1639.

In 1639 Martha, the widow of Henry Smith, died. She was related to the Chestlyon family. She left 20s. to her oldest son, Leonard, 5s. to buy him a pair of gloves, desiring him that "he will be loving and kind to his brothers and sisters and to be helpful out of the great estate that has fallen to him". This was Chestlyon, which had belonged to his grand-uncle, Leonard Wilmot.

In 1640 Mary Yeatman died. She left £10 to her son, Nicholas, to build his home at a place in Clanfield called the Coles. (This was the age of rebuilding — it was pre-Civil War.)

In 1640 Richard Clark the elder, freeholder, died. He left his house to be made into two for his son, John, and daughter, Catherine. John was to have the hall and the chamber over it. Catherine was to have the parlour and chamber over that. There was only one chimney, at John's end, by the kitchen, so he "shall help her to pay workmen for putting a chimney in the parlour".

An interesting will appeared in 1641 of Andrew Wayne, steward of a ship, the

A 1905 postcard of St Stephen's Church

The old Vicarage (since renamed Caveridge House)

Chestlion – line of ownership from 1242 to present

1242 Richard Savage

1275

Richard Chasterlon, d. 1279

1279

Hugh Chasterlon

1316–50 Richard Chasterlon

1396 Elizabeth, grand-daughter, m. Will Gernon

Joan and Elizabeth, aunts. Elizabeth m. Sir Thomas Hill

Elizabeth Hill, daughter, m. Ralph Latham

Sold in 1512 to

Richard Wenman, d. 1533, m. Ann Bush

1533

Thomas Wenman, brother

Richard and John Wenman, sons of Thomas

Richard sold in 1595 to

John Fitzherbert

Sold in 1596 to

Leonard Wilmott, d. 1608

1608

William Wilmot, brother

Leonard Smith, grandson, d. 1660

1660

Thomas Smith, son

1668

John, younger brother of Thomas

1704

Katherine and Mary Smith, daughters of John

Mary Smith • daughters of John • Katherine Smith

1729

Thomas Barnard, son | William Dawes, husband

Sold in 1753 to | **Sold to**

Alex Hogg

1774

Thomas Bennett, d. 1807

Thomas Bennett, nephew

Sold in 1835 to

William Aldworth, nephew

1846

Will Aldworth, son

Sold in 1875 to

Christ Church College, Oxford (present owner)

Expedition. The *Expedition* was built in Bermondsey in 1637. Andrew left his father and mother, John and Marjory, £5 in English money. He left his brothers, Richard and Thomas, 40s. each, and brothers William and Leonard £5 each. "I give to those who tend me in this my visitation 20s. to be paid out of the sum of 84 ryalls and 30 drs which I now have remaining in my box. To the Purser of the ship *Hart*, Tim Kendall, who came out as purser's mate in the ship *Willen*, 10s. out of the above box. To Robert Heath, purser, and John Cherurgion, 10 ryalls of eight to be equally divided between them. (30 drs make half a ryall)."

In 1649, the year Cromwell took over, Henry Adams, carpenter, died. He was probably the son of Robert, who died in 1636. His house was the same size. His estate was £2.10s.4d more than Robert's. His books were valued at £1, double Robert's. What a pity he did not write a diary of these turbulent years.

An interesting deed came to light on the property later known as Horns Cottage, by the Vicarage. In 1628 Thomas Turner, gent, died and Amy, his wife, sold Horns Cottage to Anthony Pawling of Clanfield, yeoman, now deceased, for the use of the children of John Tull, his brother-in-law, baker of Bampton. It was "all that messuage and tenement in the occupation of Adam Hedges, two lays adjacent, about two acres, one acre in common meadow, seven acres and three farendalls of arable land dispersed in the common fields of Clanfield, also occupied by Adam Hedges and also two loads of firze to be taken out of the ground called Rookahill, lying in the lordship of Alvescot and common pasture for three beasts". The two loads of firze still grow west of Batesland, and this shows the shortage of woods in 'open field' Clanfield. This property was part of Turner's Southwick estate.

Another interesting document is a Terrier or Deed of Parsonage, which dates from September 1634:

1. There belongs to the parsonage of Clanfield one yard besides the tithes corn and hay worth around £120 rented and all discharged of dues payed to the King and Church which parsonage is in the possession of Sir Edward Yeate, John Gunn, gents, and John Chapman.

2. There belongs to the vicarage of Clanfield ¼ yard besides other privy tythes worth by common judgement £30. We do certify that our vicarage house of Clanfield is kept in good repair and for any other lands belonging to our church we do certify that we have not any.

Richard Thickette, John Stevens — Church Wardens. John Sayer — Sidesman.

Often in our records parsonage means rectory. The three owners reflect the fact that John Edmunds left the rectory to be shared between his three daughters. Edward was married to Julianne, daughter of Marie and Robert Taylor. Chapman had married Elizabeth Edmunds.

During the Commonwealth, a parliamentary survey was made of all the Hundreds. That of Bampton was:

A survey of the Hundred of Bampton with the rents and issues and profits thereof lying and being in the county of Oxford — late parcell of the possessions of Charles Stuart, King of England, made and taken by us in the month of December 1652 by virtue of an act of ye Commons of England assembled in Parliament for sake of the 'Hommo Manno and lands heretofor belonging to the late King, Queen and Prince and a commission thereupon grounded under the hands and seals of five or more of the Hon. Trustees

All that the certainty money, common fine money, Tything silver or by what name or names else distinguished, due and payable by the several townships or tythings within the forsaid Hundred of Bampton at Michaels only. Is paid ann. 13s.4d.

The profits of Court Leet with the three weeks court, fines, issues and amercements of the said courts, waifes, strays, deodands, fellons goods, goods of fellons, of themselves of fugitives and of condemned persons, other convicted and outlawed persons. Hawking, hunting, fowling and fishing and also the office and officers of the Baylewick of the aforesaid Hundred of Bampton, with the serving procos, writts, judgements and out lawyers with all and singular the royalties profits and advantages belonging to the said Hundred of Bampton we estimate to be worth £6.

Memoranda.

The foresaid 3 weeks court is usually held at the town of Bampton and also the Court Leet at Michaelmas and Lady Day.

There is also one Court Leet held at Black Bourton at Micbaelmas yearly and one Leet at Alvescot Bradwell at the same time and one Leet at Ducklington or Dukleton and also one leet at Standlake at the time foresaid.

The aforesaid 3 weeks court may try and determine all actions under 40 shillings.

The inhabitants within the aforesaid Hundred are to perform their suite and service at the aforesaid courts.

The Certainty money is payable at Michaelmas only.

An Abstract.

"The certainty money is annually 13s.4d.
And the improvement is paid annually: £6.00.
Total: £6.13s.4d"

Memoranda.

That the said premises were lately enjoyed by ye Countess of Kent deceased and are now claimed by Sir George Saviles Knt. but by what grant the same is so held we know not, although required, with we refer to be cleared before the ....the trustees etc.
(Ref: PRO E317 Oxfordshire No 1, Bampton, Survey of the Hundred)

No Court Leet is noted at Clanfield. This is because it then belonged to private people. The one of Old Clanfield to the Honour of Ewelme and the one at Friars Court were now, after the dissolution in 1652, in the hands of the descendant of the three Edmund daughters.

During this same year a sad occasion was recorded at Witney. Men of Stanton Harcourt went to Witney to entertain the inhabitants and could not have the town hall, so they had a room at the White Hart Inn. When the drumbeat and the trumpet sounded at 7 o'clock, about 300 people came. The floor gradually gave way under the weight of the people with the result that one woman broke her leg, 60 people were badly bruised, and five children were killed.
(Ref: Richardson, Charles. Oxfordshire Collections, vol 1)

So came to an end a very frightening period in our history. We have no record of the men who served in the war, but all men of military age had a responsibility under national service. Some 30 or 40 of the 88 men who were registered must have been eligible. Did these fight for the King or for Parliament? As we had no powerful local lord it most probably would have been for Parliament. Did any die? We do not know.

★ ★ ★

Chapter 10

The Last of the Stuarts 1660-1714

Charles II 1660-1685

MANY, of course, feared the day when Parliament asked Charles II to come and be King, but he was more careful and wise than they gave him credit for. He did not set out to get his revenge. All except those who had condemned his father at the trial were pardoned. However, all the lands which had been confiscated, except those sold to pay royal debts, were returned to the King.

Whilst he leant towards Catholicism, he did not try and force it on the country. He accepted the Church of England as the national Church. The Puritans, who had lost power, were accepted on a lower national level. The only limitation made was that no puritan Minister could live or operate within five miles of a Borough or church he had officiated in.

Parliament kept the King short of money. He became known as the 'Chimney Sweep' because he brought in a tax on the chimneys and the Hearth Tax. People had to pay 2s. a year on a half yearly basis (at Lady day and Michaelmas) on each hearth they possessed, only the poorest were exempt. This tax originated in France, and it operated from 1662 until 1689.

All parishioners had to tell the constable of the parish the number of hearths they had, and if they did not give this information he had the power to enter their homes. The money collected was sent to the quarter sessions. The authorities felt they were being cheated so, in 1663, two other people had to visit along with the constable.

The Hearth Tax which the Restoration Parliament imposed was surely the least popular of all taxes, as every home that possessed a hearth or stove had to pay, all except the poorest were caught. The thing that really hurt was the method of collection. This was given out to private individuals who paid a fixed sum to the Exchequer for the privilege. To them it was an investment, so naturally they were eager to take every penny of it. They had the authority to enter any household, and were very harsh and insolent. If they could not get their money on the spot, they took furniture and even the family's only bed.

The original return of 1662 shows that Clanfield had 116 hearths and 40 people. This is not thought to have been very accurate. The return we have is for the year 1665, and it lists 71 hearths and 24 people or homes.

Hearth Tax returns 1665.

A tax of 2s. for each fireplace in the house (and stove).

Thomas Smith	8
Samuel Smyth	3
Hiddessey Chapman	5
Thomas Barnes	3
William Castle	5
Alex May	3

William Sperrinck	3
Thomas Adams	5
Widdow Turner	3
Nicholas Yateman	3
Richard Yateman	2
John Linzy Jun.	1
John Stevens Jun.	3
Roger Parsons	3
William Pawling	3
Widow Tomes	3
John Stevens Sen.	3
John More	4
John Palmore	5
Isaac Meisey	3

71

William Fawlkner	2
........Sprinke	
Both discharged by poverty	

Returns 1665: 71 hearths, 24 households.
(In 1662 it had been 116 hearths from 40 people)

It is thought that 1665 is more accurate, but I doubt if people paid if they did not possess a hearth, so in Clanfield it looks as if these three years saw a depression or loss of houses. With the exception of Filkins and Radcot, the whole of the Bampton Hundred shows a loss between these years.

If each house is multiplied by four and a quarter, Clanfield had a population of 170 in 1662 and 102 in 1665.

Of the names mentioned, it would appear that Thomas Smith was at Chestlyon, William Castle at Southwick, Will Pawling at Little Clanfield Osney estate and John More at Friars Court.

1665 was the year of the plague, which would explain the lowering of the returns for the Hearth Tax.

The populations for the villages of the Bampton Hundred were as follows:-

	1662	1665
Witney	171	127
Bampton	99	77
Aston	68	59
Ducklington	57	35
Hailey	47	39
Brize Norton	46	43
Clanfield	40	24
Standlake	39	33
Asthall	38	19
Curbridge	33	30
Alvescot	31	41
Filkins	31	41
Black Bourton	30	21
Lew	22	13
Bradwell	21	15
Kencot	19	25
Shifford	16	10
Kelmscott	16	10
Broughton Poggs	15	10
Grafton	14	12
Crawley	14	11
Asthall Leigh	14	9
Chimney	7	5
Holwell	7	7
Radcot	3	3
Brighthampton	9	

In this same year, the Act of Settlement appeared. If a stranger did not obtain work in the parish within 40 days he could be removed. If he just came for the harvest he had to bring a certificate from his village. Every parish had the right to send a man back to his original parish, and this affected 90 per cent of the population.

During this year Samuel Smith, Vicar, disappeared without record, presumably as a result of the plague. No parish register exists. In fact, many of the village records had been somewhat erratic since about 1640. Phatmell Denton, the Vicar at that time, must have been a very sick man. He entered nothing in 1640, for 1641 there was just one wedding and five deaths, one burial and one birth in 1642, none in 1643 and he died in April 1644, when seven deaths were recorded.

Records were made up for 1644 and 1645. Baptisms failed to be entered in 1641, with only one of the Chestlyon Smith family mentioned in 1642 and no more were entered until 1645. From that year until 1650 the records were kept up.

It would appear that a book of births from 1650 and deaths from 1644 until 1678 was lost, and a new book was started in that year. This was unfortunate, but the baptisms after that period were about the same as before. If anything, the burials increased, so it would appear that the plague did not hit Clanfield too badly.

On July 1st 1665 a watch was kept at Oxford to keep out people with plague. Also, it would appear from the parish register that two families died in Taynton, but not from the plague. However, no more deaths were mentioned.

The plague hit London badly. It was said that during the summer of 1665 nearly a thousand people a day died there. The same year, London suffered a great fire, the scourge of all early towns built mostly of wood. In less than three days it cleared 80 per cent of the city, with 13,000 homes burned. The local booksellers, carrying all the precious books into the old St. Paul's, provided the material which set it ablaze. Charles was determined to rebuild London in brick and stone.

Soon a great building programme was begun and the call for stone, which would not burn, was immense. Every quarry must have been working flat out to cash in on the boom. Burford and Taynton were loading stone at Radcot and floating if off as fast as they could get it there, or as soon as there was sufficient water.

Soon, the King led a national effort to rebuild St. Paul's. Sir Christopher Wren was given the job. The stone of the Old St. Paul's was sorted and used for the foundations and the crypt, but for the above-ground work he wanted Portland stone. However, he found great difficulty with this quarry. Much of the stone had to be drawn when the tide was out, and the quarrymen were never satisfied with their wages. In the end he increasingly looked for other stone.

Working under Wren were master masons Kempster and Strong who, no doubt, had been called in from their local quarry to help in this great project. Kempster owned a quarry at Burford, Strong owned one at Taynton. Wren decided the Burford stone would match the Portland, and because of its softness could be used for the inside carvings. Taynton, unfortunately, did not match the Portland, being too brown, but it could be used for work out of sight. The problem now was how to get it out. The quarry men were mostly part-timers, who had to work part of the year on the land. The answer was found by the King sending troops to help. So, according to an old account book of Kempster's, soldiers could be seen working in the quarries and carting the stone to Radcot.

(Ref: Pocock EA. Radcot and its Bridge, 1966)

In Kempster's diary it says:
   September 20th 1672. Then loaded into Houses boat 8 tunn 3 foot ffrom ratcat. ...September 21. Then was loaded into Humphry Duffins boat 75 ffoot of ston at ratcat... September 26. Then was loaded into Houses boat 9 tunn 2 foot ffrom ratcat pd him then fivety shillings.

(Ref: Prichard M, Carpenter HA. Thames Companion, Oxford Illustrated Press Ltd, 1975)

On the national scene, Parliament decided to pass a law in 1671 preventing all freeholders of under £100 a year (the vast majority) from killing game on their own land. Fox hunting came in after the Civil War, as so many deer parks were broken into and deer killed, and foxes were hunted as a substitute.

As far as religion was concerned the authorities tried to keep a check on all non-conformists. In the 1669 Conventicles it states:

   Charlbury in the house of Alexander Harris on Sunday and Friday most weeks about 30 Quakers. Chadlington in the house of Robert Clements an old anabaptistical soldier about 30 Presbyterians, Anabaptists, etc. For the most part, the said Robert Clements is speaker but sometime one Dunce, an itinerant non-conformist.
   Brize Norton in the house of Francis Dring on Sundays and once a month about 100 Quakers. This Francis Dring is a great ringleader of the sect and is also himself a preacher.
   North Leigh in the house of Thomas Taylor 60 or more Quakers.
   Milton-under-Wychwood in the house of Robert Seacole of Shipton meeting monthly about 80 Quakers.
   Coggs at the house of Mr. Blake of ye Fine Office once or sometimes twice every Lords day about 200 Presbyterians or Independants. Edward Wise,

*Richard Cruckfield and ye steward of ye said Blake by ye said Blake's
encouragements are great promoters of the meeting in defiance of the
authority. The teachers are a combination of non-conformist Ministry, viz. Dr.
Langley, Mr. Cornish, Mr. Dod, Mr. Troughton and Mr. Connoway.*

Then again, in 1676, the Compton Census was made. Compton was the Bishop of
London. He realised that non-conformity had increased in the early years of Charles
II, and he also wished to know how many Catholics there were.

The census for our area was as follows:-

	Conformists	Papists	Non-conformists
Black Bourton	130		2
Alvescot	100		11
Broadwell	300	4	4
Kencott	70		
Brisenorton	190	4	7
Bampton and members	899	2	45
Hanfeild (Clanfield)	200		3

*(Ref: Whiteman Anne ed. Records of Social and Economic History New Series,
The Compton Census of 1676: A critical edition. Oxford University Press, 1986)*

Clanfield's population would have been about 280 people, if we assume that there
were some 80 more children to be added to the above figure of 203. The population is
quite difficult to determine. In the Patent Rolls of 1641 we assumed a population of
296 so, if the figures are correct, a slight decrease was recorded from 1641 until 1676,
through the period of the plague.

Locally, Edward Tyler became Vicar in 1671. He began a school in the church in
1674 and married Elizabeth, daughter of William Castle of Clanfield at Black Bourton in 1678.

In 1674 Charles II married his second wife, having had no children with the first.
She was a Catholic. The leaders feared the result of Catholic children, so they began
to turn against him. He died on February 9th 1685 of a stroke, after being secretly
received into the Catholic faith.

James II (1685-1688)

Charles' brother, James, was accepted as King, although he was a Catholic, because he was 52 years old, and his daughter, Mary, was a Protestant. James was much more severe than Charles. Non-conformists were persecuted.

Will of Monmouth landed at Lyme Regis to claim the throne. The west, numbering some 5,000, rallied to him but he was defeated at Sedgemoor, captured in the New Forest and beheaded on the spot.

The brutal Judge Jefferies toured the west. Three hundred rebels (or non-conformists) were hanged, 800 were transported as slaves to the West Indies — such vengence was not seen in our land again.

James II was a frightened man. He kept a large army of 30,000 men just outside London on Hounslow Heath. He tried stealthily to reintroduce Catholicism, but the incoming Huguenots, who were bringing stories of their persecution on the Continent by the Catholics, made few want Catholicism to return to England.

James offended too many. He had a son by his second wife who would be brought up in Catholicism. The country cried "enough". They sent to Holland for William and Mary (Mary was James' daughter and William was her husband). They landed at Torbay on November 5th 1688. James tried to remove all the Catholics he had been sliding into office but it was too late. Deserted by his leaders, he fled. Some say he was captured and pushed off to the Continent by William.

William and Mary (1688-1702)

William and Mary, although not too fond of each other, served England well. They were now totally servants of Parliament. The crown was no longer to be on a Catholic head. The country needed internal peace, not strife. To finance the King and Parliament a group of Whigs formed the idea of lending one million pounds to Parliament at 8%, so forming 'The Bank of England'. Coins were milled on the edge. The national debt began. Through this financial wizardry England fought her wars and built her Empire.

Mary died in 1694, childless, a lady loved by everyone. But William people could not get on with at all. Indeed, many Ministers would have gladly exchanged him for James II. He died in 1702, when his horse stumbled over a molehill in Hampton Court. The Jacobites from there on raised their glasses to the "little gentleman with the black velvet coat".

Anne 1702-1714

Mary's sister, Anne, was sent for. She had married the kindly George of Denmark. She was a pathetic figure, having lost a dozen or more children, and her body was swollen with gout and dropsy.

During those times Marlborough was leading our troops in Spain. In 1704, letting none but the Queen know, he marched to Blenheim and won a great battle.

In 1707 the union of Scotland and England took place — one crown and one Parliament.

In 1714 Anne died.

During Anne's reign the weather again turned bad. A very severe frost of several weeks in 1709 was followed by several bad harvests. Enclosure was just beginning to become a national issue. Jethro Tull invented the horse hoe and seed drill. Thomas Newcomen had invented the steam pump and Abraham Darby had invented coke smelting. There were now gentry and yeomen, husbandmen and labourers, but the labourers' lives were much better than those on the Continent and in Scotland.

In 1704 Queen Anne's Bounty began. All the monies that had come to the Crown at the Reformation for lights and prayers, etc, were now invested to help pay the poor clergy.

Several controversial Acts were passed towards the end of Anne's reign against Dissenters, the first being the Occasional Conformity Bill (1711) which threatened ruinous fines for any man in state or municipal office who attended any non-conformist place of worship. In 1714 the Schism Act took away from Dissenters the right to educate their own children, this coming into force the same day that Anne died.

However, non-conformity was beginning to develop. The church had been slow in the built-up areas. Now in the expanding London there were more chapels than churches. John Wesley was born in 1703. When he was born, 20% were non-conformists. When he died, 25% of the people were nonconformists.

During these 54 years of the Stuart monarchy Clanfield was changing considerably.

Chestlyon

Leonard Smith died in 1660, and left Chestlyon to his son, Thomas. Thomas Smith had died with no family in 1668. The estate went to his young brother, John, who had been serving an apprenticeship when his father died in 1660. John died in 1704, thinking his wife, Katherine, was pregnant.

Presumably, she had told him that so that he would die in peace, as they had previously lost a boy and had two girls. She was not pregnant, however. The estate went to the two daughters, Katherine and Mary.

Friars Court

This had been divided into three portions in 1558 by John Edmonds, a third to each daughter, Agnes, Mary and Elizabeth. Agnes had married Walter Savage, and left her share to Francis More, son of their daughter, Agnes. Francis died in 1593, and left it to his son, Francis. The son Francis was mentioned in the Protestant Returns of 1641, but by 1651, on the Court Roll, John More, son of Francis, had a third of the manor.

In March 1663 John More, gentleman of Clanfield, and his wife, Mary, sold their part of Friars Court to John Smith, gentleman, of Eaton Hastings, Berkshire for £20. John married Anne, spinster, of Oar Chievely in 1664. They had two sons, John, born in 1665 and Richard, born in 1666.

The second portion of Friars Court belonged to Mary Edmonds. She had married John Regers and had a daughter, Marie, who had married a Warren, and by 1622 they had a son, John. In 1660, John Warren died at Friars Court, but just before that his own son, John, had apparently died at Burford and he had left his own portion to his son, John, who was the grandson. In 1683/4 John Warren sold the land to the above John Smith, who settled it in 1696 on his son, John Smith, and Martha Clyffe of Oar as a marriage settlement as 'Warrens of Clanfield'.

According to the Court Roll of Friars Court in 1685, John Smith had two-thirds of the manor. John Smith's son died, leaving, it seems, his first portion to his son, Richard. In 1704, John, Martha and Richard sold their estate, two-thirds of Friars Court to Ferdinando White. White bought it as two-thirds of the manor being 8 messuages, 12 gardens, 100 acres of arable, 60 acres of meadow, 60 acres of pasture, 7 acres of wood, yearly rent of 45s. Thus, it would seem that two portions had come together.

The third portion was Elizabeth's, who had married Robert Chapman. They had a son, John, and then it went through four generations of Johns, before the last died without issue in 1702, and left it to his sister, Katherine Turfry of Witney. So in 1714, according to the Court Rolls, Friars Court was being held by Ferdinando White and Katherine Turfry.

Southwick

Drew Turner died in 1602, and left it to his son, Thomas. In 1633, Thomas sold it to John and Will Castle of Clanfield after the death of his wife and himself for £120, as five messuages, 60 acres of land, 20 acres of meadow, 30 acres of pasture, 3 acres of 'wood, furze and heath'.

So now some 140 acres of land, 30 acres of pasture, 3 acres of wood, 100 acres of heath had gone to other members of the family. In 1637, Thomas died. In 1685, a Terrier gave Southwick the name 'Mr. Castle's living'. That same year William Castle died. He had two boys, William and John. The son William had died in 1680, so the estate went to John. In 1687, John married Ann Phillips. He died at Burford in 1720, and left 10/- to pay for a yearly sermon at Burford. He left the manor to his son, William. In 1718, William married Mary Smith of Burford, and in 1734 he died, leaving it to his son, John, aged 15 years. The estate does not appear in the records again until 1750.

Village and Area News

In 1690, in the deanery of Witney, Clanfield was rated at £7.6s.4¹/₂d and had the seat of two gents, presumably the Smiths.

In 1694, a tax was made on births of 2s, marriages 2s.6d and deaths 4s., costs rising according to wealth.

In 1696, a window tax replaced the hearth tax to help meet the cost of re-minting the damaged coinage. The cost in 1782 was 7–9 windows — 2s; 10-19 windows — 4s. In 1825, fewer than eight windows were exempt. This tax was abolished in 1851. Until recent years, some of the windows of The Gables were blocked and at the time of writing some of the North Court Cottages windows still are blocked.

In 1704, Burford Charities invested in 18 acres in Clanfield. When enclosed, this was the land at the top of Mill Lane called 'Burford Poor'.

Two very interesting Terriers exist from this period:

Terrier of ye Vicaridge of Clanfield Sept. ye 22nd, 1685

1. *Vicarage House and Homestead on 1acre bounded on the north by Mr. Gunn's, on the south by Widdow Mayor.*
2. *One pasture of 1¹/₂ acres having John Chapman's ground on the north and Mrs Mitholl's ground on the south.*
3. *1¹/₂ acres of meadow in More Mead with the meadow of widdow Laffer on the north and Mrs. Lovedon's on the south.*
4. *¹/₄ acre in Foremead with the Parsonage mead on the east, Mrs. Lovedon's on the west and other ¹/₄ acre lying in Rie Mead with Parsonage mead on the west and Mrs. Lovedon's on the east.*
5. *4 acres arable dispersed in the common fields. 1 acre in Tawney in Langly Furlong having on the east Mr. Gunn, on the west Richard Yateman Jun. ¹/₂ acre headland lying in the field called Barrowfield and in a furlong called Louse furlong having the land of John Chapman on the east. 1 acre in Linton field in a furlong called Stocklains with Robert Turner on the west and Henry Lococke on the*

east. $1/2$ acre in Mill field in Brook furlong with Mr. Smith on the east and Mr. Winnot on the west. $1/2$ acre in Mill field in Skinner's furlong with Widdow Pawling on the north and Mr. Castle on the south. $1/2$ acre in West field in Longland with Mrs. Busby on the east and Mrs. Yeatman on the west.

6. Paid yearly to the vicarage from the Parsonage 3 quarters of wheat and 3 quarters of barley.

7. Due and paid yearly out of the following livings $11 1/2$ bushels of wheat:

Mr. Castle's living	$2 1/2$ bushels	**(Southwicke)**
Sir William Coventry's living	1 bushel	**(Coventry farm)**
Mr. Winnot's living	1 bushel	**(Cumming farm)**
Clanfield Mill	2 bushels	
Richard Mayor's living	$1/2$ bushel	
Robert Turner's living	1 bushel	**(Edgerly)**
Francis Whiting's living	$1/2$ bushel	
Mrs. Lovedon's living	1 bushel	
William Faukner's living	1 bushel	
Mr. Loder's living	1 bushel	**(Friar's Court)**

(Lately purchased of Nicholas Arnold).

8. The whole Tythe of Culvery furlong in Linton field being $7 1/2$ acres of field acres by estimate, arable.

9. The Tythe of Bollam Hays in Tawney arable by estimate 10 acres of field measure.

10. The Tythe of 2 acres in West field called Butts.

11. The Tythe of 1 acre in a field called Billings field.

12. The Tythe of all More Mead except some few lots of which Bampton vicars have some part of the tythe.

13. The Tythe of Wimones adjoining the above.

14. The Tythes of Closes in Clanfield called 'The Old Enclosure'.

15. All the Privy Tythes except those going to Bampton.

16. The whole privy Tythes of the living called Spittlands (Putts) in the Liberty of Alvescot and the Tythe of several grounds there belonging to the vicarage of Clanfield (**Batesland, Southwick manor**).

Edward Tyrer, Vic.
Thomas Hoare and Absolam Panting, Ch. Wardens.

(Ref: Oxon c142, f147)

In 1685, the three Hides given to Clanfield after the Domesday Book which we call Barrow field are noted in a Bampton Terrier.

The Tyth of twelve yard land is due from Clanvill a fourth part whereof belongs to the Impropriators. But the vicars know not where the lands lie neither can they get a terrier from the Impropriators for which reason they intend to put them in Charney.

(Ref: Oxon b40 f44)

Fifteen years later was an extract from: **A Terrier of the Lands lying in Clanfield fields made by me John Gunn Sen. in January 1700 as follows:**

More tythes belonging to the Parsonage of Clanfield. The one half of the tithes which do belong to the four grounds called Bates lands lying in Alvescutt Liberty by the lane going into Clanfield and the Furzes and having John Smith of the farme his grounds lying by Clapgate on the one side and the hither part of the place called South side on the North side thereof and the furzes on the west and Alvescott Marsh in the East side and some part thereof now sowed.

Also some Leyes in South side belonging to Pittlands Livings and in some other places there and Broke Meadow. And the tithe of the Hay of Pittlands Lotts in Sharndy mead allotted every year to the same Livings. And the tithe of all the Corne belonging to all the Pittlands Livings lying in the fields there paying to the Minister of Alvescott aforesaid yearly six shillings and eight pence.

And the Vicar of Clanfield hath the Tythe of some other Closes there and the Privie Tithes thereof for which is paid by the Owners of the same Tenants £3 per annum and 6s to the Parsons besides the 6s.8d.

Memorandum. That the whole tithe of Mr. Smith of Friars Court 'now one piece, heretofore 2 pieces' by Tarney Lane doth belong to the Parsons of Clanfield. (This is Bottom Bridge close.)

(Ref: G A Oxon, c317/7, Part 1)

The Tithes belonging to the Vicarage of Clanfield.

The tithes of all the several grounds there called the Old Enclosures being those wherein the houses stand and of John Stevens late Winnetts (Coopers) Close by Bourton Marsh (Grants Hay Close) and Mr Tirers and of Simon Maiseys late Close, Nicholas Yeatmans, Richard Yeatmans, Mr. Gilberts, Coll Heyes, Thomas Stevens his, Robert and John Adams home Closes and Bushes late Close. Robert Stevens, 2 closes, John Chapman's Close, Jonathan

Yeatmans, Simon Diors home Close, Mr. Smith of Friars Court his bushey
Close, and Cowlease late Mr. Warrens except the bottom of it taken out of the
Barroe field belonging to the Parsons and the part of the Little Green Close
next to the Milking Penn belonging to the Vicars Tithe of Clanfield, and also
the tithe of Alloes heye and of all Wimans Grounds now John Mayseys, and of
the ground called Weeks his piece, and also the fourth part of the tithes of all
the several Closes belonging to Bampton Tithe, viz Mr. Loders Crofts Close by
Jonathan Yeatmans Francis Whitehornes Botts Close, Mr. Coventry home
Close Mr. Busbies home Close and the tithe of Grants Heye and Mr. Sperink's
home stall and the whole tythe of late Eliz. Laters Closes William Fauckner's,
Mr. Castles Sheephouse Close, Peter Herberts late Close, B. Kinches Close
and the tithe of the more Mead except five lotts of meadow there viz. Robert
Stevens lott Mr. Loders Lott which lott two Exchange yearly, Mr Coventries
Lott at the more Mead, one of Mr Gilberts and another of the Widdow
Pearsons, and in Little Clanfield the close called the Belham Heyes Close
(Osney) being Mr. Gilberts next to Buckrills, the widow Paulings Close
between the Belham Heyes furlong. Mr Chapmans Close and Mr. Busbies and
Mr. Coventrys heyes there, Goodwife Berries and John Addams Mr Loden,
Thomas Edwards his, Robert Turners, Mr. Gilberts, John Clarks of Bampton,
John Stevens (Loders) late Winnetts next to Grafton Green furlong, and by
Billings the close of Mr. Abell, next to it widow Paulings of Christ Church
cottage next to it.

Mr Abells close next to his house, Thomas Hore his close next, Mr. Chapmans
close next on the Mill, Blagroves homestall and the home Close Copse and
Crabtree ground, and the tythe of 9 Vase Butts viz. 2 of Robert Turners, 1 of Mr.
Greenaways a headland, 1 of John Stevens late Mr. Winnetts, 2 of Mr Busbies,
3 of John Mayseys late Shiltons and the tythe of the Culvery furlong in Linton
being 7 acres and $\frac{1}{2}$ and the tithe of the Belham heyes furlong in Tarney being
50 acres and Mr Busbies home in Billings and the tythe of Sarfords Coppice at
Boambridge belonging to Mrs. Smith of Friars Court and the tithe of Margaret
Mayes homestall and Close and the tithe of the Homestall of Robert Stevens his
Culvery Homestall and John Clarks.

Besides his Vicarage house and Homestall and his Marsh Close and 1 acre
in the More and a farindal in the Rye and another in the Foremead and 2 acres
and 4 half acres of land in the fields Tithefree and likewise 3 quarters of Barley

yearly out of the Parsonage and moreover of Composition of Wheat out of the
Town of Clanfield viz.

out of Mr. Castles living 2 bushels and one half

out of Mr. Coventries living 1 bushell
from John Stevens for Mr. Winnetts 1 bushel

from Blagrove for the mill 2 bushells
from Richard May for Coopers half a bushell
from Robert Turners living 1 bushell
from Jonathan Yeatmans half a bushell
from John Maysey for Shiltons 1 bushell
from Mr. William Franchners living 1 bushell
from Hodges his living C:V half a bushell
from Mr. Loder for Knapps Living 1 bushell whereof half a bushell lost
as is said —
    And all the Privie tithes of Clanfield save only of the living belonging to
Bampton Tithe in which Bampton is to have 3 parts and Clanfield the fourth
part of the Tithes."

(The latter contains three, first the Parsonage Tithes then the Vicar's and
then the parts of which Bampton has 3/4).
(Ref: GA Oxon c317/7 Part 1)

From Charles II's reign we have 22 wills and inventories:

In 1660 Leonard Smith of Chestlyons, gent., died. He left £1700 to his family of
eight and Chestlyons to his son, Thomas. His widow died in 1680 at Corsham, Wilts.
    The same year John Warren, gent, died at Friars Court. It appears that his son,
John, died at Burford just before him. He left two Bibles, Smith's sermons and other
books valued at 15s. His estate was valued at £44.15s.4d.
    James Hill also died in 1660 and left six books. He was a wheelwright and his
timber and his tools were worth £7. His estate was worth £82.19.0d

    John Sperrink, yeoman, son of William, died in 1661. He left an estate of
£157.16s.4d. All his estate passed to his son, William. In his cellar he had two full
hogsheads of ale (this was probably The Plough).
    John Paulings, yeoman, of Little Clanfield died in 1661 with an estate of
£187.17s.0d. He had a three-up and four-down house.
    John Laffer died in 1662, and in his inventory the willows growing on the Cause-
way are mentioned.
    John Linzey the elder, carpenter, died in 1665 leaving his business to his son,
John, and 2 acres to his daughter, Alice Whitehorn.

In 1671 there is the inventory of Richard Pryer, a man murdered at Radcot:

A true and perfect inventorie of the personal estate of Richard Pryer of

Radcote in the parish of Langford, died 15 August 1671, taken and valued by Willia n Yate sen. and Waltar Carter of Stanford in the Vale of White Horse.

His wearring apperal	2	10	0
Money due to him upon bond	90	00	0
	92	10	0

DECLARATION OF ACCOUNT

<u>*Funeral*</u>		17	0
Paid to the crown for setting on ye body of ye deceased		13	4
Expences at two times	1	9	8
Shroud		6	8
Paid for searching after Mr Sunnybank Veaysie who was supposed to have slain the ded	1	4	0
Another time going after him		11	0
Spent at ye Assize at Oxford	1	13	0
For horse hire at ye same time		2	8
For bringing in the Wittnesses at ye Assize at Oxford		1	0
For ye Lres of Aldron obligason onye said ingressing ye suven rids, other charges in side out thereouts	1	4	4
For horse hire and charges to Oxford and her coming to pay her account		1	6
For ye degree of ye Judge in examining the ac.		10	0
For the Quinotus est		10	0
For the recovering of the ac. in writing		6	8
For the jugressing of the ac.		3	4
For the appareless fee		1	0
	9	15	2

John Stevens Snr and John Stevens Jnr both died in 1675. Both had Bibles. Junior was very wealthy, owning a house in Clanfield as well as land, and his estate was valued at £244.1s.0d. His widow carried on the farm and died in 1682.

Thomas Adams, baker and yeoman, died in 1680 leaving an estate of £208.5s.0d and he owned the Masons Arms. His property had a cellar in it with three drink barrels, an old tub and three leather bottles. Will, his son, died the following year with an estate of £269.2s.0d, a wealthy yeoman.

Alex May, yeoman, died in 1684 leaving Coopers quarters land to be sold. This may be the Ball (in more recent times the Golden Ball).

William Castle junior in 1680 and then in 1685 his father, who was a yeoman, died. However, he did not leave Southwick.

During the three years of James II we had three wills and inventories. During this time the Pearson family were blacksmiths in Clanfield. In 1674, Roger Pearson died, leaving all his tools to his son, John. John died in 1686, leaving the tools to his son, Thomas. According to his inventory he left "in the shoppe and belonging to it — to grine stones one annfill (anvil) to Hisses, one pear of billes (bellows) and the working tools £2.10s".

Richard Yateman the elder died in 1686. He was the wealthiest yeoman so far, leaving an estate valued at £501. This was in Hedges land which went with Horn cots., but had £300 cash let out on a bond. His father, Solomon, left £187.13s.4d.

In 1687 Will Sperrink, the wealthy landowner of Clanfield, was elected Chief Constable of the Western Division.

During the reign of William and Mary we have eight wills and four inventories surviving. In 1689 John Adams the elder, yeoman, died leaving an estate valued at £142.2s.6d. In 1696, George Knapp died, a tenant farmer of Friars Court. He was a yeoman with an estate of £319.16s.0d. He was the first of the Knapp family who later played such a large part in the life of Clanfield. The house was mentioned as being four up and four down.

In that year Robert Adams, carpenter, died. He had an estate of £35.10s.0d and his tools were valued at 10/-. He left his trade to his son, John, who died in 1704. John's estate was valued at £47.12s.6d, and his tools were listed as follows:-

One whipsaw, 3 tennan saws, 5 old handsaws	*1*	*1*	*6*
3 Broad axes, 2 pitchery axes		*9*	*6*
1 pump with a short handle, 6 bits, 3 cramps	*1*	*3*	
2 jig planes and some little planes		*8*	
8 augers, 3 shiffells, 2 gauges, 4 spokes		*7*	
6 wedges, 1 spade, grindstone		*10*	
1 vice, 2 working benches, 6 thinges,			
lumber, old books		*11*	*6*
1 chain, wheels	*1*	*13*	

In 1702, James Breakspear, yeoman and baker and "a little indisposed in health", died. His son, James, was a baker in Langford. His estate was valued at £244.7s.4d. His crops in the field in July came to £120.

In 1702, John Taylor als Chapman, died. His sister, Katherine Turfrey, who lived in Witney later owned a third part of Friars Court Manor from the Elizabeth Edmonds side. Because John had no family and his estate was sold, she must have taken Friars Court, for she shared the manor with Ferdinando White in 1714. This estate was valued at £190.12s.3d.

During Queen Anne's reign, in 1703, John Wells died. He was the innkeeper of Radcot. He had three children with his wife, Flora, and a fourth with his mistress, Ann Davis, who lived with him.

In 1704, John Smith died at Chestlyons. He left "to Katherine my wife my house called the Great House where I live with gardens, orchard and hopyard. A close called Little Cowlease and fish ponds there, etc."

John Gunn also died in 1704. In 1623 a John Gunn of Witney, gent, married Julia Rogers at Black Bourton. She was a daughter of Marie Rogers, who owned a third of Friars Court and the rectory. This John was Marie's grandson. He was given the money left by Marie Rogers to pay 40 a year to the poor of Clanfield. It was now £25. He stated: "My will I do hereby oblige my several closes called The Parsonage lying in Clanfield (being part of the estate I lately purchased) for the true payment every year of 40s. on St. Thomas' day to be distributed amongst the poor of Clanfield."

John's father, also John, died in 1707. He was a lawyer. He left his law books to his grandson, Giles Nash, son of his daughter, Elizabeth.

In 1680, John Gunn was a Commissioner of Peace in Oxfordshire. In Monk's book, *A Ramble in Oxfordshire*, he records: "In a book belonging to the Witney Society of Friends there is a record to the effect that nine Quakers were fined 5s. for being present at a meeting in Alvescott, which was broken up by Justices John Gower of Weale and John Lunn (But it should read 'Gunn') of Clanfield with Waltar Powell, priest of Alvescott as informer, and others."

In 1705, Nicholas Yeatman, yeoman, died leaving a "messuage, dwelling house and one yard of land". He left it to his son, John, who is seen to have died in 1721 with an estate of £407.

1707 was the year in which 13 people died at Alvescot as a result of pestilential fever, which began at the Ale House.

In 1710 we see the first mention of a Blagrove, miller of Little Clanfield, who left it for the use of his mother, Joan, and his son, Thomas. John Thomas Blagrove signed as Church Warden of Clanfield in 1641.

★ ★ ★

Chapter 11

The Age of Hanover

George 1714-1727

WHEN Anne died, her sister, Sophie, granddaughter of James I and next in line for the throne, had also just died, so Sophie's son, George, came to the throne. He was a German who could speak little English. However, he could speak French, the language of the court. He left his wife behind in prison, and brought his mistress over with him. He was a very shy man who loved music and the arts, but he could not get on with his son.

He had landed at Greenwich on 18th September 1714, but within two years the Jacobites had tried to regain the throne. Few supported him in England, so within a month he went back to the Continent.

England was now in the position of having a population explosion. Until then, our population had been kept under reasonable control by manorial law. Under this regulation, a man was only allowed to marry if he had land. Thus he was often older when he came into possession, which would limit the size of his family.

Now, at last, men began to be free of the manor and so could marry earlier. Big houses were being built and added to. The poverty of the post Civil War was now long past, and towns were growing.

Religion, however, was on the decline. Pluralism was the curse of the Church of England. This was when a vicar owned more than one living and employed curates to do his work.

The old Non-conformists, the Prebyterians, the Congregationalists and the Baptists were in decline. Drink was becoming a curse of the land, as people tried to get away from their troubles and so created more difficulties. Marlborough's returning soldiers brought much of the gin drinking habit to London.

George II 1727-1760

George II was another like George I, in that he came to the throne late in life. He was crowned at the age of 44. He also loved music and the arts, also could not get on with his son, and had several mistresses. George's wife, Caroline of Anspach, was a mainstay to him and when she died in 1737 he became a different man with little life in him.

In George I's reign there had a bad harvest in 1720, and George II saw bad harvests in 1737 and 1742. Otherwise they were mostly good harvests in the 1730s and 1740s. Food was cheap and so there was a large increase in the adult population by the 1770s and 1780s.

The Jacobites tried to take over the land again in 1745. We are told that they reached Derby, where only 300 Catholics met them. Mr. Hartmann, author of *The Civil War in Faringdon*, told me that in looking up the records of this period, he found that the Jacobites were stopped not by English soldiers but by a contingent of Scottish soldiers who were waiting at the southern ports to go to the battles in Europe.

All the English soldiers were already in Europe. These Scottish soldiers were rushed back up the country, and so in the battle against the Jacobites, Scot was fighting against Scot.

It appears that the Pretender had been secretly in England seeking support. A Charlbury barber told of a visit he made to Cornbury to shave a guest who apparently held 'extraordinary' respect from the family. Also, Mr. Heber Percy told me that it is said that in his property, Faringdon House, the fir trees had been planted, as was the custom, as a secret sign that they belonged to this Jacobean movement.

In 1756, England was at war with France and this lasted until 1763, and was known as the Seven Years War. In 1747, a tax was put on carriages and this was to last for 35 years before it was abolished.

George II died in 1760, but as his son, Frederick, had died in 1751, he was followed by his grandson, George III, aged 22, who was mentally and emotionally very backward.

George III 1760-1820

George married Charlotte of Micklebury in 1761, and she pulled him together — but in 1765, a long mental illness began and after his favourite daughter, Amelia, died in 1810, he went quite mad. His wife was not very pretty. But he had 15 children. His sons were wasters, but nevertheless the people were very loyal to him. His oldest son ruled as Regent from 1812 until 1820, when his father died.

George was very interested in farming. Our farming was then being greatly influenced by the Dutch, and a four-year rotation was evolved in Norfolk. Dutch turnips were introduced for better winter feed. Farms were getting larger, rents doubled from 1720–1790 and again from 1790–1810. Enclosure was developing. Black Bourton was enclosed in 1771.

The spring of 1771 was bleak. There were eight weeks of snow, and food was terribly short. Large numbers of cows were barren.

A new road had been made to our village, staked out at 60 ft wide. Part of the old road remains at the Bourton end, but then it left its old twisting course to go straight to Clanfield. Another one from the marsh gate was staked out 60ft wide to go to Fairford. This was called Calcroft or Cowcroft Lane.

There was a gate across the road into Clanfield. There was also one on the other road described as for "private cart and carriage, branching out of the Bourton Clanfield road into and through an allotment of the Dean and Chapter of Christ Church to Turners Gate in the parish of Clanfield 20ft wide, to be used by the owners and occupiers of the land and meadows belonging to Alvescot, Kencot and Brize Norton, called by the several names of Borough way, Charney, and Charney Hurst."

Turner's gate is by the house on the parish boundary which used to be, until recently, in Black Bourton parish. This was the Turner who was a Quaker. He looked after Black Bourton cattle grazing on the marsh and kept the gate shut.

The private lane was really a continuation of Calcroft Lane to Marsh Lane. Clanfield later made sure the Black Bourton farmers used it rather than tearing up the village road. Also, there was "a footpath of the Dean and Chapters' land to a stile at Clanfield called Cooper's stile". This footpath followed the road and went into the paddock opposite the Grange, which was always called Coopers, after Nick Cooper who died in 1633 owning the Bull.

As a result of enclosure, the rents of Black Bourton were raised from about 1s.6d or 2s, per acre to 14s. by 1806. The reason for this was the fact that men farmed better any land they held freely without the constrictions of a communal farmers' court.

Further machines were being invented. The threshing machine came into being in 1788, and the chaff cutter in 1794. This latter machine cut the straw into short lengths to mix with chopped roots.

The winter of 1784 to 1785 was the severest known. From the first snows in October, England was frozen until the last snows in April. The summer of 1783 had been very heavy and foggy with many thunderstorms. There was intense heat and flies everywhere.

As the population increased, so food prices rose. Restrictions on imported goods were relaxed in 1773. Poaching increased as families grew larger. By 1795, there were so many people without land and out of work that a policy was started at Speenhamland, Berks, of subsidising wages through the poor rates, depending on the size of the family and the price of corn, and this became accepted by all.

When the Napoleonic war ended in 1814, prices fell, so imports fell and prices then rose again. Riots followed, but in 1822 the prices fell back again sharply.

From 1793 to 1802, England had been at war with Napoleon. After a short respite we were fighting again from 1803 to 1814. Napoleon was defeated, and put in exile on the Isle of Elba which he was allowed to virtually govern. He escaped, fought another 100 days and was defeated at Waterloo on 18th June 1815. He was then sent to St Helena, where he died in 1820.

It was during the reign of George III that the age of canals and railways began to flourish. Many new taxes were introduced, such as for dogs (1796–1882), female servants (1785–1792), male servants (1777–1852), hair powder (1795–98), horses (1784–1874). Income tax was introduced in 1799, originally as a temporary measure to raise money to fight the French. Public whipping of women ceased in 1817 and ducking ceased in 1809.

In 1809, Ireland joined with us to form the United Kingdom. In 1815, unemployment began to be a serious problem as a result of post war depression. Soldiers returning from the war flooded the labour market. The problem was worsened by bad harvests, high food prices and a rising population.

George IV 1820-1830

George III died in 1820, and his son, the Regent, came to the throne as George IV. He had previously been married in 1785 to Mrs Fitzherbert, a young Catholic widow, but this was later annulled and he then married Princess Caroline of Brunswick. They had a daughter, Charlotte. George grew to dislike his wife and she later left him. Ill health and laziness made him a poor King. He ended his years skulking in sullen oblivion at Windsor.

William IV 1830-1837

William was the third son of George III, and was aged 64 when he came to the throne. Previously he had had a family of 10 children with the actress Mrs Jordan, whom he left when he saw that he might become King. He loved the sea, and was rather a rough diamond, not at all diplomatic.

Mrs. Jordan had done much for his rough ways. He married Queen Adelaide, a very charming lady, in 1818, with whom he had two further daughters. Unfortunately they both died.

Although poor material for a King, it was said: "This undistinguished old gent with a head shaped like a pineapple did a good job in a perplexing time." He came to the throne when the monarchy was very low. Seven years later, when he died, by his geniality, good humour and get-at-able-ness he had restored much of the position of the monarchy. People respected his genuineness.

His illegitimate sons caused him much concern, as, deprived of any official position, they sought an economic position. In his age the old system was removed by the Reform Bill which gave everyone who held an estate of £10 or over the vote. During this time the tithe was commuted from being paid in kind to being paid in money.

Farming saw the invention of the American Reaper in 1834 which was to herald a great change.

Clanfield during the Hanovers 1714–1837

Chestlyons

As we recall, Chestlyons went to the two daughters of John Smith, who had died without a son. Mary, one of the daughters, married John Dodwell who promptly died. She married again, to Thomas Barnard. When they died, the Chestlyons share came to their son, Thomas, who sold it in 1753 to Alex Hogg. Katherine, John Smith's other daughter, who received Chestlyons on her wedding day, married a William Dawes, captain in His Majesty's Foot. She died in 1729 and left her half to her husband, who in 1761 also sold out to Alex Hogg, lacemaker, for £1,149.9s.8d.

So by 1761, Alex Hogg owned the whole estate. He offered it for sale in *Jacksons Journal* in 1764 as follows: "Estate for sale, house, barns, subject to payment of £20 charity. Enquire Rev. Middleton of Hampton." Eventually he sold it to Thomas Bennett of Dudgrove in 1774 for £3,740. The tenant then was a Mr Smith.

In 1807, Thomas Bennett died of dropsy and was buried in the east end of the churchyard at Shrivenham. He left Chestlyons to his nephew, Thomas Bennett, who, in 1835 sold it to William Aldworth for £7,000.

Friars Court

In 1704, Ferdinando White had bought two thirds of the manor off John and Martha Smith. These were the portions of Agnes Moore and Marie Rogers, two of the Edmonds daughters. Ferdinando died at Friars Court and lies buried in the chancel of Clanfield church, He was buried on 6th January 1720. He had three girls. His oldest daughter, Amy, had married Charles Collins. They had a son, Ferdinando, and in 1749 he had sold the manor to a Dr. Richard Frewin of Oxford.

Frewin was one of the well known Oxfordshire doctors. Frewin Hall, his home, is in New Inn Hall Street, Oxford. It can be seen, and has been used by Brasenose College for students. The front doorway is now blocked up, but most interestingly, under a wing adjoining this, there is a crypt with Norman pillars and arches.

Dr. Frewin's picture is in the common room of Christ Church and his bust is in the hall. In the picture he is a man full in vigour and life, but the bust is of an aged and decrepit man. When he died he left all his books, some 2,300, to form the basis of Dr. Radcliffe's library, and he also left a considerable sum to Christ Church College. He was a physician and Professor of History at Christ Church in 1698. He had his BA in 1702, his MA in 1704, his MD in 1711, and in 1727 was elected the Camden Professor of History. He married three times.

On his death, in 1760, he left his estate to three trustees, James Hawley, James Gilpin, and John Frewin, to sell and pay his debts. James Hawley and John Frewin bought the estate between them on the death of James Gilpin in 1767.

Thus, two-thirds of Friars Court was again held in two parts. James Hawley was said in *Jacksons Journal* of 1787 to be a Doctor of Physics. James Hawley's son, Henry, married a Dorothy Ashwood in 1770. Their son, Henry, died in 1822. The second son, Joseph, was to become a Knight and in 1835 he became Sir Joseph Henry Hawley.

Sir Joseph Henry Hawley, third Baronet, lived from 1813–1875. He was a patron of the turf. He became a Lieutenant of the 9th Lancers in 1833. He left the Army in 1834, and after having sold Friars Court he went on to have the winner of the Oaks in 1842. He cleared about £3,000 by winning the Derby with Beadsman in 1858, and he won the Derby again in 1859 and 1868. He owned the winner of the St. Leger in 1869.

On the Frewin side, John died in 1760 and his widow, Elizabeth, married Nathan Wright. So, in the land tax of 1785, Friars Court was owned by Hawley and Wright. In 1794, Selena, daughter of John and Elizabeth Frewin, married the Rev. James Moore. In 1816, when Selena died, she left it to her son, the Rev. John Frewin Moore. In 1835, Sir Joseph Henry Hawley and the Rev. John Frewin Moore sold their two-thirds of Friars Court to William Newman.

The remaining one third portion of Friars Court left to Elizabeth Chapman went, on the death of John Chapman, to his sister, Katherine, who had married a Francis Turfrey in the wood trade in 1667 in Witney. In 1714, Katherine stood as lord of the manor with Ferdinando White. She died in 1725 having a family of seven of which Francis, her son, was born in 1670, and John in 1675. Francis had a daughter, Sarah, in 1702, who died. John, called a blanketer, married Sarah Grey of Witney in 1701, and had two children. Elizabeth, born in 1702, died in 1708 and John was born in 1704 but died in the same year.

Southwick

John Castle of Burford died in 1720, leaving Southwick to his son, William. William died in 1734 leaving the manor to his son, John, aged 15. On 11th October 1750, John, apothecary, and grandson of John Castle of Burford, sold Southwick to Mary Bradshaw of Kelmscott, who was to marry John Howse of Winstone, Gloucestershire. She made her will in 1772 and when she died in 1779, she left it to her nephew, Edward Bradshaw. Her husband had the property for his lifetime and in the land tax of 1785 he was seen as the owner.

In 1796, Edward Bradshaw sold it to Mr. William Clarke who was farming it, although he seems to have been living at the weir by the river. He died in 1802 and left it to his son, John, providing that he paid £2,400 to the rest of his family. The debt was too heavy for John. In 1815, he sold off 45 acres to William Collett. John was called a maltster. Southwick was advertised in *Jackson's Journal* in 1814 as freehold land, 45 acres, 1 r., arable in the common fields of Clanfield in the ownership of Mr. John Clarke in lots.

In 1817 he passed what was left on to his daughter, Priscilla. She had been left £1,500 by her grandfather, Thomas Pope of Whelford, and had married a Dan Edmonds, so she paid her father £1,400. In 1830, Priscilla and her husband stood as owners.

In 1785, our first records of the Land Tax appear. The record for Clanfield was as follows:

Elliott	£17.17s.0d	*Owner of Brooks Farm, Pound Lane and Rectory Farm, and ²/₃ rectorial tithes (Gunns and Chapmans)*
Tuckewell	£3.6s.0d	*Little Clanfield Manor*
Hawley	17s.6d	*Friars Court*
Howes	9s	*Southwick*
Pearsons	1s.8d	
Coventry	£8.0s.4d	*Coventry Farm, Lower Green*
Boucher	£5.0s.8d	*¹/₃ rectorial tithe*
	8s	*Pigeon House (Possibly Rectory Farm)*
Adams	£5.2s.4³/₄d	*Adams Yard (Wicks and Little Clanfield Estates)*
Collinson	£3.0s.0d	*Vicarage*
Thomas Adams	£2.15s.	*Lower Farm*
Higgins	£10.15s.7d	*Post Office and Garage Site*
John Pawlin	£2.14s	*Part of Osney land adjacent to Little Clanfield Manor House*
Hower	£1.0s.0d	
Boucher	£2.15s	*Clanfield 'Manor' Farm*
Stevens	£13.4s	*High House Farm*
Nordon	£3.3s.4d	
Adams	£1.0s.0d	
Waine	£4.13s	*Another part of Osney*
Cox	£8.10s	*Windmill Farm*
Cummings	£7.4s	*Adjacent to Coventry in Lower Green*
Yells	£1.3s.2d	
Collett	19s	*Yew Tree House*
Withers	£3.8s	
Butts	£2.0s.0d	
Holcombe	£1.12s	
Colston	£3.10s	*Edgerly*

Nicholls		
Yateman	*£2.8s*	
Richard Chessus	*£1.0s.4d*	*Friars Court Cottages, Old Chapel*
Clarke	*£1.0s.6d*	
Blagrove	*£1.0s.0d*	*Tenant – Arthur Lay, Little Clanfield Mill*
R. Knapp	*4s*	*House behind the Pond*

An interesting sale took place in 1817 and 1818. Clanfield, in the Domesday Book, had been the estate of Roger d'Ivry. This was now part of the vast Honour of Ewelme, and the Court Leet had always belonged to that, rather than to the Bampton Hundred. This manor court in 1827 met at the Masons Arms, the house of John Furze, when "all males over 12 years had to attend, and three householders were to be elected as Jury. Various odd references to this court exist.

In 1691 Clanfield had to pay 1s., in 1692 – 3s., 1694 – 15s., 1695 – 3s.4d. These were the income of the Court. A Roll says that from Michaelmas 1680 to Lady Day 1681, Clanfield paid 4s., Bourton 7s.3d, Southwick 3s.2d, Putts Fee 3s.11d, Abbots Fee 3s.2d, Norton Bruern 23s.10d, Carswell 2s.4d. These were all members of the Honour who attended the court at Clanfield.

William Ward of Clanfield acquired the Manor Farm, as it is called. Manor Farm was actually part of Southwick Manor, but from then on it became known as Manor Farm.

The Quarter Session records hold a few interesting facts about court cases of the time which affected the inhabitants of our area. In 1706, Robert Clarke of Bampton, fellmonger, George Wells of Radcot, yeoman, and Richard Clarke of Clanfield, butcher, appeared in court for stealing two casting nets from Lord Rochester. This shows the importance of fishing in our area.

In 1714, Anthony Stevens, living at the Vicarage, had a wife, Margaret, who was insane. She had threatened to kill Sarah Whitehorn. Stevens was ordered to restrain her.

In 1720 Cal Johnson of Oxford, bargeman, John Gardener of Oxford, bargemaster, and Thomas Roger Buckland, fisherman, were in court for trying to steal Amy White's fowls at Clanfield and assaulting Richard Coxter jun. Again, another reference to the importance of Radcot as a canal. Also, it shows the temptation of stealing for the men who were here today and gone tomorrow. These men were caught, but it was a very dangerous age.

In 1758, the trial took place at Oxford Assizes of Edward Wheeler. He was charged on 6th June by Will Seiger of Coleshill, Berks, of having stolen a black gelding worth £7 out of Seiger's yard on the previous day. Wheeler said that he bought the horse off a stranger on the road, as they were coming to Chipping Norton, near Shipton Downs, about seven o'clock in the morning, and the saddle with it, and that there was no person present as witness, and he could not find the man who accepted three pounds for him. He later pleaded guilty, and was sentenced to hang. This was later commuted to transportation for seven years. Wheeler was said to be of "Clandon", Oxfordshire.

James Clack, a labourer of 33 years, was sentenced to seven years transportation at Oxford on 5th January, 1835. He had stolen beans and peas from Thomas Adams. He was transported on the "Bandasten" and arrived in Van Diemans Land on 7th September 1835, where he died in 1836.
(Ref: HO 27/50 fo. 108 and HO 11/10, fo. 80v)

Jackson's Journal is also a mine of information. This paper began as a leaflet for the 1735 election. It had such a good sale that Jackson continued to publish it weekly. At first, only a few reports about Clanfield appeared, but they increased over the years. In 1757, Edward Wheeler, victualler, of Clanfield, was committed to the castle at Oxford for breaking into Richard Miles' house and stealing £40. He was acquitted. In 1758, Mr. Edward Wheeler was condemned to death for horse stealing, reprieved and transported for 14 years. It is possible that this was the same man who was charged with both offences.

On 12th May 1757 Samuel Johnson, of Bampton, claimed to have been robbed by a single highwayman of £24, chiefly in gold, on his way from Lechlade market. In 1759 there was an advertisement for his arrest by the parish officer in the paper. He had run away and left his wife on the parish for 18 months. He must have been a corn merchant, not a farmer, having sold nearly five tons of corn.

In an inquest in 1759 on Will Ilot of Filkins, farmer, a verdict of "accidentally drowned" in a ditch at Radcot was given. He probably had had too much to drink. In 1757, there had been reports of risings and mobbings at Oxford and Abingdon and the adjacent markets. A later report said this had been untrue, and that it was in fact quite safe to frequent these markets. In May, 1758, smallpox was reported in Burford. People were staying away from markets and fairs.

In the years 1735-40, the Great Frost occurred. The Thames was frozen over. In July 1762, there was a sale at Faringdon of some cottages which would be sold to the best bidder at the burning of one inch of the candle. This was a common way of taking bids. In January, 1764, there were very bad floods, and in November of the same year an earthquake was felt early one morning.

On December 1st, 1764, it was said that several locks on the river between Oxford and Lechlade should be kept open for the space of three hours from Lady Day until Michaelmas, and for two hours from Michaelmas to Lady Day. In May, 1765, it was said that from May 20th to 20th November no boat should draw more than 3' 8" and the tonnage should be marked on each boat. The stranded boats blocked the river.

It was during this time that a coach started running from Highworth to London for 13s.6d, leaving at 2.00 a.m. from Highworth on Mondays, Wednesdays and Fridays, and returning at 4.00 a.m. Tuesdays, Thursdays and Saturdays. It arrived in Highworth at 7.00 p.m. It was half-price for children and those sitting outside.

In September 1766, riots took place at Oxford and Abingdon. Corn was very expensive, because so much was exported.

In January 1767, Dan Eckland, one of the rioters at Abingdon, was executed at Reading. During this same year Bampton market, which had been shut for many years, reopened.

The Radcliffe Infirmary was completed in Oxford.

In June 1771, there was a meeting at the Horse and Jockey, Black Bourton, in which the proprietors of the Thames meadows, belonging to the parishes of Clanfield, Black Bourton, Brize Norton, Elscott and Kencot, met to consider repairing the lane leading to the meadows — this was Marsh Lane.

In 1772, there was an inquest at Curbridge on John Clarke of Clanfield, baker, who fell off his horse drunk after coming home from Witney market.

In June 1773, a property was let in Clanfield — 70 acres of arable, 30 acres of meadow and enclosed pasture ground with communal pasture, large farmhouse, barn, stables in good repair. The tenant farmer was Mr. James, and the owner was Mr. Cox of Letcombe Regis. The property was Windmill Farm.

In 1779, the turnpike road from Pidnal Bridge (the northernmost of Radcot's three bridges) through Clanfield was raised above the flood water level.

In 1782, the Rev. Middleton died, aged 80 years. He and his predecessor Edward Tyler had between them held the living for 113 years.

In November, 1783, the sale took place of the Red Lion and 19 acres of arable, and 1½ acres of meadow which was let at £12.10s.

In July, 1784, there was a large fire at Faringdon during which 15 houses were burnt down. A public subscription was to be used to raise money to help those who lost homes in the fire.

In January, 1785, there were extremely bad floods which happened when the thaw from the severe winter was followed by very heavy rains.

In September, 1786, the sale took place of a freehold estate and dwelling house, three rooms on the first floor, three on the second, two on the third. It had a large barn and stable, and four acres of arable. It was said to be "in good repair, and will do for any business, but especially for a bakers as it has a large new bread oven". This was probably The Plough.

In 1797, there was a report of Bampton Fair, which was suffering a lot of trouble from pickpockets. One farmer, of Gaunt House, was said to have lost a pocket book containing £50.6s. Another lost £40.

In December, 1796, the Duke of Marlborough gave seven fat oxen and 1,000 loaves of bread to the poor around Blenheim for Christmas.

In 1803, William Wilkinson, labourer, of Clanfield was a substitute for Richard Hanks of Stanton Harcourt for the Oxford Regiment of the militia. He did not turn up, and a 20s. reward was offered for information of his whereabouts.

In October, 1804, T. Davis was induced by his friends to take the house of the late Thomas Stephen, gent, as a boarding school. The cost was fourteen guineas per annum for board. This may have been The Plough.

In 1809, on October 25th, there were great celebrations everywhere for the Jubilee of George III. The bells in Faringdon rang. Six cannons fired a salute. Two large balloons set off at 2.00 p.m.

During 1812, the Bampton enclosure boundaries of the parish were to be determined. On April 21st, 1813, the Commissioners eventually met at Charney Meadow to check the Bampton boundary against Charney and Burroway. It had been too wet to do it previously. There was also a reference to the road from Yatt in Weald along Welcome Way (presumably this meant Welton Way) to Cowleaze Corner.

In February 1814, the Thames froze over again. This was another of the years that a Great Frost Fair was held on the river in London. During the same year, in March, there was the sale of a leasehold estate of 600 acres, the lease having 600 years to run, in the occupation of Mrs Clarke. It consisted of a farmhouse with barn, stables and yard, garden, all standing in 1½ acres of ground, conveniently sited in Clanfield, together with 18¼ acres of arable, two enclosed grounds, 4½ acres of meadow. It was subject to 4s.6d rent per annum. This was 'Manor Farm'.

During July, 1818, seven acres of land was sold at Bampton by the Shrewsbury estate to meet the cost of the enclosure award, and this generally cost about £1 per acre.

1819-20 was a very severe winter. During this same year, a reward of 20s. was offered for deserters James Radhourn and James Nicholas of Clanfield, aged 23 and 30 respectively.

On 30th, June, 1821, there was an advertisement to let .... "Clanfield vicarage. Two front rooms good cellar, three good bedrooms, small brewhouse, barn, stable for two horses, ¾ acre of garden". This had been rebuilt by John Farmer of Clanfield for £233.5s.8d. The Vicar, the Rev. John Dimmocks, was living at Uppingham, Rutlandshire. The patrons were G. H. Elliott Esq, of Bracknell, Berks, and Thomas Bennett of Castle Eaton, Highworth, Wilts. The house had apparently been in ruins before that.

The winter of 1823-4 was the mildest winter ever known. This was followed by a very good harvest in 1824.

In January 1828, there were very high floods. Faringdon was like an island. All the meadows in the neighbourhood of Radcot, Clanfield, Buscot and Lechlade were completely inundated. At the end of this year, the inhabitants of Faringdon were awoken at 2.00 a.m. to the sound of "Fire, fire". Upward of 300 people assembled in the street, many with hardly anything on. It was raining in torrents. Despite all the fuss, it was a false alarm!

The winter of 1830 was very hard, and there was a severe fuel shortage. Radcot was the last hope of Faringdon for fuel, but it soon ran out.

It was during this time that there was a minor revolution amongst the agricultural labourers. Until recently, England had been full of peasant people who owned a bit of land and had common rights. As farms became larger, and commons were enclosed more and more, people had to become agricultural labourers working for others, particularly as families grew in size and manorial powers waned. During the bad years, it was these people who suffered the most, although they were not quite so badly off as those who inhabited the appalling slums. Moreover, by and large, they were illiterate and unable to express their thoughts easily.

During the Napoleonic wars, owing to a labour shortage, machines increased, especially threshing machines powered by horses. During the winter, a barn full of corn to be threshed by hand made winter's work for seven men. The threshing machines took away this work.

Trouble broke out in Kent during August 1830. By November it had reached Berks. During this month, a man called Swing was making trouble, threatening to destroy all the machines. A group of men destroyed machines at Childrey, and they had to be dispersed by the Yeomen and 'Specials'.

On November 29th, Mr Faulkner of Broadwell had his machine broken. In fact, the following extract from Thomas Banting's diary in 1846 shows how bad the situation was:

"I think it was in November 1832, as the machine breaking and rioting was. People drawed all their four horse power threshing machines out into their grounds away from their homes for fear of having their farms set afire as every night parties went out somewhere or other to break up the threshing machines, till at last they all agreed to have a regular riot so all men of several villages all round met together on Southrop Bridge by hundreds, and I can just remember hearing the horn being blown before it was scarcely light in the morning, but before night all dispersed in all directions some went clean away and never came back and very many went to prison and a great many came home and was taken up and tried afterwards and sent to prison for various terms of imprisonment. But the ringleader of that day was never caught, as one Tub of Tultlup was the head man. I understand he came home many years afterwards and died."

There were more riots in December. Fifty rioters assembled at Southrop to destroy machinery in a paper mill at Quenington. On receiving information that in Faringdon a man was trying to raise a group to go to Southrop, a large body of men set out at 7.00 a.m. on horse from Faringdon, and went to Southrop where they dispersed the mob, who showed no fight.

In fact, because of all this discontent, the Allotment Act was pushed through Parliament in 1831–32 to give all who wanted it a portion of land to grow vegetables on.

In 1833, during October, the sale of the Masons Arms took place on the death of John Farmer.

In 1834, the sale of Chestlyon took place.

In November 1835, the poor house was being built in Witney.

In 1835, James Clark went overseas for seven years.

In 1836, a railway was planned to be built, passing through Clanfield and Little Clanfield.

Wills and Inventories of the Era

In 1715, Mary Goodenough left her estate in trust to her daughter, Mary, to be kept separate and apart from her husband. However, it does not appear she needed to worry too much. He died a yeoman after five years — and left his wife well cared for. His estate was valued at £96.9.6d.

John Clarke the elder, yeoman, died in 1714. He left his estate to his son, William. William died at The Weir, Borroway, in 1783, leaving to his wife all stocks of beer, ale and other liquor and two enclosed meadows at Clanfield for life. It was their son, William, who bought Southwick in 1796, and he was already the tenant. It was his son, John, who, when living there, was called the maltster.

Robert Turner died in 1718 at Edgerley. He left his estate to his brother, Thomas, who was then living at Prospect House, on the south side of the school.

John Yateman died in 1721, a large farmer with an estate worth £407.1s 10d. His will survives. In the register he was called John Yateman junior. He was born in 1691, nine years after his sisters. His father, Nicholas, died in 1701 and left to him his messuage, dwelling house, 1¼ acres in Clanfield. He evidently thought that his son was not too well and made provision, if he died, to leave it to his sister, Mary, and her family.

Joseph May died in 1727, a yeoman with an estate worth £303.14s.6d. He was a wealthy tenant farmer. His father, Richard, a yeoman, had left lands in Clanfield to his family which Richard the older boy could have, if he paid the others £120 between them.

John Norden, a wheelwright, left property in Clanfield and Langford, and an estate to his son, John, on condition that "if any or either of my own sons or daughters shall keep themselves single and happen to be afflicted either with sickness or lameness so as to be incapable of work, they shall have free liberty of a kitchen belonging to the said premises in Clanfield and a little patch of ground belonging thereto". His son died in 1729, a wheelwright, leaving an estate worth £120.

Simon Blagrove died in 1736. He had his brother Thomas's mill, who, when Thomas's son, John, died, left it to his cousin — Simon Blagrove. He left it to his son, John and this mill remained in the family's hands for 100 years.

Mary Sperrinck died in 1739. She held a cottage by lease from Ferdinando White, gent, and John Smith, both deceased. These were the lords of the manor of Friars Court, which suggests that Ferdinando bought each one-third at different times.

Benjamin Sperrinck died in 1766, leaving the Masons Arms to his mother, Mary, providing that she did not marry again. She died in 1769, and left it to Mary Yateman and her husband, William. They only had one daughter, Winifred, born in 1785.

Elizabeth Breakspear died in 1766, leaving to her sister and her son William the messuage Bakehouse Barn in trust for her son before marriage, Robert Yateman. (This was the Poplars).

Richard Knapp, carpenter, died in 1804 and also Richard Knapp, shop keeper died in 1832. We shall refer to these later.

James Stephens, gent, died in 1804. He lived at the Plough and had no family. Richard, his brother, gent, died in 1828 at the Plough — and he lived there with his brother, Anthony, and he left it to his granddaughter, Phoebe Adams.

John Miles, gent, died in 1826, aged 78 years. He had been a butcher in Clanfield, and had done well. He bought part of Mary Stephens' estate in 1792, of which he was under-tenant. It was a messuage in Clanfield with a garden, croft, 4½ acres, 3 acres in Lintern field, 25½ acres in Barrow field, 11¼ acres in Tarney, 31¼ acres in West field, 1 acre in Rye, 20 purchases in Bourton at Morford, 2 acres 2 roods 30 purchases in Moor Meadow, 3 acres 2 roods 28 purchases in Four Meadow for £2,240. This was The Firs.

Clanfield Village
(1714–1837)

The population of Clanfield was now rising. During the first ten years of George I's reign the average births had been 10.7 per thousand a year, and deaths 7.9. In the last ten years of George IV's reign, the births were averaging 17.7, and deaths were 8.7. A visitation of 1738 says that the number of houses was forty. The next visitation of 1759 said the number was seventy, and the one in 1771 said sixty. These, of course, were estimates.

In 1676 we remember we thought that the population would be about 280. At the first census of 1801 it was 455. In 1811, it was 458, in 1821 it was 490 and in the

1831 census it was 525. Therefore, it would appear that in 1714 there were about 310 people and in 1738 about 340, which would make the figure of 40 houses in 1738 something of an underestimate.

The number of deaths varied considerably. In 1715, only one person from Clanfield was buried. In 1720, there were 14 deaths, of which two came from Grafton. However, in 1729 there were 24 burials, three from outside the village. Five children and six adults died in October alone. In the following year the Vicar, Mr. Edward Tyler, died. He had been the Vicar for 59 years and 9 months.

Thereafter deaths were more consistent until 1755, when 18 people died, only one being a child.

From that year onwards the new year, that is running from January to December, was used, not the old year, which ran from April to March. Deaths began to increase from 1766, which was, perhaps, a reflection of the population boom from 1717 onwards. By 1773, the number of deaths had eased off, but they increased again in 1785.

From 1784, the word "poor" was entered against names in the register to save the cost of the registration fee, about half the people being so called until this practice ended in 1794. The ages of people were entered from 1784 onwards, very few actually reaching 80 years.

Many of the people who had left and were living outside the village were brought back to be buried there.

The causes of death were also shown. Edward Clack of Langford, aged 19 years, died as a result of a sickle running into his eye. During the same year, Richard Dix, 54 years, was killed by a wagon. In January 1814, Robert Breakspear, 44 years old, froze to death on the road near Bampton. The same month John Hambridge, aged 9, met his death after having his leg cut by a scythe wielded by another boy.

Visitations from 1738 to 1831

Visitations were the Parish Returns made in that era. In 1738, the Bishop of Oxford, Dr. Thomas Secker, sent out a questionnaire in order to discover the state of each parish. The report for Clanfield was made by Thomas Middleton, ordained in 1731. He said the inhabitants were all husbandmen and labourers, and that there was no papist nor popish priest in the parish. Neither were there any dissenters nor meeting house.

He said that there were too many who absented themselves from public worship on the Lord's Day, and those "chiefly servants, employing themselves in fishing, fowling and such like exercises".

Mr. Middleton resided at Bampton, being Master of the free school there. The curate looking after Clanfield was Henry Shepherd, who resided at Oxford. His salary was £20 per annum. Services were performed twice on two Sundays out of three, and on the third once only in the afternoon. There were no prayers on weekdays, the catechism was expounded every third Sunday. The sacraments were given four times a year, and about 20 people received them.

There was no free school, hospital nor alms house. There was no charity school. The money from the offertory was disposed of to the poor of the parish by the Minister and the Church Wardens. The Bishop was not satisfied with this, as clearly Clanfield had no vicar during the week. He wrote to Thomas Middleton about this. We do not have the letter he sent, but we do have the reply he received: "Mr Shepherd is the vice principal of Edmund Hall where he lived and also second master of Magdalene school. He is not licensed. The reason why Clanfield is served every third Sunday in the afternoon only is because Mr Shepherd does duty at the chapel of Shifford that morning where there are prayers and a sermon as there are also at Clanfield in the afternoon, and an exposition of the church catechism one of these Sundays.

"My parish being but a mile from Bampton I am ready to perform all occasional duties in it. The true reason for my residing in Bampton is my being master of the free school there where I have lived upwards of two years before I had the curacy, the statutes of the school so requiring. My vicarage house at Clanfield is indeed a very mean one but in good repair and inhabited. I shall carefully observe your Lordship's directions and personally exhort my parish to a better observation of the Lord's Day, and if any shall continue refractory I shall present them to your Lordship's court. — My Lord, your most dutiful and obedient servant, I. Middleton."

The situation did not improve. Indeed, some twelve years later there was trouble again. A re-arrangement had to be made in the area because Mr. Reynolds, Vicar of Bampton, had to move to Bristol for health reasons. In the new arrangement, Shifford was being taken from Mr Middleton as they were not being looked after well enough. In a letter from Mr Reynolds to the Bishop, referring to Shifford's complaint, he said: "When Mr. Middleton had Shifford, he had only had Clanfield before, now he had the living of Baden Berks school at Bampton (£20), a sinecure of and rents from two or three farms. He is the greatest pluralist in these parts." (A pluralist being one who owns many livings.)

According to the 1759 visitation, Mr. Middleton was still living at Bampton as schoolmaster. Now there were two anabaptists, no quakers, 70 houses, but no curate.

In 1768 two women anabaptists went to a meeting house at Bampton, and there were now 50 houses.

In the years 1771, 1778 and 1781 there was one family of anabaptists and Mr. Middleton was still living at Bampton.

By 1784 things were better for Clanfield, as Mr. Collinson had become vicar and we now had a curate, Mr. Johnson, living at Bampton. By 1787, a Sunday School was mentioned, partly paid for by the Society of London.

In 1790, the visitation said that Great Clanfield had 100 houses, nearly 600 people, and one family of anabaptists, when taken together with Little Clanfield. Mr Collinson lived in a house at Long Ashton, near Bristol. Mr. Johnson lived at Langford, his salary being £25 per annum and he sometimes served Broadwell.

In 1796, Mr Johnson still lived at Langford, the vicarage of Clanfield being in need of repairs. In 1800, Mr Johnson resigned, on November 28th. In 1801, the vicar, Mr John Giles Dimock, lived at Stonehouse near Stroud, and also had a curacy at Eastington, Gloucestershire. His stipend was £30. There were no papists nor dissenters mentioned.

In 1802, Mr G Johnson wrote: "I have served the cure for 18 years, first as under a title for priest orders, next by virtue of a licence from the Bishop, afterwards as a vicar, now as a curate. I reside in Langford, but have a lodgings in the village. My stipend is £30. No dissenting teacher has ever preached in the parish for the last 20 years. There is a morning service, four sacraments, 20-30 communicants. Even service takes place when there are sacraments. There is a Sunday school with about 40 scholars."

In 1807, there was no vicarage, just ruins of a cottage and outbuildings.

In 1808, there were two dame schools and a writing school. Services took place morning and afternoon alternately — when it was in the morning, prayers were in the afternoon, Mr. Johnson being at Langford. In 1812, Mr Johnson, who served from 1785, was now replaced as curate by Mr J. Thorold, who lived and also served at Kencot.

In 1814, a few people met to worship outside the parish Divine Service, once a Sunday at 1.30 p.m., the communicants numbering 36-37. The parish clerk's stipend was £3s12d per annum, one of his duties was winding up the church clock. (The clock having been installed in the previous three years).

In 1815, the parish returns said that there were two day schools, one having 9 boys and 18 girls and the other having 22 boys and 17 girls. The Sunday school had 15 boys and 20 girls on average. This Sunday school is thought to have started in 1810. There was a mention of the ruins of an old vicarage house which had "not been habitable for the past 50 years". There was one service every Sunday.

Confirmation of the state of the vicarage was found in a letter from Mr Dimock to the Bishop in which he said: "There is no vicarage house at this time on the living. There were the ruins of a cottage and outbuildings when I was presented to it. I do think I am correct in saying it has not been inhabited by any clergy for nearly 40 years. I say this from what I was told on the spot nearly 10 years ago and therefore my memory may fail me. For several years I continued to be undetermined whether to put myself to the expense of a complete building, for nothing less than that would have answered my purpose. I was recommended not to do so and therefore I had the stone of the ruined walls preserved for the use of the repairs upon the Glebe."

By 1826, things had changed. Vicar J W Huntley wrote: "I am resident in my own house in the parish which is about 200 yards from the church and 5 from the vicarage for the time preserved by law this last year, serving Shilton also for Mr. Graham. There are services once every Sunday morning and evening alternately."

However, by 1831 a curate was in charge — Mr. Walter P. Powell of Bampton Grammar School house. The parsonage house was occupied by a labourer and his wife. He had two services each Sunday, in the morning at 10.30 and the evening (in winter) or 2.30/3.00 p.m. (in summer). The average congregation was 200. The sacraments were four times a year. The last three times there were 34, 40 and 49 people respectively. There was no poor house.

In 1773, an Act had been passed encouraging villages to set up their own workhouse. Nothing stands in the Clanfield records, but tradition has it that, for a time at least, a part of the Gables was so used.

The Land Tax of 1785 shows that we had about 36 property owning families. This, including the tenants of distant landlords, would account for some 200 people, therefore at least 100 in this period were labouring class. Of the artisans shown in the wills of this period were the Blagrove family, millers at Clanfield, the Breakspear family, bakers, P. Cockhill, wheelwright in 1818, farmers, masons, Thomas Greenway, cord wainer, John Gunn, lawyer, Richard Knapp, carpenter and joiner, Richard Knapp, shopkeeper, John Northern, wheelwright who died in 1727, the Pearson family, blacksmiths, R. Underhill, gardener, N. Yateman, shopkeeper in 1815, and the Adams family, who were bakers and carpenters.

A Terrier from 1805 was drawn up for the village. It dates from May 19th, 1805 about the vicarage. *(Ref: Oxon c448 f34).* A Terrier is a document which sets out rights in land.

> *1. Vicarage on 1 acre stone built and thatched, on the north the Rectory, on the west Chest Lion, on the south a close of William Collett, on the east a road to Black Bourton.*
>
> *2. 15½ acres in the Parish of Alvescot (enclosed 1796) instead of small tythes and 2½ yard lands bounded on the east and north by the boundary hedge of Alvescot and Black Bourton and on the west by William Colletts allotment, and on the south by Calcroft Lane. Corn rent of 1.074 bushels of wheat valued at 8s.6¾ d per annum charged on the barn.*
>
> *3. 1½ acres of pasture in Marsh Close bounded on the north by Mr Thos. Guy's close and on the south by Mr. Richard Clark's close. 172 acres in the common meadow. 4 acres arable in the common fields. The above two items are tythe free.*

4. The whole tythes of several grounds called the old enclosure being those wherein the houses stand. Also the tythe of Alice Hay, all Winmans grounds, Weeks piece. All the parish part of the tythe of several closes belonging to Bampton tythe. Also tythes of certain closes in the Hamlet of Little Clanfield and Blagrove Mill with Homstall and closes annexed. Also the tythe of Moor mead except 5 lots in which the vicars of Bampton have three and the vicar of Clanfield have one part. [But no mention of this is made in the endowment.] *Also corn and all other tythes of Nine Page Butts in the West field: of Culvery furlong in Linton field; of Bellam Hays furlong in Tawny field; of 1 acre in Billing field called Busby's; of Garford coppice; of Bownbridges Coppice at Friars Court; of certain other Homestalls and closes there. Also all the privy tythes of Clanfield, except the livings belonging to Bampton of which Bampton is to have 3 parts and Clanfield one part.* [Although no mention is made of Bampton in the Endowment dated 4th November 1276 in the Bishops Register at Lincoln.]

5. Three quarters of wheat and three quarters of barley are paid yearly out of the rectory. Two thirds by Elliot Esq., and one third by William Collett, the responsible proprietors thereof. Also 1 1/2 bushels of wheat are paid yearly out of certain Homestalls or livings in the said parish, 1/2 a bushel of which is said to be lost.

6. Land tax of Vicarage and Allotment in Alvescot being £3.14.6d purchased by certain private individuals among the Governers of Queen Anne's Bounty in the year 1802.

7. Twelve small elms in the Vicar's allotment of Alvescot and the same number in Marsh Close. The Communion plate consists of one small silver chalice holding somewhat more than 1/2 pint with a cover dated 1575 and one Patten, the gift of Mrs. Margaret Allworth. Also a large pewter tankard, a large Folio Bible, Folio Prayer Book and two surplices. Repairs of the Chancel belong to the Rectory and the repairs of the Church and churchyard to the parish.

Vicar John Dimock
Curate G. Johnson
Church warden Richard Hart
Thomas Pope, WilliamTuckwell, WilliamCollet, JohnHiggins, JohnPauling

(Ref: Oxon C448, f34)

A questionnaire regarding tithes survives for 1808. The value of the living was £75 averaged over seven years. They had a glebe of 247 acres of corn and hay tithes of 567 acres. Privy tithes came from the whole parish, except that which belonged to

Bampton. Easter dues amounted to about 2 guineas,and surplice fees were 10s. There was no Prebend Stipend . When these were redeemed in 1839 the value put on these was £50. The Bampton vicars had £100, the two lay rectors had £300, being a total of £450 a year which the farmers had to find — a very heavy burden. It was probably as much as the total rent paid on the land.

['Glebe'means soil. The Glebe is the land owned and farmed by the vicar. The Privy tithes were the private ones or the small tithes which belonged to the vicar. Easter dues were those paid by the parish to the vicar at Easter, usually by a collection. Surplice fees were those paid at marriages, burials and on the other occasions when the vicar officiated. The Prebend Stipend was a pension payment.]

Roads

The roads were now improving. The old idea of each person in the village giving four days of eight hours each year to repair the roads had given way to the turnpikes. These were private companies set up to repair stretches of the road and they used to put up gates to charge people who used the roads.

We, at Clanfield, had two of these turnpikes. One went from Faringdon to Burford and was set up in 1770–1771, and the other went from Clanfield Cross to Galley Hill, Witney and was set up in the same year. The only gate we had in the village was one leading to Langley Lane. Another gate, just outside us in the Black Bourton parish, stood on the Calcroft Lane entrance.

The valley crossing had always been a problem because the road, although continually built up, never seemed high enough. Low hollows in the Langley meadow show where one time the gravel was dug to build up the causeway. Along its side from Tawney to Radcot lies a wide hollow from which, at one time, soil was taken. In clearing the ditch by the Moors Bridge, it was found that hard core was still present at a depth of five or six feet below ground level.

In 1779, the turnpike again made up the road from Pidnell Bridge up and through Clanfield. This must have been the time when the old road, passing west of Radcot House, was diverted in a straight course east of it from Pidnell Bridge to Clanfield. The following account of the Turnpike Company in Radcot appears in my book 'Radcot and its Bridge':-

The company in charge of the road through Radcot was called the Faringdon & Burford Turnpike Trust. One of its toll gates was placed on the south side of Pidnell Bridge. The stone shed with the chimney there was built for the benefit of the operator.

The right to charge tolls at this gate was put up by auction annually. The charges were fixed. the collector expected to make a profit. The auction price of Radcot Bridge (with Langley Lane side gate) increased from £134 in 1834 to £361 in 1867, showing

Friars Court – line of ownership from pre-1529 to present

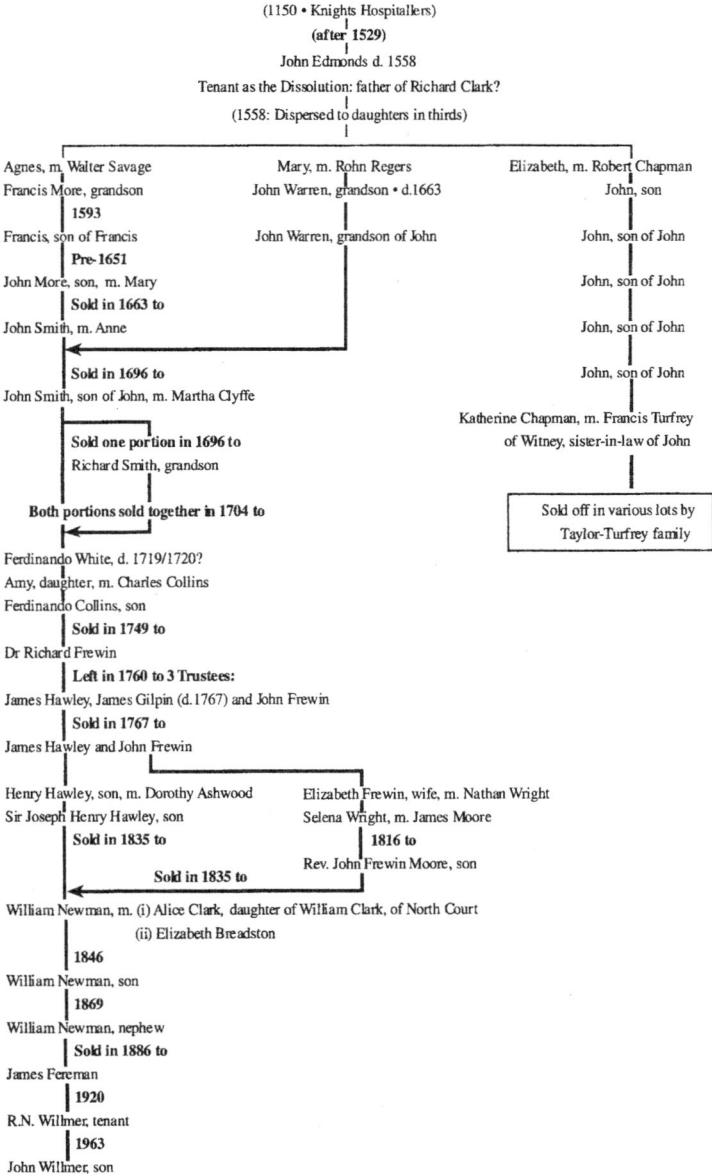

(1150 • Knights Hospitallers)

(after 1529)

John Edmonds d. 1558
Tenant as the Dissolution: father of Richard Clark?

(1558: Dispersed to daughters in thirds)

Agnes, m. Walter Savage	Mary, m. Rohn Regers	Elizabeth, m. Robert Chapman
Francis More, grandson	John Warren, grandson • d.1663	John, son
1593		
Francis, son of Francis	John Warren, grandson of John	John, son of John
Pre-1651		
John More, son, m. Mary		John, son of John
Sold in 1663 to		
John Smith, m. Anne		John, son of John

Sold in 1696 to
John Smith, son of John, m. Martha Clyffe

Sold one portion in 1696 to
Richard Smith, grandson

John, son of John

Katherine Chapman, m. Francis Turfrey
of Witney, sister-in-law of John

Both portions sold together in 1704 to

Sold off in various lots by
Taylor-Turfrey family

Ferdinando White, d. 1719/1720?
Amy, daughter, m. Charles Collins
Ferdinando Collins, son
Sold in 1749 to
Dr Richard Frewin
Left in 1760 to 3 Trustees:
James Hawley, James Gilpin (d.1767) and John Frewin
Sold in 1767 to
James Hawley and John Frewin

Henry Hawley, son, m. Dorothy Ashwood	Elizabeth Frewin, wife, m. Nathan Wright
Sir Joseph Henry Hawley, son	Selena Wright, m. James Moore
Sold in 1835 to	1816 to
	Rev. John Frewin Moore, son
Sold in 1835 to	

William Newman, m. (i) Alice Clark, daughter of William Clark, of North Court
(ii) Elizabeth Breadston
1846
William Newman, son
1869
William Newman, nephew
Sold in 1886 to
James Fereman
1920
R.N. Wilmer, tenant
1963
John Wilmer, son

A view towards the Institute from the Faringdon end of the village, with Windmill House, formerly Elm Tree House, on the left

Repairing one of the village roads

how the traffic increased.
The rates to be charged were:

> '*Horse and cart 4d.*
> *Waggon with wheels 6 inches or more wide 27d. per horse*
> *ditto if 4½ inches to 6 inches 3d per horse*
> *ditto if less than 4½ inches 4d per horse*
> *4 wheel coach empty 8d, loaded 1s.4d.*
> *Empty chair cart or two wheeled vehicle 4d. if loaded 8d.*
> *Ox drawn vehicle to be half a horse drawn one mule or ass laden or un-*
> *laden 2d.*
> *Every drove of cattle 10d. per score.*
> *Pigs ditto.*
> *Sheep 5d. per score.*
> *No further charge if return the same day.'*

(Ref: Pocock EA. Radcot and Its Bridge. 1966)

Now the grassy muddy road through Clanfield became a much better gravelled one. Other turnpikes were planned. A map of Gloucestershire shows plans made in 1813 to go east from Clanfield across to Fairford. Three alternative routes were planned across West Field and Tarney, which never matured. Perhaps the most interesting part of this is the drawing of the small cross at Clanfield. This is most likely an imaginary drawing of the church, but obviously at one time it stood on the top green.

★ ★ ★

Chapter 12

Queen Victoria 1837-1901

AFTER the death of her uncle Bill, the young Victoria, daughter of his younger brother Edward, Duke of Kent, came to the throne. All the many sons of his original marriage to Mrs Jordan, the actress, were passed over. But she was well served by good leaders.

After the Battle of Waterloo in 1815, Britain had become the most powerful nation in the world. Without any planning, she had become the first industrial country to supply the world. Within ten years of the beginning of Victoria's reign, our land was covered with a network of railways joining all the important centres. Canals and coaches had had a short life, and railways ruled then.

They had been built in an unbelievably short time, by good engineers using all the spare labour of the increasing population — including Ireland, where the priests who dominated the land had a vested interest in getting people to marry young and have large families: a policy which led to the terrible tragedy of later years when the potato blight decimated the crops.

In 1834, the New Poor Law was introduced, and that resulted in the separation of families. Under the terms of Gilbert's Act of 1782 the unemployed man requesting poor relief from the parish had to be found work near his home. But with the advent of the industrial revolution, this meant there was little work to be found anywhere, let alone in a man's own parish. When Great Britain went to war with France in 1793, food prices rose drastically, whilst wages declined. Poverty was becoming widespread, and in 1795, to avoid unrest, the magistrates of Speenhamland in Berkshire decided to implement a new system of poor relief by supplementing labourers' wages with grants of food and money to be paid for out of the rates. However, because of the worsening situation, the Poor Law Amendment Act was passed in 1834.

This was extremely harsh, and had the effect of forcing the unemployed into workhouses and even separating and dividing husbands, wives and children to prevent the births of more children who would, in turn, have to be supported by the rates. In the north, especially, there were rebellious outbreaks and demonstrations of the dislike of the new system, and many workhouses were burned down.

The 1840s became the age of papers, postage and railways. In 1844, the Government decreed that on every railway line trains should run each way at least once a day. They should stop at all stations, and there should be a third class fare of 1d a mile. Now, factory needs could be met, farming needs could be met, and people who could afford to travel became much less insular. In fact, the railways killed the large houses as local social centres, and they lost the great importance which they hitherto had enjoyed.

The troubles of the 1830s had been contained chiefly because of the Primitive Methodist movement between 1829-36. In the trouble spots its numbers had increased fourfold. It gave the labourers a status in life. It called for discipline against breaking the law. It offered hope in the life hereafter.

Victoria came to the throne in the epoch of Evangelical and Methodist power which gave the country the moral lead it needed, but which previous Kings had failed to achieve. She reflected the new middle class standards, and from this time government ministers could no longer ape these kings in their personal lives.

In the 1840s, the Oxford Movement began. The Church of England was finding a new zeal as a spin-off from the Evangelical movement. A few dons at Oxford began what was really a reaction against the evangelical movement, bringing back the authority of the priest. Originally, they did not advocate the ritualistic side, which did, however, come in later. But their cause was divided when their leader, Newman, moved across to Rome.

Victoria came in bad social times. One in ten people were paupers. Poverty in the countryside among the agricultural labourers was bad, but in the towns it was even worse. After the French Wars the economy stagnated. Agricultural depression set in as demand fell. Over two million acres which had been ploughed up for the war fell back to grass. But by 1841, the worst was over and things in the countryside gradually began to improve, leading up to the golden years of 1850-75. Money was put back into the land.

Perhaps the zenith was reached in the exhibition year of 1851, to which "all the world came" to see our country and what we had to sell. One farmer spotted the new factory-made round pipes, and saw possibilities. From then on, they were to be used extensively in land drainage, replacing the old shock drains which consisted of two flat stones pitched one against the other with a third underneath forming a triangle, or the old handmade horseshoe-type which was also laid on a flat stone. There was also at the exhibition a forbidding display of one particular machine which after a while was to play havoc with English agriculture. This was the MacCormick Reaper. By means of this machine and the modern transport, corn was soon to flow into our country from the new lands.

The census of 1851 showed one interesting factor. Now, over 50 per cent of people lived in towns. This had never happened in any nation before, and boded ill for the countryside.

After 1851, Victoria's reign began to lose steam. In 1854, we began a two-year war trying to stop Russian influence in the Crimea. Russia was trying to gain access to the Mediterranean by agreements with Turkey, giving Russia virtually free use of the Straits. It became obvious that the Czar Nicholas was intent on the destruction of the Turkish empire. A *Times* war correspondent, William Russell, brought the war to people's doorsteps for the first time. The bad planning and the shortages caused by sunken ships showed the agony that our soldiers had to put up with in such a severe winter. The country was stirred. Florence Nightingale became a legend. The Crimea showed that the organisation of the army was dreadfully out of date, and led to many changes.

In 1861, there had been a lot of rural depopulation. Previously, men had grumbled about the agricultural depopulation caused by enclosures, but now it was accepted as a natural part of life.

The country was helped by many new government Acts. In 1870, the Education Act, making schooling compulsory for everyone, was passed; and in 1875, the Public Health Act made water and sewage the responsibility of the local authorities, which resulted in a sharp decline in the death rate. In London in 1870 this had been 24 per 1,000, but by 1900 it was only 19 per 1,000. By this time our factories had been overtaken by those of Europe and America. No longer was Britain the most powerful industrial nation in the world.

In 1872, the Agricultural Workers Union was formed to get better conditions for the farm labourers. It met with great responses, but the tide turned against agriculture in total. In 1875, the depression started to come to our countryside. It started with a series of bad seasons. With the weakening of the manorial system, our ancient method of birth control — that a man could only marry when he had land to farm — fell away. People could now marry whenever they wanted, and were no longer restricted to the constraints of the manorial system. And marry they did — at a much younger age than before. Large families appeared in a fast-growing population.

These young people became the pioneers of the new territories in Australia, Canada and America. There was plenty of land on the prairies, and they were within reach of the English market. There, people could grow vast quanitities of corn at a much cheaper price than we were able to, using much less labour. Trains and ships poured grain into our land.

In Germany and France the governments would not let their farmers go under so easily. They introduced tariffs to ward off the influx of cheaper American food. In England, the Government was not interested, as we had become a town-orientated society. The British Government did not even seriously consider such a policy. The belief was that 'Free Trade' was the secret of Britain's prosperity, and also the reminder of the catastrophic results of the Corn Laws of 1815 which meant that bread became too dear for the poor to buy.

In 1879 came a terrible year as far as the weather was concerned. It was the wettest and most sunless that anyone could remember — so bad that much of the corn stayed in the fields. The 13,700,000 qts. of wheat grown in 1874 became in 1879 just

5,990,000 qts. Yet food prices fell, because of the quantities of imported food. That same year, foot-and-mouth disease and pneumonia ran riot among stock, and footrot killed off three million sheep. A late harvest meant that land was ploughed late and sown late, so repercussions were inevitably felt the following year. Then, in 1881, came a very severe winter and drifting snow blocked the land. From then on, agriculture drifted downwards, and many farmers went bankrupt. Land again fell to grass, and from 1881-1900 two million acres went wild, and between 1875 and 1895 wheat prices halved.

In 1884, the Government gave the vote to the masses, and agricultural labourers could now take part in the elections. When an election was held the following year, the leader of the agricultural workers, Joseph Arch, a Methodist local preacher, was elected Member of Parliament.

In 1899 the Boer War began, and lasted until May 1902, but Queen Victoria did not live to see its outcome; she died in January 1901, aged 83.

She left behind a great nation, with her people more cared for than before she came to the throne. Community life was very strong, and the churches were well attended. The greatest sadness was the Poor Law system, with its workhouses. The Poor Law was very inhuman, causing couples who had been married for years to see each other only across the floor of the chapel. However, two things were of great help.

The first was the tackling of the drink problem by the churches with their bands of hope. Their aim was to educate the young, so that instead of drowning their sorrows at the pub, they took their money home and made life that much happier. The other main source of help was the formation of clubs. Accidents, sickness, widowhood, orphans — these were terrible problems, and the clubs gave people back their dignity. As of right, without going cap in hand to the Poor Officer, they had an income provided when tragedy hit them — but it cost them a lot of money each week in subscriptions.

News about the Area

In 1837, there was a large fire at Edward Early's mill in Witney.

In 1839, farmers who had lost their goods because they had been commandeered by the Army could charge £4.10s per ton for hay, £1.3s.6d per qtr for oats. A waggon with four horses was 1s for the first mile and then 4d a mile thereafter; the same for a wain with six oxen, or four oxen and two horses. In May 1839, times were so bad that one man took his wife to Witney Market and sold her for £10. In September of the same year, there were 2,993 sheep and lambs sold at Faringdon Market.

In March 1840, the Leather and Bottle (Challow) Station opened on the Great Western line, and in July of that year a railway was proposed between Witney and

Faringdon, going through a tunnel at Buckland. In September 1840, the Witney Races at Curbridge Common ended because the land was enclosed.

In 1842, the threshing machine for wheat was being demonstrated at Bampton.

In January 1846, prize-fighting took place in Dudds Plain, Wychwood.

In August, after a thunderous rainstorm, a pile of money (50s) was washed out of a dung heap in Faringdon.

In March 1848, a Mr Whittaker was taking teeth out at Bampton, using ether as an anaesthetic.

In May of that year a barrel of gunpowder, soaked in the terrible storm of August 1, 1846, was stored in Mr Belcher's cellar at Faringdon. A shopkeeper, out of curiosity, took a bit out and put a match to it to see if it was dry. It was — the front of the shop was blown out!

In December, Roman relics were found by a workman at Mr Bradshaw's in Lew. They were in a box — 14 in all.

In March 1849, the west wing of Minster Lovell ruins fell down.

In September, there was an epidemic of cholera. As a result, a day of prayer was proclaimed.

In May 1852, Hussey's new reaper was on trial at Bampton. In July 1853, the steam engine was being used at Bampton to drive a thresher.

In October 1854, the trial of Dr Giles, of Bampton, took place at Oxford Assizes. This young curate had obliged the wish of a young girl to get married. She was free before she started work, so he married her before 8.00am. This was regarded as a terrible crime at that time. No-one was allowed to marry in darkness as marriage was a contract and a person might be marrying someone entirely different to the one intended. The curate was given six months' hard labour — but it could easily have been as much as 12 years' transportation. He lived to be a great scholar and translator. He wrote the history of Bampton and the history of Witney.

In January 1856, a meteor was seen in the sky before 5 o'clock in the evening, leaving a great trail of smoke.

In November 1858, a photographic salon was opened in Bampton market place.

In July 1859, stocks were used in Witney for a six-hour sentence.

In January 1861, it was so cold that 'ground ice' formed in the Thames. It was said that the river froze at the top and bottom. In May of the same year there was a riot at Leafield. Apparently between three hundred and four hundred people assembled to pull down a wall built across a footpath.

In the June, steam ploughing took place at Mr Akers' in Black Bourton.

In 1862, the Great Western Railway train journey from Oxford to London, with a stop at Reading, took one hour and 32 minutes. The return journey took one hour and 25 minutes.

In January 1865, a threshing machine was smashed at Ducklington.

In July, Spurgeon was at Ringwood. This preacher, who had a massive Baptist church in London, came to stay with the Abrahams family at Ringwood each year. In the evening he preached from a waggon in the field to large crowds who had come from all over the area by horse and trap.

In September the stocks were removed from Bampton.

In June 1866, the stocks were used at Faringdon for a drunk who would not pay a fine. In September, there was a female preacher at Faringdon in the Corn Exchange. She appeared to the Faringdon people like a popular actress of the Metropolis, and drew a large crowd.

In March 1868, at Brize Norton, Mr Thomas Smith — a watchman — was the stopper of the Old Berks Hounds. When the hounds were going to meet in the area, he went out early, after the foxes had left their earths, and blocked up the entrances so that the foxes would not run to ground when being hunted.

On 31st November, there was an earthquake at 10.45pm.

In July, Mr Richard Weaver, the converted collier, preached at Aston. Between three thousand and four thousand people attended and between five hundred and six hundred people had tea between the meetings.

In February 1870, a new screw steamer was taken up the Thames to Lechlade. In that same month, a large stone coffin, about eight feet long, was found under the floor of Bampton church.

In September 1871, a man was put in the stocks on Witney Green for six hours for not paying the fine after being drunk. (He had probably spent all his money on drink).

In April 1872, the Ordnance Surveyors were working from Faringdon Folly Hill. In the May, Bampton spire was hit by lightning.

In November 1875, terrible floods came up in Witney during a church service at the Wesleyan Chapel. The chapel keeper fetched members of the congregation home by carts and then went to St Mary's Church, and then to the Congregational.

In February 1876, false teeth were on sale locally for the first time!

In August, 12 adults were baptised in the stream at Alvescot.

In June 1877, Blenheim monument was cleaned. The lowest tender for the contract came from a Frenchman. others came to see how he would manage the work. Instead of using scaffolding, as was thought, he flew a line over the top with a kite and proceeded, with a block and tackle, to get up and clean it. On the top he found a penny, and on the statue were the words "G. Austin, 1871".

In July, a statue of King Alfred was unveiled at Wantage by the Prince and Princess of Wales. The statue had been in the grounds of St James' on show for three weeks.

On January 2, 1877, two men from Oxford caught 12 pike at Radcot, the total weight being 89lb. The largest fish weighed 19½lb. In the August of that year the Sunday School centenary was held at the White Horse Hill, with 1,500 and 10,000 adults attending. In November, 1882, Moody and Sankey, the great American evangelists, were at Oxford.

In November, 1883, a Court Leet was held at Witney. W.G. Collier, the town crier, opened the Court under an apple tree in the grounds of Moat (Mount) House, which was on the southern boundary of the parish. The following month a Salvation Army officer of Witney was sent to the prison in Oxford for creating a disturbance, but he was later released.

In December, 1884, soup kitchens were opened in Faringdon for 40-50 labourers.

In September, 1886, the sale of farm stock took place in Wales for tithe arrears. The auctioneer was surrounded by police. Three cows in the ring were driven off by the crowd, the bailiffs followed the cows, the police followed the bailiffs and the mob followed the police. Someone at last bid 6d for a cow, and it was finally sold to the brother-in-law of the man in arrears for £20. The auctioneer left in such a hurry that he forgot to collect any money, but it was sent on later.

In February, 1888, a train with two engines was stuck all night in the snow between Bampton and Alvescot stations.

In August a mouse appeared in St Mary's Church, Witney, and the ladies held their skirts very tightly and watched the clock!

In January, 1891, the river was frozen solid, and a coach-and-four drove across the Thames at Oxford. The same month, a band in Bampton had to stop playing as the valves on their instruments had frozen solid.

In March, 1892, the first corridor train ran from London to Birmingham. It was made in Swindon.

Clanfield in the Victorian Era

Chestlyon

Chestlyon was owned by William Aldworth, of Frilford, and had been tenanted. Aldworth died in 1846, and left it to his nephew Will Aldworth, of Frilford. This William died in 1874, and left it to his son to be sold. It was offered for sale, and in 1875 Christ Church, Oxford, bought it for £12,000. They are the present owners.

Friars Court

Two thirds of Friars Court had passed into the hands of William Newman. He had married Alice Clark, daughter of William of North Court, and after their son was born they went to live in Faringdon. Will set out to buy a lot of land in Clanfield. He bought Stevens farm in 1802, rented part of Osney land in Clanfield from Christ Church, bought two properties and land from the Adams family, and in 1835 had bought Friars

Court, followed by the purchase of Southwick just two years later. Alice died in 1830, aged 68, and he remarried. Elizabeth Breadston, his new wife, was a local girl, and no doubt he rebuilt Friars Court to bring his new bride home. William Newman died in 1846, aged 78. He left Friars Court to his second son, Will. Henry, the first son, was left Stevens Farm. The second son was presumably living with him, as was his daughter, Priscilla. Neither of these two married, and Will died in 1869, aged 69. Priscilla died before him in 1864, aged 62.

Will left Friars Court to his nephew, Henry, the second son of his elder brother, Henry. It was this second Henry who made a name for himself. In 1881, he was farming 900 acres, employing 23 men, six boys and five women. To obtain Friars Court, Henry had had to pay £1,000 each to his brother and three sisters. Most of the land he bought in addition to Friars Court he had obtained by means of a mortgage. All the land he had was his, on condition that he paid off about £4,000 for Friars Court and £12,000 from Adams and Stevens Farm.

In 1885, the family took him to court in London to get their money out of him. That same year, one of his chief mortgagers, Mr James Fereman of Swindon, died. The bad weather of the 1880s broke him, and he had to sell up in 1886.

James Fereman, the mortgagor's son, being unable to sell the farm, took possession. Abraham became the tenant. The remaining one-third of Friars Court appears to have been sold off in odd lots by the Taylor/Turfrey family.

Southwick

The manor was owned by the Edmonds family. Priscilla, the wife, was the daughter of John Clark who had previously owned it. In 1842, it was settled on their twins, John and Ann, at 21 years of age. They then sold it to Will Newman of Friars Court in 1843, but it was now only some 40 acres. Alice, Will Newman's late wife, had been their great-aunt. When Will Newman died in 1846, he left Southwick to his two boys, Will and Henry. These, in turn, left it to their families, who sold it to Charles White for £3,400. In 1898, Charles White died, and in 1903 Southwick was sold to Ernest White, his youngest son.

Meanwhile, in the village itself, much was happening. The Coronation of Victoria was duly celebrated.

The poor were entertained with an excellent supper, the men being busily employed during the day with agricultural pursuits. Tables were set out along the valley, and covered with plenty of meat and pudding, of which 200 people partook, with a plentiful supply of strong beer. Members of the band gave their attendance to join their musical friends at Clanfield, and considerably enlivened the scene. The evening concluded with a merry dance.

The thing that filled the minds of the village people most of all was the imminent enclosure of its fields. All around, they had seen it happening — in Black Bourton in 1771, and Alvescot in 1801. For a long time they had talked about it.

In 1825, Mary Waine, tenant of Christ Church's Osney land wrote to the Treasurer saying that she had heard from Mr Ward, lord of the manor, that the proprietors of the land in Clanfield were going to apply to Parliament for an Act of Enclosure. She was 76, and said she "hoped it would happen in her time" and if it did she hoped that the College would pay the expenses. The College replied that they had heard nothing.

Things came to a head in 1836, when the Government passed the Tithe Commutation Act. This was to transfer all payment by kind into a payment by cash. In October that year, a letter appeared in the Press signed by Will Newman, James Clark and Henry Collett, saying that as they owned more than a quarter of the parish, they would call a parochial meeting to get the tithes commuted within the parish.

Most likely, this came from the Vestry Meeting, but unfortunately we only possess the vestry books from after 1849. The meeting was duly held at the Masons Arms on Wednesday November 9th at 1.00pm and was adjourned for another meeting to be called in April 1837 to consider not only the tithes, but the enclosure of the village fields. The agreement was signed by James Haines, a member of the legal family that had for so long served the area from Faringdon (The last member of this family died tragically in 1982, when he missed his bus stop in the bad snows of that year, started to walk back but fell into a ditch and perished).

The enclosure was put in hand, and Francis Attwood of Old Sarum, Salisbury, was given the job. He was sworn in at Great Milton, Oxon, on July 12th 1837, before Mr R. Ashurst J.P. of Oxford to handle a number of parishes, among which was Clanfield. He called the first meeting on Wednesday October 4th 1837 at the Masons Arms, the house of Richard Clark, to start work on the enclosure. He came again on October 28th to hear objections, and on December 20th the new map was on show.

His men had surveyed the village, worked out what each owned, and made a plan of fields equal to their ownership in just six to seven weeks — quite an achievement. It was done, of course, immediately after the harvest was over, and it must have been good weather.

It is to be noted that the Bampton landlord of the Shrewsbury estate, Thomas Denton, and also Christ Church, who were the trustees of the Osney land, did not get involved. For his own personal reasons Thomas Denton had paid to have a survey made of his large estate which was scattered over the Clanfield fields some 12 years before. When we mapped out our open fields (at Windmill Farm) in 1961 we did not have the map, and thought it had been lost — but it turned up in the late 1970s with Denton's estate deeds, and is now held at the Oxfordshire Record Office.

At this point it would be interesting to look at the village that was mostly destined to disappear. We left our vision of Clanfield in very early days, you will remember, as a village that had developed around three large ploughable fields — West Field

(Clanfield Field) where it all began, Tarny (which joined it) and Barrow Field (which had been brought into Clanfield between the time of the Domesday Book and the Hundred Rolls. While Barrow came into the control of the village farmers' court, its manorial loyalty lay to Weald, and most of its tithes remained with Bampton Church. At Little Clanfield, the Osney lands had been centred on a messuage just south of the present Little Clanfield Manor, and these were operated through their court at Black Bourton.

Three manorial courts operated within the village — Chestlyon, Friars Court and North Court at Southwick's property. The Court Leet was still in private hands, belonging in later days to the Crown. It came from the great estates of Roger d'Ivry, to which Clanfield belonged at the Domesday period. The court was held in later days at the Masons Arms, and villages outside, which were held by the Crown, attended this court like the inhabitants of Clanfield.

In the earliest times, in the 13th Century, we have records that Clanfield's three fields were operated under a two-year rotation, corn and fallow, being called East and West Fields. The East Field brought in all those other than the original West Field. We do not know when the two-year rotation became three, but in the inventory of William Clack in 1580 it mentioned that he had half an acre of barley and half an acre of wheat, suggesting that he had a three-year rotation of fallow, wheat and barley.

In 1715, Mary Goodenough had ten acres of wheat and ten more acres, half of which was barley and the other half vetches, suggesting that the three-year rotation was on its way to becoming four. The village court of 1752 says that the village consisted of three corn fields. When the tithes were commuted, the village was divided equally into wheat, beans, barley and fallow — about 212 acres of each on a four-year rotation.

To the north of Barrow Field against the village lay Linton Field. This was a late field, as its ridge and furrow shows. They were very neat, and the headlands were small. The name tells us that it grew flax, and the 17th century inventories have flax, linen and linen wheels mentioned in them.

Very little of the arable land had been enclosed. Besides the furlongs through the village against the road, only two other small portions were there. Both of these were at the end of a furlong including the Gores as well as perhaps one full land. One was at the back of the Football (or Line) Field. It was the end of Brook furlong, and this had then been divided crosswise into two portions called the Lays. The other is at the junction of Marsh and Stocks Lane. Here in Barrow Field, on the north end of Marsh furlong against the junction, a similar thing happened — two gores and a long land became a private field.

Around the three islands of arable lay the grass. The marshes lay all down the east side of Marsh Lane. It was the lane to the marshes. Through this ran the Maw or Marl Brook. It was an old brook which had been re-dug as a relief stream for Bourton Mill after the Bourton enclosure of 1771. In their parish it goes across a field, but in ours it is a boundary brook.

In Clanfield's enclosure map, the new work can be seen with odd bends left out in the field where it ran through the marshes. Clanfield called its side Marshes, but Weald called its side the Moor. Our lane was Marsh Lane, Weald's was Moor Lane. We, however, called their side Gypsy Lane for obvious reasons!

These marshes had, for as long as our records tell (from the early 17th century) been enclosed. It was a manorial venture. They were enclosed from each end. Where they met in the centre, the last field was cross-boundaried and, presumably, each shared a portion. In the southern enclosure the vicar had been given a portion of about 1.5 acres.

A similar situation existed on the south side of Tarny. Here, Langley is a long meadow which has been enclosed from both ends, meeting in the centre. We have records from the 17th century referring to meer stones being set up to mark out the meadow. A stream used to run through this, and its beginning can still be seen in the field east of the house there — and it returns to New Brook beside the moors. The causeway of the Radcot Road cut across this meadow and Wymonds, an ancient settlement site, stands on this eastern portion. Many gravel pits can still be seen in the Langley on the west side, suggesting where at one time the spoil for the causeway came from.

Below the main village a long expanse of meadow leaves the Withy Beds, beginning as Green Close. The north end, as far as Friars Court and ending in Ryemead or Rye Mead, was still held in furlong and strips of grass. Between these and the Wymonds lay the Moors, another shared meadow.

At the end of Marsh Lane lay an interesting set-up. The old settlement at Burroway died out, with only the Fox and Hounds pub, serving the bargees, remaining. The old encampment became 'extra parochial', and the remainder became meadows shared between the parishes of Alvescot, Kencot, Brize Norton and Black Bourton. After the hay had been taken, the grazings were shared between Clanfield and Weald. A similar situation existed at Nippenham, just to the north of the Clanfield/Bampton Road, where, after the hay had been cut, Clanfield and Weald shared the latter mass of grazings.

Of all this area of grass, the tithe award tells us that 128 acres and 200 acres respectively were cut for hay, and 200 acres fed — a rather exact figure. Besides all of this, Clanfield still retained two woods — the copse by Little Clanfield and that by Friars Court, both planted with hazel for making hurdles. The former had been a cottage site according to early maps.

Long before the Clanfield enclosure came, all free rights of common land had been extinguished. Prior to the enclosure, all grazings were determined by the acreage a man held in the arable fields.

Southwick – line of ownership from pre-1538 to present

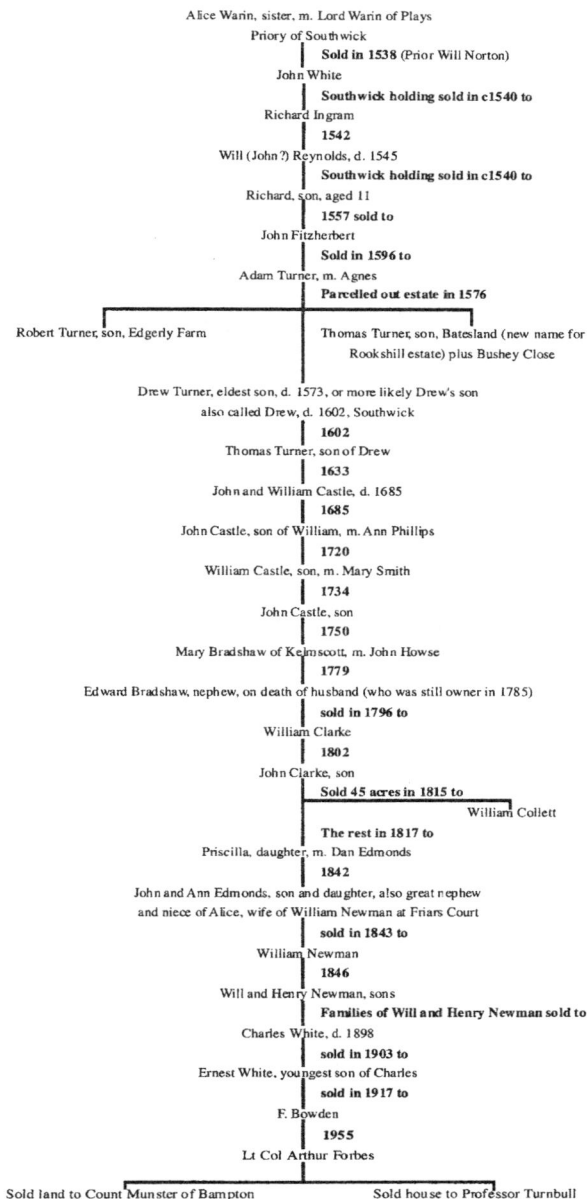

Alice Warin, sister, m. Lord Warin of Plays

Priory of Southwick

| Sold in 1538 (Prior Will Norton)

John White

| Southwick holding sold in c1540 to

Richard Ingram

| 1542

Will (John?) Reynolds, d. 1545

| Southwick holding sold in c1540 to

Richard, son, aged 11

| 1557 sold to

John Fitzherbert

| Sold in 1596 to

Adam Turner, m. Agnes

| Parcelled out estate in 1576

Robert Turner, son, Edgerly Farm   Thomas Turner, son, Batesland (new name for
                                      Rookshill estate) plus Bushey Close

Drew Turner, eldest son, d. 1573, or more likely Drew's son
also called Drew, d. 1602, Southwick

| 1602

Thomas Turner, son of Drew

| 1633

John and William Castle, d. 1685

| 1685

John Castle, son of William, m. Ann Phillips

| 1720

William Castle, son, m. Mary Smith

| 1734

John Castle, son

| 1750

Mary Bradshaw of Kelmscott, m. John Howse

| 1779

Edward Bradshaw, nephew, on death of husband (who was still owner in 1785)

| sold in 1796 to

William Clarke

| 1802

John Clarke, son

| Sold 45 acres in 1815 to

William Collett

| The rest in 1817 to

Priscilla, daughter, m. Dan Edmonds

| 1842

John and Ann Edmonds, son and daughter, also great nephew
and niece of Alice, wife of William Newman at Friars Court

| sold in 1843 to

William Newman

| 1846

Will and Henry Newman, sons

| Families of Will and Henry Newman sold to

Charles White, d. 1898

| sold in 1903 to

Ernest White, youngest son of Charles

| sold in 1917 to

F. Bowden

| 1955

Lt Col Arthur Forbes

Sold land to Count Munster of Bampton   Sold house to Professor Turnbull

The ruined windmill,Windmill Farm, 1907

Working at Little Clanfield Mill

Of the early manorial courts we have remaining a series belonging to Friars Court — part in the early 16th century, and part of the early 18th century. Of the Court Leet, we have two years — 1715 and 1716. Of the Farmers Court we have remaining only a portion of one court. It is on the back of the parish register for 1752. The top had completely gone, and we appear to have two-thirds of the remainder, the right third having been cut off.

It says:

5. *That no horse shall be tied there at night nor any other cattle backed there till appointed on pain of 1/- for... only 3 to the yard land and so in proportion.*

6. *It is agreed that no Commoner of Clanfield aforesaid shall lett any common (save summer sheep common) to a ... save to any Commoner and refused so to do, but if such commoner cannot let his common to any Commoner before the first... till after the 10th day of May yearly.*

7. *It is agreed that the grass growing around the outside of the fields of Clanfield aforesaid shall be cut the... of one shilling for every Hade or Furrow that shall be cut contrary to the meaning of this article.*

8. *It is agreed that the Mead hedge shall be well amended and kept during the said term by the own... hedge shall be kept in good repair by the owners as aforesaid responsible all the summer on pain of 2/6d.*

10. *It is agreed that any man may sow vetches in any of the three cornfields to tye his horse on and that...*

11. *It is agreed that every owner and occupier of lands of or in Clanfield aforesaid shall sufficiently ring... shal continue the same so ringed on paid of 4d for every pigg every time offending.*

12. *It is agreed that no occupier or owner of lands in Clanfield aforesaid shall bait anymore than one... greens or highways till they have taken commons at 16th August in the Mead.*

13. *It is agreed that the Constable of Clanfield aforesaid for the time being shall provide hurdels...*

14. *It is agreed that whosoever shall agist or let out the Commoning or pasturage for any cattle within the...*

The ditches and roads had been formerly looked after at the manorial courts. The Friars Court Rolls of 1512 say that *John Lococke has a ditch next to the road called St Leonard's in bad state of repair. John Clark is the same. The Mill Brook as far as Charney needs cleaning. It is the villagers' responsibility to repair the causeway by St Leonard's. Ashenbridge needs repairing. A bridge near the land of John Turfry needs repair.*

By 1714 the manors had weakened, so it seems the Court Leet had taken over responsibility.

William Faulkner — Constable Jonathan Yeatman elected in place of Faulkner.
Princes Fee: Robert Hicks — Henry Bishey elected in place of Hicks.
Southwicks Fee: Richard Clark — Robert Lanarkshire elected in place of Clark.
Pitts Fee: Arthur May — Dead.
Abbot's Fee: William Taylor — Richard Peasons in place of Taylor.
(This document also refers to Brize Norton, Black Bourton and Casswell near Astrop).
Names on the document were:
Will Faulkner, Arthur Toms, Chris Lord, Sims Denton, Robert Haines, Francis Edwards, Richard May, Jacob Champe, Richard Butler, Thos. Beckinsale, John Dow, Benjamin Sperrinke, John Stevens, Thos. Smithier, Rich. Meysey, George Capell.
(Ref: MS DD Ewelme Honour d2 item 5/20/8, Clanfield View of Frankpledge 11th May 1715 Ref 5/20/8)

The following are extracts from the Court Leet records of 1715 and 1716:

1. *Wee doo present the mill brocke to be well skouord up and to shouor the banke well and to begein att Blagros mill and doun to the mour bridge and to mend the mound well begin att the over end of the Long Ground and to ye end of John Stephens line and to bee doun by the 10th day of May. Every man against is oun ground and if not don the penelty 2 shilins a Loge.*
2. *Wee doo present the mound and dich begin at Apsolin paling grin close to be mended and to skouor up doun to the over ind of the four med and to be don by the 20th day of May, and if not don the penelty 1 shilin a Loge.*
3. *Wee doo present the watercost from Grafton Green doune to Mr White peses to bee well slouored up by the 20th day of October next. Every man against his own ground and if not donn the penelty of one shilin a Louge.*
4. *Wee doo present the Chasway from ye upper green down to the lower green to be well covered up a both sides. Every man against is owne ground and to be grasiled in the midle and if not don the penelty 2/6 a Loge and to be don bey 20th day of October next.*
   Signed Will Faulkner, Foreman
(Ref: MS DD Ewelme Honour d2 item 5/20/6 and 5/20/7, The Presentment of Clanfield for 1715)

Jonathan Yeatman: Constable John Adams elected in place of Yeatman.
Princes Fee: Henry Bishey — Tithing man as before.
Southwicke Fee: Robert Lankashire — Tithing man James Clampe in place
of Lankashire.
Pits Fee: Anthony May — Tithing man dead.
Abbots Fee: Richard Peasons — Thos. Goddenough elected in his place.
(Document also refers to Brize Norton, Norton Brewere, Black Bourton and
Casswell near Astrop).
Names on the document were: Will Faulkner, John Adams, John Mayfield,
Richard May, Richard Clark, Simon Denton, Thos. Beckinsale, Benjamin
Sperwick, John Stevens, George Capple, Richard Meysey, John Clarke.
(Ref: MS DD Ewelme Honour d2 item 7/8/8, Clanfield view of Frankpledge 25th
April, 2nd year of George I (1716) before Philip Diaper, Dep. Steward)

1. *Wee doo present the Mill brocke to bee well skouord up and to shouor the*
   banke well and to men the mound well against Thomos Mays Long ground
   and John Stephens Line and to begein att Blagros Mill and doun to the Mour
   Bridge, every man against is oune ground and to bee dun by the 10th day of
   May and if not done the penelty 2 shilins a Loge.
2. *Wee doo present the mound and ditch begin att Apslon paling green close,*
   bee well mende and skouored up down to the ovor Ind of the fore med. and to
   be dun by the 20th day of May and if not don the penelty 1 shillin a Loge.
3. *Wee doue present the water cost begining att Thomas May Piors bridge down*
   to Yatemans bridge and to bee doun by the 10th day of May and if not doun
   the penelty 1 shillin a Loge.
4. *Wee doue present the water cost been going at Alishay down to the More*
   Lake to be skouored up well and to mend the mound against Bengemen
   Sperinke Lange and to be doun by the 10th day of Agos and if not don the
   penelty 1 shiling a Loge.
5. *Wee doue present the Langly brooke beging at Grafon gree down to the Ind*
   of the More Lacke next to the fore mead and to be cot and draged by the 10th
   day of May and to be skouored down to the bodom by the 30th of September.
   Every man against is oune ground and if not done the penelty 3 shiling a
   loge.

Signed William Faulkner, Foreman.
(Ref: MS DD Ewelme Honour d2 item 7/8/7, The Presentment of Clanfield for
the Year 1716)

Whilst Futts Fee was still under this court, by now this had long been in Alvescot parish and was a dying or dead community.

From the document surviving from 1715 we see mention of:

1. *Mill Brook from Little Clanfield Mill down to the Moor (Bottom bridge).*
2. *The brook from Stocks Lane behind Green Close going all around Barrow field to the Sharney brook.*
3. *The old 'New Brook' from Grafton Green to Mr White's.*
4. *The causeway between the Upper and Lower green needed repairs.*

From the 1716 document we can see that the stream from the Weir bridge came through the village, so it had been dug by then. Our earliest maps show that it had not been dug.

All of this was the old village which was about to end when Francis Attwood hung up his map in the Masons on December 20th. He did his best to make it not only a fair award but a convenient one. He tried to give every man the largest part of his share against his property. He did this very well, as the map shows.

Of course, the largest farmers had to give odd pieces of land away. He gave all a chance to swap around. Will Newman did a lot of this. One portion was three acres that he had been given in Tarny opposite the Langley Lane house. He swapped this with the village for the Haywards Ham by his copse at Friars Court. They had the better deal with acreage, but he by convenience. This was the portion later sold for the school.

The rearrangement of the roads was, perhaps, the most interesting. Of course, many of the access roads through the fields disappeared. One case is at Chestlyon. The old road went right through the farm and fields to the west. This was now ended at the back gate of the churchyard.

The back road to Friars Court, along the west of Barrow field leading to the entrance of Friars Court, disappeared. The lane past Foundry House to Linton disappeared, as did the lane from Stocks Lane to Linton. Mill Lane, or Weeks Lane, began by a bit of straightening, but at the parish allotments it took a new course to West South West. The old road can still be seen wandering off to West North West.

At the top of Mill Lane the old Asom way is straightened out. It came from Alvescot as a green drift lane. It was now planned on a straight course across West field and on to the ford at Little Clanfield Mill, and so on across the Grafton common.

Linton or Stocks Lane was extended. Originally it served the lane north into Linton field, south into Friars Court, east into Stocks Close. Now, with the former two being done away, it was extended past Stocks Close to Marsh Lane.

Various footpaths were confirmed. The church path from Little Clanfield is interesting. It originally went in a straight line from the cottage by the mill stream to the church. The north-east end across the allotments remained of this. On the tithe map it is shown on the same course to Mill Lane. But this was finally changed so that it went on its present course to Mill Lane, up that lane to Green Benny, and then south to the cottage on the mill stream.

The years 1837 and 1838 were used to sort out problems and to finalise the plans. On August 28th, 1838, at 11 o'clock, the final meeting to sign the enclosure was held at The Crown, Faringdon. Various meetings had been held in Clanfield on 27th April, 29th August and 15th November 1837.

Now, men suddenly possessed a new world. No longer were they tied and restricted by the farmers' court. They could plan, act and plant as they wished — freely and without restraint. No longer did they set out to plough and plant a strip. Now, they had a field to tackle, and they were there, in the same spot, day after day.

Of course, men jumped the gun with the official blessing of the surveyor. If that man's field lay within the fallow portion, he could mark it out in the summer. Presumably the other villagers had to plough their portions, but his fields were ready. So, as we note, they had begin to put up their fences. If, of course, their field lay after corn it was another matter. But in some measure, they must have tried to follow the same rotation.

However, time sorted things out. Where they could, the old hands still ploughed the old ridge and furrow. In the 1920s, when Mr Bowden came here from Hampshire, he sent his men out to plough new wide lands. He went down, and found they were still, despite his orders, ploughing the old ridge and furrow. He almost had a strike on his hands before he could get them to so to do.

In my earliest days, in the 1930s, we still ploughed the old ridge and furrow in Lower Farm, before it was part of Windmill Farm, because it was heavy land and at the end of each furrow a trench could be dug into the Mill ditch to let off the surface water. Only when tractors came in, and the land was tile drained, did we give it up.

The Enclosure Award also had the effect of showing who owned the boundaries. So, as soon as men had planted their Autumn corn, they would have spent much of the winter planting the new hedges on the spoil they had thrown up from their new ditches, because a man's boundary was marked by his ditch. The cost of our enclosure was not stated, but Will Newman said that it cost about £1 per acre — that is just over £1,000 for the whole village — when he wrote to Christ Church about the Osney land he held from them by lease. The college also allowed him £15 for planting a quick hedge around their land.

At about the same time as the enclosure, the Commutation of the Tithe was taking place. They made their own map, copying it off the enclosure map, but using the map before it was finalised, so that it differs in small details.

The details we have of our village are:

Clanfield:
£

			£
Ar. 935	21 Turnips	Covered by Modus	nil
Enc. 85	21 Barley	4 qrs per acre 84 at 32s	134
850		14 mown, 1 ton p.a.	
		14 tons at 60s	42
	21 t seeds		
		7 eaton owned my Modus	nil
	22 wheat	3qr 66qrs at 56s	184
Open field	212 wheat	3qr 636qrs at 56s	1,780
	212 beans	2½ qr 530qrs at 35s	927
	213 barley	4qr 852 qrs at 32s	1,363
		213 fallow	nil
	straw	468 tons at 25s	585
		128 meadows mown ¾ ton	150
146 tons 50s 615			
		200 eaton covered by Modus	nil
Woods	6		
Common	3	Covered by	nil
Total	1,472		_____
			5,636
		One tenth	563
		One quarter collecting	141
			_____
			422

Add the Moduses which are said to have produced only about 7

£429

On grassland they used a calculation of 2d per milk cow, 6d per calf, 4s a score of lambs, ¾d a score of sheep, 4s a score of pigs.

Certain lands were held as Glebe lands. The vicarage was given 7 acres, 3 roods, 26 poles. This was the allotment land at the end of Pound Lane and the 1½ acres down Marsh Lane. G.H. Elliot had 27 acres, 1 rood, 29 poles, Henry Collett 9 acres, 1 rood and 26 poles, Rev. J.W. Huntley at the parsonage had 3 acres, 2 roods, 29 poles, and Thomas Guy had 2 acres and 9 poles, all holding as lay rectors.

The tithes were finally valued at £450. The lay rectors — G.H. Elliot, holding ⅔ and Henry Collet holding ⅓ — had £200 and £100 respectively. The three Bampton vicars had £100, and our vicar had £50.

This tithe became a great burden to farmers in the years of Depression. There was great feeling in our area in the 1830s when it became as high as the rent. The tithe was redeemed by the Government, who invested a large sum into the account called Queen Anne's Bounty. This fund had been set up in her reign to put into it all the church rights taken by Henry VIII for Lights and Prayers, and together with the interest, helped to pay the salaries of the clergy. This increased sum was used to pay them instead of the tithes, and monies from the farmers were to be redeemed over so many years.

Machines were now appearing. In February 1842, the Clanfield farmers went to see a demonstration of a machine being used to thresh wheat. As we noted, threshing machines drawn by horses came in during the Napoleonic wars. After the war in the 1830s, the labourers broke up many machines. Indeed, it really was as economic to thresh by hand as to buy an expensive machine.

Until this point, it had been done in flail-out barns, which were so designed that two wide doors faced each other. The sheaves were put in the bays, and all winter a man literally threshed out the corn from the sheaves. It was a skilled and laborious task, but it paid the wages. The doors were opened enough to let a breeze through, so that when the pile of corn and chaff was tossed into the air the wind separated it. The best corn fell first, and the tail — or worth on the tail — fell on the line. But no doubt a lot of corn was never extracted from the straw. In Clanfield a Mr Neville persisted in using a flail to thresh his corn until the 1939-45 War on his council holding, because he could not afford a threshing machine. Unfortunately, I never saw him.

Things were still hard for the countryside in these 'Hungry Forties'. A letter in the *Witney Gazette* of 1912 recalls:

In 1849, I was a boy 8½ years old, and lived at Kelmscott. My first employment was scaring small birds off a piece of turnip seed, and in June and July I worked from sunrise to sunset (16 hours a day) and was paid 1s 6d for a week of seven days.

The farm labourer's pay at that time and place was 7s a week (7–day week). For mowing and reaping hay and harvest (piece work) he was paid 2s to 2s 6d per acre for the former and 8–10s for the latter, with an occasional 12s for an extra heavy crop. For turnip and swede hoeing the pay was: setting out, 5s; seconding, 3s 6d – 4s an acre. Harvest and haycarting and stacking were paid 2s per day, and the men worked from 6am to dark with the usual portion of beer, 6-8 pints a day.

Bread at that time was 4d for a 4lb loaf, good village-made fresh butter was 7d a pound, eggs 24 a shilling in summer and 12 in winter. Cheese was from 1d to 3d a pound. Potatoes etc. were all grown in the garden. Rent of a cottage and garden was up to 1/6d per week.

Four years later, at from 12–13 years old, I was receiving 4/- per week of seven days, with free breakfast at the Master's house on Sunday morning, as undershepherd. The head shepherd received 10/- per week with free cottage and garden and breakfast on Sunday, with 1/6d per score extra for shearing the flock, and a pound extra for the lambing season — which, of course, demanded attention night and day.

Carters were paid 10/- to 12/- per week with free cottage and garden, and 40/- extra for hay and harvest with probably 50-100 bavins (faggots) of firewood worth 1d to 1½d each.

At this latter period (the Crimean War) bread was a shilling a 4lb loaf. Meat to us was out of the question, save a very small quantity of American bacon which began to arrive here in a very poor condition indeed. It would not be looked at now.

The local miller bought up some of the best barley and dressed it as wheat flour, which we were glad to buy at 10/- a bushel for pudding-making. The flour was spread out, bacon, pepper, slat and sliced onions were placed on top, and the pudding — a foot long — was rolled up in a cloth and well boiled in a pot swung over a wood fire in the wide chimney place.

In the very severe winters of that time, we used at midday to run home cold, and with an excellent appetite, and partake of the pudding with thanks and joy. Hunger was appeased that day far better than with bread, and indigestion was unknown to us. The farm labourer's pay at that time was 10s with harvest and hay pay much the same. There was much content and peace, one among the other.

In March 1842 the village saw a noble lord racing through Clanfield on a horse. The Great Western railway came through Challow in 1840, and this lord, for a bet, came by early train from London, got off at the *Leather Bottle*, hired a horse and galloped through to Burford for breakfast. He went to Sherbourne, eight miles away, for the meet, then went back home the same way for dinner at night in London. He must have had a remarkable seat!

The year 1843 was a sad one for Clanfield, as can be seen from these notes of Mr George Swinford in Filkins:

I often heard my father talk as a little boy how he went with his grandfather to the quarry in College Road. One summer morning in August, it was warm and close. After working some time, the old man looked up at the sky in an apprehensive way and said: "Can you hear thunder?" I said: "No," and as the sun was shining, I thought it was a foolish question. After a while he said: "I hear it, now put the tools away, we must start home at once."

Coming down the road, they saw cloud hanging in the sky like an elephant's trunk. The old man said: "There will be a lot of damage where that bursts." They had barely reached home when the storm broke in fury.

The cloud emptied itself over Clanfield and the river. The cut corn floated about in the fields. A farmer had his peas just ready for carting, and they swam about like boats. Two men hoeing in a field did not return home in the evening: James Joy and Robert Cross had been struck by lightning.

The following report from *Jackson's Oxford Journal* on August 12th, 1843, was of that same event

Inquest at Burford on Robert Cross and James Joy. Wednesday last, a violent thunderstorm. The deceased were turnip hoeing in a field near the village and appeared to be leaving the field for shelter, when they were struck by the electric fluid. They were found after the storm, laying three yards apart.

The body of Cross, a young man of 28 years, appeared to be uninjured and his countenance calm and placid. Joy was lying on his face, the hair burnt entirely off the right side of his head, and his body much burnt; his hat was lying at some distance, much torn, his gaiters, shoes and stockings much torn to shreds, his watch pocket, in which he had a watch, seemed as if gunpowder had exploded in it and the case of the watch was found some distance away. Some links of the chain still remained in his pocket, the rest could not be found.

Close to the body was a large hole in the ground caused by the electric fluid, and appeared as if some heavy substance had been driven and forced the soil up. Joy leaves a wife and one child, Cross a wife and five children of which two are deaf and dumb. Appeal started for families. Mr Clark paid for the funerals.

A stone plaque commemorating these deaths was put in the church tower in Clanfield.

The same newspaper, in lighter vein, reported an amusing wager in 1844. The village turned out to see a man, for a trifling wager, undertake to wheel another man from Clanfield to Lechlade, six miles in 1½ hours. A crowd followed him. Unfortunately, he took 20 minutes extra.

Grafton was now being enclosed. One field was set aside for a recreation and sports field. Their cost was £1,441. 5s 1d, seemingly much more than ours.

1844 was the year the Primitive Chapel was built in Bampton Road. There was also talk of enclosing Burroway and Nippenham, which were still farmed in the old way.

1848 saw the first of our vestry books that survive. The meeting was held on 31st March at the Masons Arms to elect parish officers. Present were the Vicar, the Rev. J.P. Penson, Mr Henry Collett, Mr James Clark, Mr Will Newman, Mr John Higgons, Mr Will Green and Mr Amos Shylor. Mr W. Green was elected parish church warden, Mr Henry Collett and Mr Amos Shaylor were elected overseers of the poor, and Mr John Higgons, together with Mr W. Newman, were elected surveyors. The next meeting, in June of that year, was in the school room across the green.

No cattle were allowed to graze loose in the village. In the November meeting James Adams, watchman, was to be paid 10s per week and 2s for each journey to the magistrates. Often the vestry started in the old school, and finished in the Masons Arms.

People began applying for assistance to emigrate in December of that year. David Mobey, 25, and his wife, 29, together with their three children, 10, 5 and 2 years old, applied. John Laugher, single, aged 21, and his twin brother Henry applied, as did Will Adams, single, aged 22, Thomas Adams, single, aged 21, Will Wilson, single, aged 20, Emma Joys, single, aged 23. The following year, £30 was granted out of the poor funds to assist Will Wilson and the Laugher twins.

In 1849, the Postmaster General began a foot post from Bampton to Shilton, taking in Clanfield and Black Bourton.The post office was by the Masons Arms.

In 1850, the vestry sparrows were to be taken at ½d each for April and May. This was a village pastime. The sparrows did so much damage around the farm to the crops. The lads went out at night with a long net, hung it up one side of a hedge quietly, and then went in the dark round to the other side, to shine a light and frighten the sparrows into the net.

In 1851, Burroway and Nippenham were enclosed. The vestry also decided to sell one cottage that it owned — the one next to the village's 'bottom shop' (formerly

Clare's Stores, later 'The Granary').

In 1852 it was decided to elect two church wardens, one for the parish and the other for the vicarage. In that same year, £26.4s.9d was paid to send three men to Australia.

In 1854, the year the Crimean War ended, Mr Thos. White, church warden, applied to the Postmaster General for a Post Office receiving house, an application which was granted.

We know of no-one in the village being at the Crimean War, which ended in 1856. No doubt some walked to Faringdon hoping to see the Malvern beacon, and the following extract from Jackson's Oxford Journal from June 14th 1856 shows how peace was celebrated:

The poor of Clanfield were not forgotten by their wealthier neighbours in the celebrating of the peace. Mr John Higgons originated the movement for the feast, and was seconded by Mr Henry Newman and Mr John Watkins, and with the assistance of the general body of the inhabitants it was soon well arranged. An ample supply of beef and mutton with other edibles, and a good quantity of strong ale, was provided, and distributed to about 400. Alvescot Band played during the dinner time.

In March 1858, a full eclipse of the sun was observed. This same year, the sale of the effects of John Wells took place at Radcot. This was the Wharfage. His goods — 70 tons of block coal, 18 tons of forest coal, 6 tons of Welsh coal, boat, nets, quantity of rushes, were mentioned in the inventory. This was of great service to the area, and showed that the Thames was still at this time used as a canal. The railways had not killed it thus far.

1859 was the year of the great whirlwind. It was reported in **Jackson's Journal**:
On Monday night a storm (which for its virulence and the damage it occasioned has never before been equalled here in the memory of any living) passed over this town (Bampton) and district. In the morning, the barometer read 28.13. As night approached, the wind became unusually boisterous, and the hoarse roaring of the storm was accompanied by heavy showers of rain, wind, flashes of lightning and loud peals of thunder. This state of things continued until 1.30am, when the storm appeared to be at its height.
At this time the fury of the elements was frightful in the extreme. A shower of hail, with the howl of the hurricane, woke many from their slumbers, and immediately the crash of falling trees, chimney pots, slates, barns, hovels and other erections, gave startling evidence to many of the awful force of the wind.

Persons in extreme terror rose from their beds, fearing that their houses were about to share the fate of less substantial fabrics. This night was intensely dark, and the wind south west. Daylight revealed the extent of the damage inflicted which was the work of but a minute; and from the examination of the wreck, not a doubt remained but that the immediate agent was a whirlwind, and that it had been exceedingly erratic in its course. From what we have been enabled to learn, no damage of any consequence was experienced until the storm reached Clanfield, a village two miles to the south west of this place...

...At Clanfield, the whirlwind exhibited even more violence than it did at Bampton. Much timber was prostrated on the estate of Messrs W. & H. Newman, while large numbers of trees were denuded of their limbs. The cornstacks on the homestead of Mr John Higgons sustained much damage by being distributed in almost every direction, some as far as half a mile. Much corn and also some buildings belonging to Mr R. Lay were similarly treated.

A building near to the turnpike road, at the entrance to the village (from Bampton), the property of Mr White, was entirely destroyed, the roof thatch being spread almost all the way to Bampton. Great fears were entertained for the safety of the cattle in the home yards and pastures; several persons went out with lanterns, but it was found the course of it was limited in the area, and the cattle and sheep had met no harm.

Since the above account was written, we have visited Clanfield, where the evidences of the peculiar and terrible effects of the storm are literally without number. At about one mile on the Bampton side of the village, the spectator first witnesses the strange destruction which is on either side so apparent. Trees, hovels and every kind of agricultural construction is levelled with the earth. The timber is scattered towards every point of the compass, showing that a whirlwind and not just a mere wind had done it. In a field of Miss Newman's, in the occupation of Mr C. White, on only $4^1/_2$ acres lie more than 40 trees, and on his premises many buildings were destroyed, also of Mrs Steward.

A portion of one of Mr Higgons' wheat ricks was carried over a dwelling house, across the turnpike road, and left in a field more than a furlong away from the rickyard.

Mr G. Knapp and Mr J. Watkins have also had much damage done to their property. Upwards of 200 trees have been uprooted; a large number partly so, not a single tree in the line of the storm escaped damage. The unroofing of ricks and cottages, the breaking of windows, etc., are all but of universal occurrence. As the storm came at night, a serious loss of human life was *averted. The village wears a very melancholy appearance indeed. The impression made upon the minds of the villagers will not be easily removed from their memories.*

The Clanfield Friendly Society began in 1858 at the Masons Arms in the month of August. Some 50 people joined. The village felt it needed more security in times of sickness. Thereafter they had a yearly day, with a band going to church, then a meal afterwards, and a parade around the village followed by swings and roundabouts.

In 1860, a new Wesleyan chapel was built beside the main road in the centre of the village. The congregation left the small hall let to them by G.H. Butler behind the Institute in the council farm, for this more commodious building.

In 1861, Clanfield was very excited when workmen putting underground drains in Mr H. Collett's field, called Lappers, above the council estate, claimed they had found 400-500 skeletons. However, when the site was inspected the next week by a Mr Stone of Brighthampton, only one was to be seen. They opened out previous places, but found no more.

Mr Stone noted that the ground was covered with Romano-British pottery, and this was the spot which was called Killingsworth, or Cilla's Worth. There had been a British settlement here, which Cilla's people had possibly taken over. However, by the time the Open Field passed over the area, they were gone.

In that year steam ploughing was used for the first time in the area at Mr Acker's, Black Bourton. Although no-one in Clanfield could afford it, this foretold of the way things would happen in the future, when four or five furrows were pulled up and down the field with a steam engine each end, instead of the single or double furrowed ploughs. This was also the year that the railway reached Witney. There were great celebrations.

In the north of England at this time, there was great poverty. The cloth mills depended on cotton from North America, but because the civil war was raging there, they could send none. At church in Clanfield on October 18, a retiring collection of £10 was sent to help them.

The roads had always been a problem. The Turnpike Acts looked after the main ones. Clanfield had two. One went from Faringdon to Burford, and was begun in 1770, and the other one began at Clanfield Cross and went to Galley Hill, and this began in the same year. Luckily we had no gate on these main roads, but the village of Black Bourton was plagued with one, and Radcot the other. But we did have two side gates. One was on the entrance to Langley Lane, and the other on the entrance to Calcroft.

The side roads were still the responsibility of the village, however. In 1863, the Bampton West Highway Board was founded to look after these roads. Marsh Lane,

Langley Lane, Mill Lane and Calcroft Lane now ceased to be the village's roads. Funds came from the Poor Rate for this. We had no village record of our rates until 1970, when a Poor Rate book for the year 1890 was found in the roof of the cottage behind the Post Office. This was duly photocopied and returned to the finder.

It was during Victoria's reign that organised sports began for the first time in the village. Cricket teams were being reported. Clanfield formed a team which played in Mr Clinch's field, possibly the feeding ground behind Chestlyon, and they had a meal afterwards in the Masons Arms, the only pub being registered at this time. Bell ringing was also in full swing. It appears a new team had started. C.H. Clinch, W. Clinch, R. Brooks and T. Collett rang for one hour and five minutes, and they rang for the club the following year.

In 1864 there was a tragic accident at the Vicarage. The vicar's son had just arrived home from the sea. He had been shooting at Langford, came home and then went out with his father. The *Jackson's Oxford Journal* reported the incident on Saturday June 4th 1864:

On Monday last a shocking accident occurred to the Rev J.P. Penson, vicar of Clanfield. He had been out walking with his son and had just returned home, when by some accident the gun which his son was carrying went off, discharging the contents through the upper part of the right arm, close to the shoulder joint, and shattering the bone into complete fragments. Medical aid was promptly procured, and as soon as the system had recovered from the immediate shock, chloroform was administered, and the limb amputated at the shoulder joint. We are sorry to hear that much prostration of the vital powers still continues, and that great fears are entertained as to his recovery.

Mr Clinch, a neighbour, sat up with the Vicar all night, but he died the next day. *Jackson's Oxford Journal*, Saturday June 11th, 1864:

Report and inquest and funeral of Rev. J.P. Penson. Inquest at Plough Inn, W. Newman foreman of the jury. Eldest son had been to Langford. On return he went out with father, son with gun, father with broomstick. Broomstick hit gun and set it off. Mr Clinch, neighbouring farmer, sat up with him all night, next day arm was taken off. Funeral on Thursday, followed by all local clergy. Most of private residences and shops were shut.
Quite a gloom was cast over the village.

The *Oxford Times* reported the election of the new vicar. It was held in the schoolroom. The Rev. Dawson, curate of Little Coxwell, and Rev. W. Palmer, curate of Bampton, applied. The Rev. R. Piggott, Baptist Minister, took the chair and 14 of the most influential were present.

The Rev. Dawson was elected, subject to the approval of Captain Elliott, in whose gift the living was. The greater proportion of the meeting was non-conformists. This is quite an interesting report insofar as a Baptist minister was in the chair, and non-conformists were now amongst the most influential people in the village. This approval, however, was not granted, and Captain Elliott gave his approval to the Rev. York of Witney, curate of Ducklington and Chaplain to Witney Union.

The upkeep of the footpaths had now become the responsibility of the vestry. The meeting had to consider the surveyor's report, as £29 3s.2d was required to repair Rye Bridge. They did not accept this because the bridge, having a footpath over it, was used by farmers. They agreed to pay half, the farmers paying the rent.

In September 1869 a fire was raging at Mr James Clark's, whither an engine was taken from Bampton. Mr Clark was insured with the Liverpool Globe. The house was completely destroyed, as there was no water, and the insurance did not cover the cost.

Influenced, no doubt, by the Methodist revival that followed John Wesley's life, the Oxford movement began to bring new life into the Anglican church. Its effects were being felt in the villages in the mid-19th century, and Clanfield had a meeting in June 1867 to see about rebuilding the church, or at least part of it. The work began in 1869, and was unofficially opened in December 1869.

Will Newman, of Friars Court, who, it seems, had been the driving force by giving £100 to start it off, died in the October. He saw the last load of corn in, and fell down dead. He was buried with the scaffolding around the church. The service was held either in the open, or in the chancel. His death cast quite a gloom over the official opening the following year.

Civilisation was approaching Clanfield. In October 1868, it was reported that the railway through Alvescot from Witney to Fairford was about to begin. All the next year, the navvies were working on it, and were too busy to attend Filkins Feast. In April 1870, the navvies went on strike.

By July 1871, it had reached Alvescot, and the 50 labourers were given a meal in the Red Lion. But in September 1872 it was still not finished. It was finally finished in the January of 1873.

When the first train ran through, the people of Bampton were worried because someone said that the speed would affect the passengers' eyes, presumably because some were sitting outside. So the Bampton doctor met the train — and they could still see as much as was good for them!

In 1869, the Thames Conservancy was busy working on the river. The Old Nan's bridge was straightened out and the weir taken out. The same was done at Old Man's, but a footbridge was built over the river here by the Fox and Hounds. This pub was rather in the way so, as shown in Taunt's photograph, the bridge had to descend rather steeply on the north side.

The Knapp family now became important to the village. Although Knapps had owned land in Clanfield, the first record of a resident was George Knapp or Napp in 1696, who died at Friars Court and was a wealthy tenant farmer. Of this family, one part became shopkeepers and pub owners, while the others became builders and machinery makers. In 1866, Leonard Knapp took over from his son, John Thomas, and began to advertise in all the papers. However, the census forms of 1871 and 1881 show that he only employed about three men. The real expansion came when he bought Norton's foundry at Faringdon, and brought it to Clanfield later.

In 1872, John Wright applied for a licence to sell petrol. The new school was also built. Later that year the parish boundaries were officially surveyed. The following is an extract from the Ordnance Survey in Southampton:

The original ascertaining of this parish boundary was in the year 1872, and it was carried out by a team of specialised surveyors working ahead of the main survey. The procedure at that time was as follows: a Mereman (local man acquainted with the boundary) sometimes the overseer of the parish, was appointed for each parish by the local Justices in Quarter Session under the Ordnance Survey Act, 1841, to point out the true position of the boundary to the Ordnance Surveyor (who was armed with the local tithe map, any Enclosure Award documents, and had access to any local estate maps, etc.)

The name of the Mereman for the parish of Clanfield was Henry Newman, and for the adjoining parishes William Cox (Black Bourton), John Clark (Bampton and Weald parish), F.H. Barfield (Great Faringdon parish), Thomas Morse (Radcot parish) and William May (Grafton parish). The last two were amalgamated in 1932 to form the new parish of Grafton and Radcot.

The two adjacent Meremen walked (or perambulated) the boundary, pointing out the boundary to the Ordnance Surveyor. If any disagreement was registered, a report was then made to the Officer in charge of boundaries, at that time the Director General personally. The position was then investigated and the final position of the boundary is that which was shown on a map depicting the boundaries (of each parish) and publicly exhibited at the following places: the County Hall, Oxford, on 23rd and 24th February 1874, to which no objection was made, the resulting boundaries were then published as part of the survey (in due course).

In September 1892, the 12th Royal Lancers, 98 men and 107 horses, passed through Clanfield going from Faringdon to Chipping Norton. Those passing through on the Monday were followed the next day by Royal Horse Artillery, 116 men, 119 horses and 5 guns. This must have caused considerable excitement.

In the December, the postal arrangements were increased by a walking messenger, leaving Bampton in the morning for Faringdon, calling at Clanfield and Radcot, and returning at 3.30pm.

The years of unrest among the labourers now began. The trouble was economic. The years were better for farming, so the labourers wanted better wages. The unrest reached our area in May 1873.

A meeting was held at Bampton which was badly organised. Others followed in June at Faringdon Corn Exchange, and The Lamb at Filkins. They met at Aston outside the public house, as the cricket ground was refused them. About 50 men joined the Union. In July they met at Milton, where Joseph Arch addressed them. He was a piece worker from Warwick who moved around the area during his jobs. He was also a Primitive Methodist local preacher able to express himself clearly. He rose to be head of the Union, and later became a Member of Parliament.

In August, 2,000 people met in a field between Clanfield and Bampton and had tea there. In November, they met at Faringdon, then the next year at Filkins, again in February. It was so cold, that they went into the Methodist Church. Such was the feeling, that it was reported one speaker said: "In the case of invasion, the Union men had nothing to lose, and would sooner aid the invaders than fight against them."

In March, Mr Arch spoke to a large number at Faringdon. In December, he had been to Canada and he appealed to the men there. In January 1874, the Union lecturers Bryant, Winter and Morse were speaking outside Bampton Town Hall, and membership was still growing. In April 1874 a Mr Pill spoke at Bampton, and a cap was passed round for those locked out. In June of that year, 10 emigrants left Bampton, led by John Bryant of the labour union. In the east there had been a big lock-out. These men had been tramping the countryside, but the union now had to say it could not go on paying forever, and that the men should emigrate.

It was not as easy as that for many, however. In Clanfield, G. Wilson, a labourer who worked at Puckety Farm over the river for Mr Harris, had run away — but he was tied to a contract. In his absence he was taken to court and ordered to return and pay 10s costs.

By 1875, the labourers' activities were not so active. A large central meeting was held in Wesley Memorial Church Hall in Oxford, but local meetings had lost their appeal and the leadership became divided.

The turnpikes that had served the land so well were now coming to an end. In the beginning, men willingly paid at each gate, but a generation arose which had not seen the bad roads and they began to take them for granted. They assumed the right of free passage, and wanted the gates gone. In the courts, actions were now being taken.

In Clanfield during 1875, the Witney Galley Hill to Clanfield Cross turnpike came to an end. It had never paid so well as the other one.

All the gates were taken up and sold. The Burford to Faringdon road lasted longer, and then all the gates and side gates and sheds were sold. In our parish there was a shed and side gate at both Langley and Calcroft Lane.

1875 was also the year of the Cridland 'murder'. Mrs Cath Cridland was found by Postman Lee bruised and beaten at the bottom of the stairs. She had a fractured skull. It was thought that her husband, a 60-year-old collar maker, had beaten her and tried to put her down the well. However her husband, who spent most of his money on drink, after arranging some alterations to his house, had gone off on the Thursday before her death to Bath, and had sent a postcard asking for some money.

When the police found him he was hard up, having sold his coat. He suggested that his wife had got up early to feed the ducks, and driven them back into the orchard, and then had a fit, like her brother, and fallen down the stairs. The jury, under James Clark of Clanfield, could find no answer, and returned a verdict of 'violent death, but by who or when not known'.

A court case followed in which Mr Townsend, who made the coffin, tried to get his money. Cridland replied that he had been in custody, and that as the parish ordered it they should pay for it. The judge, however, thought otherwise, and ordered him to pay 18s. In March 1877 John Davis Cridland, collar maker of Bampton, was found with his throat cut. He was ordered to be buried without Christian rites, between the hours of 9pm-12pm. He was buried at 10pm.

In November 1875 the floods were as bad as ever known, despite the Thames Conservancy works. On a Sunday morning, two boats were rowed from Radcot Bridge to Mr Baston's at the Masons Arms, all up the turnpike road. This was a very wet period.

In August the following year, a three-hour tempest and thunderstorm was endured in Witney. Floods were everywhere. In January 1877, there was 1ft 7in of water in Bampton houses. The Thames Conservancy, however, said that as there were only four such floods in the past 56 years, it therefore did not warrant any extreme expense.

Drink was a problem in Clanfield. In July 1876, John Edy was summoned for being drunk, fined 1s 6d and 3s 6d costs, or seven days in prison. Dan Bowls, Thos. Illot and Joseph Pemfield, all of Langford, were also summoned on the same occasion in Clanfield.

In September, Lance Collet was charged at Burford with furiously driving a horse at Clanfield, fined 10s,plus 1s 6d costs and, for being drunk in charge, 1s and 6s costs. There must have been a check-up in Clanfield, for in December Thos. Beckingsale, a beer house keeper residing in Clanfield, was summoned for selling half a pint of beer to be consumed on his premises, without a licence. He was fined £5. Thos. Beckingsale, baker of Clanfield, was also in court at Burford in October, drunk in charge of a horse and fined 14s with 26s for furiously driving at Brize Norton.

In May 1878, being early closing day on Wednesday, a few friends from Clanfield visited White Horse Hill. They found embedded in a chalk quarry about 20ft below the top, a cannon ball! (Mr J.H. Tanner, the grocer, held it for anyone who wished to see it).

Accidents always lie close at hand. In October of that year Henry Comley, shepherd for Mrs White, fell under a sack of corn which he was carrying to feed his sheep. It was a heavy load and that, together with a rough floor and a darkish building, caused him to fracture his leg. He had a family of young children to keep.

In March 1879, the old Fox and Hounds was burned down at High Bridge.

The Mill at Little Clanfield was up for sale. It had been built up a lot, but trade had become bad again.

The headmaster, Mr Webb, left the school. In the two-and-a-half years he had been there, the pupils had increased in number from 40 to 106.

A sporting collar maker said he could run one mile in five minutes for a sovereign. He took six, and lost.

The same month, the inquest took place at the Masons Arms of a schoolboy who committed suicide.

The bad years were now upon Clanfield. The tragic year of rain in 1879 was followed by the severe snow of 1881. Mr Blagrove of the Mill and his horse were frozen to death on the side of the Radcot Road, and a sweep died between Aston and Brighthampton.

American corn killed the prices, and men began to go broke — such a person being Henry Newman, of Friars Court. He owned a very large estate of some 900 acres in his prime, resulting from land owned by his family in 1874. He was the fourth generation of farmers of that family in our village. He sold Rock Farm of Black Bourton, where Carterton now stands.

He still went on buying land in the hope that bad times would soon be over, and in 1881 he bought Lower Farm. In 1886, however, his creditors foreclosed as he could not pay the interest. In the end he had to sell up and leave the village.

The situation was not helped by the fact that his father had left him to pay £1,000 each to a brother and three sisters, but profits did not pay the interest on all the mortgage he held. In 1886 it was all over, and it was a stunning blow for the village. He had two lots of money to pay, amounting to thousands of pounds. The village was shocked, the church having lost a most generous friend and giver. The Vicar, writing to the Church for help, spoke of the "tragedy of the village".

Mr George Adams of Hailey, a very shrewd man, took over many of the vacant farms of the area. He obtained them at very low rents, thus disposing of Newman's weakness of holding the land by mortgage. He could deal direct with the landlord to adjust his rent according to the years. He took over Windmill Farm.

In May 1882 a fete was held at Rushey Lock. Boats went from Radcot pulled by a horse. Feasts were lively occasions — Clanfield having its swings, roundabouts and shooting gallery.

In September 1890, Mr Will Clare, Mr Abrahams (Friars Court) and John White took their staff on an outing to White Horse Hill, to see the manouevres.

In 1891, three cottages belonging to Mr Will Clare at the end of Pound Lane were burned down.

In January 1892, a young lady from Oxford County Council came to speak at the school. When crossing over the road, a youth frightened her horse and it backed her conveyance into the brook. She was wet through, but after putting on dry clothes she apparently spoke well!

In 1894, the Local Government Act came into effect concerning the election of a Parochial Parish Council. The old vestry ceased to look after the village affairs. It was quite a day for Clanfield, as it was for other villages. There were plenty of bills stuck up, and two boys paraded with a huge Union Jack.

Allotments were the issue of the moment. The school was crowded. The Vicar took the chair. Sixteen men were put up for election, and of these W. Clare, J. Reason, T. Clare, L.R. Knapp and J. Parrot were elected. The first four, called the Moderate Party, were all businessmen. The latter, called a Progressive, was a farm worker, and a man who had great knowledge of the village.

The village was very excited, and after the election was announced the church bells were rung. From now on, the Parish Council minutes as well as the local papers tell us about the village. The Parish Council set about its work, and the question of allotments was raised, but nothing was done for a few years.

The village wanted its own policemen instead of having to go to Black Bourton. The village wastes were let — these consisted of the top green down to the Hollies, including the lettings of the top green to fair people (1s for the first night, 6d for the second, but no longer); then from the Hollies, down to Green Close including the lower green and Withy Bed; finally, from Bottom Bridge down the roadsides to Ashton Pill Bridge.

The village overseers elected were Mr L.R. Knapp and Troilys Clare. At this meeting, Mr Rhymes was asked to trim Green Close hedge, as it was hanging over the church path. The clerk was to write to ask who controlled the trees and ponds. Stanks were to be put in the stream to hold back the water in case of fire, and to keep the wells up in dry times.

In 1895, an earthquake was felt strongly in the Cotswolds.

That same year, there was a disruption at the Feast. The following year they wanted extra police. They also wanted a light outside the Post Office, and a telegraph (as the wires went by). They tried to get the District Council to take over the stream, but they would not. They allowed people to dig gravel on the greens, and the holes were used as refuse places. In 1897, they proposed that Mr Faulks, "a man of property and means" be Postmaster of Clanfield to look after the telegraph service. They also asked for the Post Office to be a money order office.

In 1897, the Diamond Jubilee of Queen Victoria was celebrated. There were special services on Sunday and a meat tea for children, old men and old women, and Mr Reason loaned his field for sports.

The village wondered what to do to commemorate the occasion — whether to rehang the bells, or to repair the clock. From this occasion it is interesting to note that people were now getting too proud to sit down as a village together, because children and the old were pushed into prominence to give a face to the occasion. To begin with, as no celebration had been arranged, whilst the people were at church some of the lads made fire by the Weir Bridge with a large pot on it, and in it some bacon and potatoes. They tied a large apron to the side part, and then dressed up in old clothes and began to eat the forbidden meal as the people came out of church.

The hint was taken, and the celebration was hastily arranged. The enthusiasm over the bell ringing had revealed limitations. The old bell frame was in very bad shape, and some bells could not be rung. Mention of the possibility of repairing the clock is interesting — for it was taken down at the restoration of the church, and as no clock exists today, it would appear that the old clock still existed somewhere at that time in bad need of repair.

In 1898, another large landowner had problems — William White. He was a local man who had gone to Rugby and made some money out of the wine trade. He had married Ann Newman, sister of Henry, who also had troubles. She had been left various large sums of money by her father, and after her brother went broke she and her husband bought up part of the estate — viz. High House, Little Clanfield and Cummings, owning also the Manor of Aston. Now he died insolvent, so the poor girl had seen her brother go insolvent and now her own husband. She had helped to ruin her brother by a court case.

In 1898, an attempt was made to get the Thames/Severn Canal going again, the Great Western Railway having previously bought up all the shares to kill it. However, as their position was secure, now they put it into a trust and it was able to be used again. Obviously, no one would really take it seriously and re-equip it with new boats, now that the railways were able to give it a much faster delivery.

This same year was also a rather sad one for Clanfield. A young couple, Mr Rand and his wife, came to the village where he had been appointed headmaster of the school. They had a young child. They threw themselves into village life, and he became choir master at the church, where she was the organist. Suddenly, the village heard that he had another wife, an invalid who for some reason had left him. He was a bigamist. This was a serious offence, and he had to go to the Assizes. He was given two years, but without hard labour. Perhaps the jury felt that there had been some cause. They left Clanfield.

Also in 1898 there was a bad fire at Horns Cottage, by the vicarage. There had been fires before in these thatched houses, but they had been contained as water was so handy. This time, however, it was too late and the whole cottage burned down. The families were put up all round the village.

In August 1899, the following report appeared in the **Witney Gazette (August 12th 1899)** about an incident in our meadows:

> There is nothing better in hot weather than a refreshing dip in the river —
> so at least thought two gents living not a hundred miles from Bampton one
> day last week, as they were walking along the river bank. No sooner the
> thought expressed, than it was acted upon, although they were minus towels
> and other necessary things.
> A quiet secluded spot was found, and soon the two friends were enjoying a
> swim, but the further they went the shallower got the river. They were on the
> point of returning when — oh horror! Just behind them was a boat filled
> with ladies and gentlemen. What was to be done? They had no time to get
> into deep water, and barbed wire on both sides of the bank prevented them
> from taking refuge on terra firma.
> At last, in the madness of despair, they made a rush for the wire and
> scrambled through it and were safe. But the sight they presented on freeing
> themselves from the barbed wire was a very sorry one. Scratched and
> bleeding in many parts of their bodies, they eventually returned to their

clothes, and afterwards wended their way homewards, sadder but wiser for this adventure.

On August 30, 1900, the first regatta was held at Radcot at 2.30pm. There was racing in sculls, canoes and punts, a tug-o-war, a duck hunt — the duck was human, though in later years it was a real duck. This regatta survived over the years into living memory, finishing some time before the last war. A greasy pole stuck out over the river, and it was a popular sport to see who could go out the furthest.

In the November, Mr Alf Radburn, the village rag-and-bone man, died. He was the Primitive Sunday School Superintendent, and greatly respected in the village. He gave the children small wooden dolls for their rags.

In the Parish Council minutes, the issue being raised was who owned the wastelands in the village, and who owned or controlled the withy trees.

By 1901, the year Queen Victoria died, Clanfield had become a fully developed and lively village. During the Queen's reign, the last of the old village disappeared, the Open Field system went, and the modern fields were formed. The land which was formerly irreligious was now filled with people zealous for the Church. Every village activity was well supported. The bad years of the 1890s were over.

Perhaps the saddest part was the handling of the old and the poor. Now, they were sent to Witney to new and frightening surroundings where they would not daily see their friends and families. Moreover, it is said that when they got there they were split up, men on one side and women the other. Long years of married companionship, which must have meant something to most, was suddenly shattered. It was also said that they were at once given a bath, something they were most probably not accustomed to, and whilst in one sense it may have been necessary, it could also have brought on early deaths through pneumonia.

Perhaps the greatest hope was the tackling of the drink problem responsible for so much poverty, and also the clubs which tackled the illness problems. The Band of Hope was begun by all churches, both Church of England and Non Conformists. Its aim was to show people how much home life could be improved if the bread winner took his wages home rather than first stopping off at the pub and spending much of it.

They wanted to show people that self-imposed poverty could be dealt with. Obviously those who made a living out of the trade objected, and when the Salvation Army came out fighting it head-on, as one of the main thrusts of its campaign, resistance became hostile. A few free drinks, plenty of ammunition at hand, and many people could be found to attack them.

As late as about 1930, Mr Beard of Bampton, who raised a list of names to get pubs closed at 10pm instead of 11pm had a riot outside his house west of the town hall. Police with truncheons had to protect his home.

The 'clubs' were also a great boon. Accident, sickness, early death, all brought terrible problems. The parish tried to look after these people, but seemingly rather coldly. Now, with these clubs they felt that they had their own rights, without going cap-in-hand. The money came in. They had more dignity. Of course, there were still many people who were prepared to say if they thought anyone was pulling a fast one. At the end of the year, at least at first, they had an annual share-out of monies not spent. It was very costly in 1907, at 2s a week, but it was incredibly helpful.

In general, everyone was better off when Victoria died, than they had been financially when she came to the throne. It was a wonderful reign.

★ ★ ★

Chapter 13

The 20th Century

ENGLAND had passed its peak, but was still a very powerful nation, envied by all. In Europe, Germany was rising in economic wealth and demanding a place in the world. In our land, life was secure, every man knew his place.

Not until ten years had passed did organised labour begin to rock the boat. Then, in the mines and factories, men began to demand a better position in life, relief from their intolerable conditions.

Southern England was in decline, as more and more of its population moved West to the Welsh mines or North into the factories. Travel was now so easy, with the railway system all over the land. Others, taking the future of themselves and their families into their own hands, emigrated. Canada was offering, for a £2 passage, free farms of 164 acres. If a man ploughed so much, built a log cabin, and lived on it for so long, then he wuld be given free title.

My own grandfather went out whilst his eldest son, who had added years to his age, had gone to join the Boer War. But conditions were bad in Canada. The Prairies were 1,000 feet above sea level. The wet 19th century gave way to a dry 20th century, with all its dust bowls. Ploughing, as they later discovered, was the wrong method, because it lost the fibre and the moisture. Log cabins did not keep out the severe weather which came in spells, sometimes 40 degrees below zero.

Early in the 20th century we were sucked into a European squabble. We began to fear Germany's expansion. War came upon us, but the saying "It will be over by Christmas" was wrong. Four long years followed, with even the Americans being finally drawn in.

This terrible war changed our life. We felt it here a little in bombing, shelling of the coast, in food shortages, but the main things were the changes that came to stay. Women now felt their freedom to earn and be independent. Men were to come back who had seen a world larger than their own villages, to a land they were told would be "fit for heroes to live in".

When the war ended, elections were held, but due to a government muddle most of the returning troops were not on the voting lists. Trouble blew up as men could not get home fast enough. Around 50,000 men were released each month.

A temporary boom, as immediate shortages were replenished, saved the Government for a while, but soon more difficulties arose. In 1926, the restless labour force came out in a general strike, and the years of depression followed right through into the 1930s. England staggered into another situation in which a reborn Germany under Hitler tried once again to regain its position and dominate the world. Another even longer war followed, but this time with less loss of life for Britain.

Since the War the country has run more and more out of steam: more wanting to share the fruits, fewer willing to pay the price. The 1960s saw the appearance of the mysterious 'Fifth Column' which seemed determined to break up the factory life of our land. Even at Clanfield we became victims of the phenomenon in the 1970s, with the Withy Beds issue.

The country's situation was saved economically by the discovery of North Sea oil and although at the time of writing a worse depression exists with more people than ever out of work, conditions are not comparable with the 1930s.

Village life has now had to come to terms with a situation in which, more and more, it serves as the dormitory of the local towns. The midday dinner has now moved into the evening, and after a journey back from work, then a meal, it is often too late for any village activity later in the evening. The net result is that the village has now become but a loose-knit community with little loyalty to itself.

Local news

In February 1903, a complaint was made about Faringdon Market. At one time men sold their own cattle, but now auctioneers have taken over and have to be paid. In 1904, the harvest was terribly wet. There was a cyclone on Salisbury Plain. The harvest was not in until November. In August 1905, General Booth visited Faringdon.

In July 1906, Will Gardener of Witney, aged 93, recalled seeing the master of the workhouse going around Witney with an inmate, pushing a barrow into which the Poor Rate was collected.

In the September of that same year, Irishmen came into the area to help cut the corn.

In April 1909, there was an awful dust at Witney, and shops had to close their doors and windows. A water cart was needed to dampen everything down.

In February 1910, George Adams died. He was a great farmer who took over all the vacant farms in the late 1880s. He lived at Wadley.

In June 1911, the White Horse Hill was used to start the beacon fires, lighted with red, white and blue magnesium lights. At 10pm, a rocket was fired. This year Mr T. Clark of Witney died. He was born at Burford in 1813, and was a clever inventor. He owned a velocipede in the mid-19th century which caused great excitement in the area.

In October 1912, a cinema opened in Faringdon. In May 1914, Langley Wireless Station was built near Leafield. In July 1917, the Witney Workhouse was closed.

Clanfield in the 20th Century

Chestlion

Christ Church still remained the owners. They added to their estate by buying the adjacent Elliotts at the end of Pound Lane.

Friars Court

This was left in the hands of the Fereman family of Swindon. In 1920, they sold it to my father in law, Mr R.N. Willmer, who was the tenant. He was a very prosperous hay and straw merchant who, at one time, bought all the hay for the GWR pit ponies in Wales. In 1963 he passed it to his son, Mr John H. Willmer, having enlarged it with land bought from Mr Bowden, of North Court and Radcot Farm.

Southwick

Charles White died in 1898, and in 1903 it was sold with other family lands. Mr Ernest White bought it. He was a ram dealer, and ended up very well off, enlarging the farm and buying up other land. In 1917 he sold it to a Mr F. Bowden from Basingstoke, who retired in 1955 and sold it to Lt Col. Arthur Forbes. Later the land was sold to Count Munster of Bampton, and the house to Professor Turnbull, so the manor property now stands devoid of all land.

On February 9, 1901, a special service was held in our church for the Queen's funeral. The church was full. The year passed as preparations were made for the Coronation. In the meantime, on Feast Day in August, there was a bad fire. Two cottages in Busby Close, adjacent to the road, were on fire.

The clerk of Knapps broke his leg falling off a ladder as he fought the fire. In the Close behind were parked all the caravans. In one of them Mr Ben Smith, who was later to own large estates around Wantage, was born. His father owned some of the fair equipment.

The Coronation was planned for June 1902. Everyone was busy preparing for it. The inhabitants of Clanfield went to Witney to buy a beast for the village beef tea.

A splendid beast was bought on Thursday last for supplying beef to the inhabitants of Clanfield on Coronation Day.

Unfortunately, the King went down with appendicitis. He was operated on, the first person on whom this operation was performed. The meat would not keep, so it was distributed around the village.

Two Clanfield men had gone to the Boer War, Bert Blunsdon and George Holloway. These, with others, were rushed back for the celebrations. They were met at Alvescot station by the Barnets, of The Plough, and brought back to Clanfield in a landau. A large banner crossed the street by Clare's stores which said 'Welcome'.

The Coronation was postponed until August, when the village celebrated. The Faringdon band had been booked. At one o'clock it paraded through the village to Mr Clare's, Busby Close, where the sports were held, and then afterwards a tea was held in Mr Reason's barn at Chestlion. Mugs were given to the children to commemorate the occasion. At night, a huge bonfire was held on the top green. Mr E. White, who was then of North Court, was pleased to see men putting faggots onto the fire and congratulated them — until he found out that they were his faggots! A Mrs Shaylor was present, aged 95 years. She was said to have remembered four coronations.

In 1903 there was a great concern about the bad bend by the vicarage. There had been many accidents there. The latest was the mail coach. The horse shied at the wall there, and threw the driver out. The driver's face was cut. The horse went galloping through the village and was eventually found by Mr W. Clare, the postmaster's man, with the cart turned over near Radcot.

The Rural Council at last agreed to do something about it. They would buy the land for £10 if Clanfield would pull down the trees and remove the soil. Knapps and Clares, who at the time were in business together, had a large steam engine. This was used to pull down the elms which were all sold off as timber and firewood. The farmers dug away the dirt, and the gravel was used on the village paths. The Council then proceeded to wall the bank, remove the ditch and build the road.

In June 1903, a medal was presented to the parents of Trooper Fred Tilby of Radcot, who died at Johannesburg on April 14, 1901. In this same month there were terrible floods in the valley. There were 5.8 inches of rain in eight days — it rained for 60 hours without stopping. The hay was spoilt, harvest was a battle. Clanfield farmers were amongst those who suffered. It rained right through the winter. People did not know where to put their cattle, the fields were under so much water.

In March 1904, Jesse Jones and Charles Hutchings, who were delivering drills for Knapps to the station, were caught by the police picking up the odd lumps of coal that had fallen off the rail trucks. They were taken by the police to Burford in handcuffs and fined 10s, but the magistrate said that the handcuffs had not really been necessary.

In 1905, the village got about the rehanging of its bells and the tower was rebuilt. The name F.W. Farmer on the side of the tower at the top comes from this work. In 1905, Mrs Carter died. Muffled bells were rung. In April 1906, James Clark died, casting 'quite a gloom' over the village. A tablet to his life stands on the wall in the Methodist hall.

In August the foundation stone of the Institute was laid. The bells which were now all in good order were rung for the occasion. The following year, March 1907, the keenness of the bell ringers resulted in 1260 changes of the Grandsire Triples being rung for Mrs Knapp's birthday. No doubt this was followed by beer all round. Later

The Carter Institute — with exposed timbers

The procession on its way from St Stephen's Church to the opening ceremony for the Carter Institute, photographed outside the Foundry in Main Street, with the Post Office seen opposite, and the Old Forge cottages to the right.

The walk from the original Weslyan chapel, beside Willow Farm

The 'new' Methodist chapel, built in 1907

that year a team, including two Clanfield ringers, rang the full Grandsire Triples of 5040 in 2 hours and 57 minutes. In November that year, the village ringers took it on, and they took 3 hours and 5 minutes.

In the April of 1907, Mrs Rainey, the Vicar's wife, died in childbirth. A new east window was put up in her memory in the church. The Vicar left the village.

The day school visited the White Horse Hill one summer's day in 1908. They were taken by vans and horse, and left at 9.30am, arriving at 11.00am, and returned at 6pm — very hot. This local spot was very popular, being just within reach for a day's outing.

In January 1909, the new covert was drawn at Clanfield by the Old Berkshire Hounds. This was the fox cover down Marsh Lane. The late Mr Amos Comley said he ploughed it for the last time. The trees came from Tuckers in Faringdon.

In 1909, the pig club held its supper at The Plough. It had been started in 1907. The cottage pig in these later years played a very important part in village life. Cottagers kept two pigs, which they bought as piglets from some local breeder, in the bottom of their garden. They fed these on house waste and upon rough toppings or grain that they had bought or gleaned and had milled.

They kept these pigs to a good size, much larger than we do today, not being frightened of plenty of fat in that age of needing great physical energy. When they were large enough, they sold one to pay expenses and had the other indoors.

Some local person would go around pig-killing. It was a very special occasion, and a child's delight. A pile of straw would be obtained, and as soon as the pig had been killed, it would be rolled onto the straw and burnt. This removed all the hairs.

If by chance it was a porker, a young pig, that was killed, it would be scalded with three buckets of boiling water to one of cold to fetch off all the hairs. After the pig had been burnt, it was hung up, the blood was caught to make blood pies or to feed the grape vine or special rose tree. The one at The Plough was fed on this over the years.

The insides of the pig were carefully removed. Everything was used. The intestines were cleaned, often in the village stream, and when cold were eaten as 'chitlings', being most tasty when mustard was added. The internal fat was boiled down and put into a large pan, forming its own surface pattern when cold, and later eaten as dripping on bread.

The bladder was always given to a waiting boy. This would be his first football when it was blown up. The old 'fools' of a past age used these, as the fool of the Bampton Morris dancers did, to put on a stick with which to go around banging everyone.

Nothing was wasted from the pig. However, in the days when there were no fridges a group of friends or families shared in turn the fresh joints. When anyone killed his pig, everyone had a part to play. After the insides and all were taken, the pig was hung to cool and harden. The hams were then cut off, and the sides with these hams were then treated or salted, each person having his own special way taught by his parents. The parts were then hung in the cottage instead of pictures!

I remember seeing my grandfather making up the fire every morning when he came back from milking. He would go to the side of bacon and cut off a good rasher about a quarter of an inch thick all across. Then, putting it on a large slice of bread, he took a large expanding fork, stuck it into the rasher, and held it over the newly lit fire. As the flames grew, so the fat ran. Some ran into the flames, most was dabbed onto the bread. When the operation was over, the rasher was cooked, the bread covered with a lovely fat, and the fire was burning fiercely. Again, nothing was wasted. A lovely meal in a laborious age.

In that year the new Wesleyan church was opened next door to the old one. The site had been bought by a Mrs Browning, daughter of J.T. Knapp, who became a member there. She sold it to the chapel. The foundation stone was laid within three days of purchase, and in four months it was built and opened. Men in those days got on with the job!

The year 1906 was when the manoeuvres came to Clanfield. These were held in September, and from the papers and the memory of our older people an interesting story emerges. The 'reds' had their local headquarters at Shipton-under-Wychwood, the 'blues' at Marlborough. War was declared on Sunday at 6pm, and hostilities began on Monday at 4am.

During the night, the reds moved into Clanfield and the village awoke to find soldiers everywhere and men asleep along the causeway, having marched all night. About one thousand men and officers filled the village and fields. The guns were drawn up on the lower green, and all day were firing at the Faringdon's Folly Hill, which was held by the blues.

Up at the Post Office, the Landers had their horses which they fed and watered there. In the meantime, they had sent 60 cyclists off as an advance guard to take Radcot Bridge and then to attack Folly Hill. The blues, attacking from the south, came to Tadpole and found the bridge blown up. Following the river to Radcot, they fell into an ambush — proceeded to Lechlade, and also found the bridge blown up there.

They crossed over the river east of the bridge, and built up a line from Kelmscot through Langford to Kencot, and on the Tuesday advanced on Clanfield and Radcot. The reds lined Radcot Road, with their guns firing west, but the blues had 16 divisions to the reds' 12 divisions, and also more guns.

At Langford, the blues were in such a hurry that the gun crews took off at full gallop for Clanfield, and in the process knocked one Langford man off his bike. A full description was given in the *Witney Gazette*:

'The Battle of Clanfield'

While the reds were busy capturing the Folly the blues were making a determined onslaught of Clanfield. The scene of the battle was perfectly flat land lying along the left bank of the Thames, and closely intersected by high hedges and many small watercourses. So close was the country that it was impossible to see more than 200-300 yards in any direction. This, together with the fact that there were no artillery positions, accounted for the extraordinary confusion which prevailed during the later stages of the fight, when the attack was pressed home.

General Grierson sent the 10th Infantry Brigade forward against the centre of the red position with portions of the 7th and 9th against the flanks.

The 7th Brigade was to the north, facing the village of Clanfield. The 1st Infantry Brigade, comprising the 1st Grenadier Guards, 1st Coldstream Guards, 2nd West Yorks, 2nd South Wales Borderers under Brigadier General Henniker-Major, had strongly entrenched themselves during the night.

The village proved a hard nut to crack and was not taken until after the red troops between there and Radcot Bridge had been swept off the field. Advancing steadily across the fields by alternate companies, the 10th Brigade slowly drove back the 2nd Royal Irish and the 2nd Dublin Fusiliers who were holding this part of the red line.

The tall hedges afforded cover from view, and judging by the way the defenders stood up behind them, they evidently thought that they also afforded cover from fire, but the bullets would have swept through the hedges as if they were made of paper, and whole companies of the gallant Irish, fighting for red land, would have been mowed down as they stood thick as bees behind their screens.

The officers tried hard to get the men to lie down, but the desire of the Irishmen to get a crack at the enemy was stronger than the desire for cover, and the 'boys' stood up and slated the foe with a pelting rifle fire that would have been hard to face in the 'real thing'. But it was all no use. Numbers told, and the blues steadily pressed the reds back until a bare 500 yards separated the attackers from the Clanfield/Radcot road by which the East Yorks and 11th Battalion RHA, who were holding the bridge, could escape.

Then followed a scene of confusion. The 7th Infantry Brigade of the blues forced its way into the streets from the west almost simultaneously with their commander of the 10th Brigade from the south, and soon friend and foe were inextricably mixed in the roadways and gardens and farmyards, all blazing away for dear life.

A battery of red artillery at one end of the village street fired into the mass of fighting men, regardless of whether they killed friend or foe. Some 300-400 yards down the same street, another red battery was equally hard at work firing into the same mob. The gunners would undoubtedly have blown the intervening mingled mass of friend and foe off the face of the earth, but they would have equally destroyed each other.

Frantic umpires rode hither and thither, vainly endeavouring to stop the firing — while the villagers from all the countryside sat on the walls and fences and cheered frantically. The wild melée will give them something to talk about for many a day to come.

At last, after an hour's exhausting effort, the distracted umpires got the firing to stop and the officers set to work to disentangle the combatants. Kilted Cameron Highlanders and wildly excited Irishmen were mixed up with stately Guardsmen, the cockneys of the Royal Fusiliers and the peasant lads of Devon and Cornwall were entangled with sturdy Yorkshiremen, until all semblance of order was lost, and only by the white bands of the caps of the blue soldiers could friends be distinguished from foes. When, at length, the battalions had been sifted apart the umpire decided that the blues had carried the village and the reds must fall back to Bampton.

The ***Faringdon Advertiser*** takes up the story:

Soldiers lined walls and ditches, fences and every place that offered a cover. Towards 2.00pm, the Infantry moved off towards Faringdon, and their places were taken by the Cavalry. The chief regiments occupying Clanfield were the 11th and 19th hussars, 2nd Dragoons and the 5th Lancers. These halted until about 5.00pm, then went off towards Lechlade.

The soldiers behaved throughout with splendid thought, both for their fellow comrades and the villagers. They were amply provided for at intervals with apples, tea and coffee, by the people who seemed not to be able to do enough for the gallant defenders.

In the meantime, the reds had crossed the river at Duxford, got to Radcot, and had a ding-dong battle with the blues. The Swan was supposed to be in ruins. One gun was placed so close to the pub that it blew out all the windows, emptied the Mulberry tree of fruit, and, it was said, so frightened one old woman that she turned a somersault.

The blues now retreated, as they found their lines were being cut. The final battle took place on Wednesday in a field of turnips near Coleshill, where the troops ended up throwing turnips at each other.

The whole campaign cost £123,000. Clanfield Parish Council wrote to the Army a letter of appreciation for the courtesy of all officers and ranks. The villagers on the lower green, who had brewed tea for the soldiers, looked at their well stocked larders. The reds left in such a hurry that they had abandoned many tins of meat and fresh food.

The old Post Office

The military manoeuvres in 1906

The Clanfield (Knapp's foundry) Band

The Clanfield Band at Chestlion Farm

— XIX —

Royal death and a Coronation

In 1910 the King died unexpectedly. A muffled peal was rung on the church bells, and the death march was played both at church and chapel.

The Coronation of King George V took place in June 1911. It began with a church service at 11.00am, and at 1.30pm a cold meat lunch was given. Three hundred people sat down for a meal. The children's tea, races, fireworks and a huge bonfire were held on the green. Mr Wallis was now at Chestlion, having moved from Friars Court. His barns and fields were used. Messrs Clunch and Garnes from the Masons Arms and the Plough offered free beer, 18 and 36 gallons respectively, and the fireworks cost five guineas. The total cost was £23. Faringdon held an ox roast in the market place.

It was this same year that the village school was extended. September of that year was the hottest for 43 years, and on September 7th it was 82 degrees Farenheit in the shade. In the August, the Bishop had died. Muffled bells were rung, and the death march was played in the church.

A pack of Boy Scouts was started under Mr Fred Clare, but they did not persevere in the village. Alvescot troop served the area instead.

There had been a fire in Clanfield, in the rickyard where the blacksmith later was, close to two ricks and the buildings of the Masons Arms. Water was very short, the stanks were not holding enough back. Mr Farmer was asked to rebuild them, which he did for £15.

In December 1911, Mr Charles Stevens died. He was the man who, by saying the right thing and by his kindly deed, helped to get Mrs Carter interested in Clanfield. He was a loyal churchman. He served in, and led the choir, was a bellringer, sexton, parish clerk and organist. He was buried on Sunday at 2.30pm. A peal of muffled bells was rung as a sign of respect.

In 1912, the village at last got around to the question of village allotments, which had been raised in the first election of 1894. Those which were rented from the Vicar in Pound Lane were not enough. It was decided to raise a loan to buy 10 acres in Mill Lane from Mr Walker, at £30 per acre. These allotments, when pegged out, were drawn for by those wanting them. They were never fully used, but the remaining portion was farmed as one.

In March, prayers were said in church for peace. The coal strike had stopped the trains running. In April prayers were said in church and chapel for the victims of the sinking of the Titanic.

In March 1912, a ditch was dug across the top green, as pipes from the pond were blocked.

In August, the lock keeper's wife was drowned. Agnes Beechy of Radcot Lock had come in the dark, apparently, to fetch mineral drinks by boat from the Swan.

On Christmas Day 1912, Reginald Marchant of Buckland drowned himself at By

Ashton Pill Bridge. He was to have been married at 2.30pm. (The event is recorded in the stone at the top of the bridge).

A band played around the village on Boxing Day at 6.00am for the first time. It had just been formed, and they were keen! They collected £5-£6.

In February 1913, the first flying machine was seen over the village.

In March, Richard Adams died. This family had, over the years, played a great part in the life of Clanfield. They owned Lower Farm, Wicks, the Masons, and many other parts in their time. They had served the village as carpenters as well as farmers. Richard had given a life of service to the Wesleyan Chapel as Sunday School teacher and steward, with his wife looking after the ministers and preachers who came to the chapel.

In November 1913, Mr Charles Horne and Mrs Amelia Comley married — their combined ages being 175 years. The day started foggy, but the sun came through for the wedding. Knapps shut at 11.00am, and Barnett's carriage from the Plough took them to church. After the wedding, the carriage was unhitched from the horse and pulled through the village by 18 men. Clanfield Band, led by Allen Parrot in full uniform, went in front, and they played outside their house on Lower Green. Charles died in 1916, aged 89, and Amelia died the same year, aged 90. They were members of the Methodist Church.

In July 1914, George Horne died just as the band was playing the National Anthem. He had been the village carpenter and wheelwright, and Mr F.W. Farmer took on the business.

The year 1914 saw a village in full activity. The chapel choir had already sung around the village at Christmas, and the band, led by Allen Parrot, paraded on every possible occasion. The Band of Hope was going strong at the Wesleyan Chapel, for young people. There was a full house for services on Good Friday and the tea which followed. The Primitives were holding their camp meetings on the Green. The school held a supper to pay for an outing. The Football Club held its annual dinner, and the church choir and bellringers went on a trip to Portsmouth, together with those from Witney. The Liberals were holding regular meetings. The chapel held a fête at Bushey Farm, and raised £21.16s.7d. And then, in August, came the news that war was declared...

A change now came over the village. All remained busy, but now with a different purpose. When the Wesleyan Sunday School had their treat in Mr T. Austin's field, after they were given an apple and a biscuit the National Anthem was played. A Ladies Territorial Committee was formed. In September £20 was raised for war families. Twenty men from the village enlisted. The band paraded around the village and £6.10s.8d was collected for soldiers' and sailors' families. At the school, a sale was held, and of the £8.10s which was raised, £6 was for the church and the rest went to the Territorial funds. Garments the ladies had made for the soldiers went on show.

By the October, one officer and 37 men had enlisted. In November, the Institute was being prepared as a convalescent home. The village entertained the patients with a concert.

At the Feast of 1915, Mr Benny Smith, one of the leading showmen, appeared with all his games and equipment. But while Benny Smith was there on the Green, an officer appeared with orders to take possession of all his horses. He could do nothing. They were all taken off for the Army. All the equipment had to be manhandled off the road onto the greens. After all that, and because he took such a long time to remove everything, he was summonsed to court at Burford. Eventually, he found enough old animals, not fit for Army service, to remove it all.

The first casualty of the village was announced in March. Private Will Messenger of the Wiltshire Regiment died of wounds on March 13th, and was buried in the churchyard at Lochre, Ypres, aged 28.

By May, 50 men had joined up. Eleven soldiers were then in the Institute. In June, £22.15s.11d was collected and sent to the Belgian refugees.

One soldier who came to the Institute soon married a local girl from Radcot who, no doubt, had been nursing him.

In August, a sale of work for the Red Cross at Friars Court raised £20 3s. In October, Allen Parrot, bandleader and Wesleyan Sunday School teacher, was given a pocket bible by the Sunday School teachers on the occasion of his joining the RAMC.

Will Gould, a Lieutenant of the 5th Northern Regiment, was killed in action near Armesfer in August. He was buried in a cemetery at Hooplains, aged 20. His parents lived at the Grange.

In November, William Tuckwell Clare, a Lance Corporal of the Royal Berkshire Yeomanry, was killed in action at Hill 70 on the Gallipoli Peninsula, aged 28. He had been a choirboy, and was a very go-ahead type. By the end of the year, 60 men from the village had joined up.

In 1916, the village was very busy. Every Wednesday, a sewing meeting was held at Mrs Goddard's at Friars Court to make things for the St John's Order. A special memorial service was held in the church for the fallen. In February, owing to lighting restrictions, evening service at the chapel was advanced to 5.30pm instead of 6.00pm. If an air raid was imminent, the large and small bells would be rung together.

Further bad news arrived in June. On the last day of May, the Battle of Jutland had been fought in the North Sea. Albert (Bert) Whipp, Able Seaman on HMS Invincible, went down with his ship. On May 15, Bill Horne, a Private in the 1st Royal Berkshires, was sent back from the front to the dressing station, after being wounded in the arm. But he was never heard of again...

The church services were very well attended. The Wesleyan chapel held its Good Friday service, and 104 people sat down to tea. The evening meeting was full.

A 20lb pike was caught at Radcot in November, 1916. It was 3ft 9ins long, and had a girth of 1ft 7ins. On Empire Day the church collected 10s. On Whit Monday there were special services. The dead march watch was played for Lord Kitchener and our own Bert Whipp.

In July, the headmaster, Mr Lucas, joined the Royal Army Medical Corps. The Wesleyan Chapel sent £2 10s from its Harvest Festival sale of fruit and vegetables to the Radcliffe Infirmary at Oxford. In December, Sergeant James Eagle of Edgerly, aged 23 and the third son of Jesse Eagle, was killed. And so this sad year came to an end.

The following year was just as bad. In February, the Military Medal was awarded to Lance Corporal E.C. Goodaway of the Gloucester machine gun section. In November, during an attack on his position, all his crew were killed except him. He kept firing until ordered to retreat. He was wounded and sent to hospital.

This was a bad winter and, particularly between October 1916 and mid-April 1917, the cold was intense. However, life had to go on in our village. Services at church and chapel were well attended. In June, a well and pump were installed on the allotments. In July, the Witney workhouse was closed, and its inmates were dispersed to other workhouses. It was about this time that Alfred and Mildred Cohen had quads — Alfred, Katherine, Vera and Gwen.

More sad news came with the news that Private Radbourne of the Royal Berks was killed in action on August 1, 1917, aged 19. One soldier came home, and could not face the trenches again. He had been through the agony of the severe cold and the slaughters of the front. He hanged himself. In November, Private George Savage, of the Hants Regiment, died of wounds at Alexandria, aged 34.

The year 1918 came in as black as ever, with the effects of the war hanging heavy on the village.

A lecture was given in the school in February on the work of the Church Army amongst the troops. A meeting of the Women's Land Army was held at the Institute in March, to discuss the starting of the Women's Institute in the village. It was founded with 50 members two months later. In April, a whist drive in the school raised 15 guineas for the army recreation huts.

My uncle, Ernest Austin, married Gladys Smith in July, and had to go straight back to his ship, the Wear. He died of Spanish Flu on October 1, 1918, and lies buried in Malta. The *Witney Gazette* reported that the death of "this bright and promising young man" had cast a gloom over the whole village. Such could be said of all who died.

Frank Butler, Private of the 8th Glos., who had been wounded and taken prisoner, died in a German hospital aged 19. Will Neville, Lance Corporal in the Australian Army 34 Battalion, was killed in action in France on June 24, aged 30. Jesse Comley, a Private in the 7th Wilts, went missing on April 24, assumed killed in the Salonica forces. Alban Clack, Corporal in the Welsh Guards, was killed in action on September 3, aged 35.

On November 11, 1918, it was all over. But of Clanfield, it was said: "It seemed almost incredible to the people of the village that the wonderful news had come at last. For some time no one dared to believe it to be true, and were afraid to show any signs of rejoicing. But when the beautiful old church bells clashed out the best and most joyful tidings they ever had to tell, we felt indeed the terrible strain of the four long years of war was over. Flags were immediately flown." A Thanksgiving service was held in the church at 7pm the next day. All rejoiced, but some 15 families were left in sorrow. There follows the list of those who served — an incredible number from such a small village:

CLANFIELD ROLL OF HONOUR
(as recorded in St Stephen's Church)

Lt. C. Arkell, RASC, MT
Lt. W.H. Farmer, 5th Leic. Reg.
Capt. A. Gee, RFA
Capt. H.R. Gould, Ind. Army Reserve
Lt. W.J. Gould, N'hants Reg. Killed in action.
Lt. W.H. Phillips, RASC
Austin, A.B.E.W., RN. Died on active service.
Barnett Pte T/RAF
G.R. Baston, Pte RAF
E. Betterton, Dvr RFA
P. Betterton, Cpl Wilts Reg. Wounded.
R. Betterton, Gnr RHA
J.E. Blake, AVC
F. Boulter, Pte Glos. Reg. Died of wounds.
G. Blunsdon, Dvr RFA
P. Cane, Pte RASC MT
A. Clack, Cpl Welsh Guards. Killed in action.
N. Clack, Pte Gren. Guards. Wounded.
W. Clack, Pte Royal Berks
H. Clack, Serg. Kings Own Pion. Wounded.
C.A. Clack, Gnr RGA
F.W. Clare, Tpr QOOH
W.T. Clare, L. Cpl Royal Berks Yeo. Killed in action.
G. Clark, Cpl RFA
A.R. Cohen, Pte OBLI
A. Comley, Pte OBLI
A. Comley, Pte Somerset L.I.

J. Comley, Pte Hants. Cyclist C.

J.G. Comley, Pte Wilts Reg. Assumed killed.

G. Cross, Dvr RFA

H. Cross, Bdr RFA

W. Cross, Pte OBLI. Wounded.

J. Cross, Sgt.

E. Eagles, Serg. Royal Berks. Wounded.

W. Eagles, Col.

S. Eeles, Cock's Mate RN

F.W. Farmer, Spr RE

G. Farmer, Gnr RFA

W. Farmer, Spr RE

C. Gardener, Pte OBLI. Wounded.

J. Gardener, Dvr RFA

W. Gardener, Dvr RFA

W. Gardener, Dvr RFA

C. Goodway, Sgt, MM DCM Glos. Reg.

C. Harrison, Gnr RFA

A. Hatton, Bdr RGA

G Hill, Bdr RGA

R. Hill, Sgt OBLI, MG. Wounded.

W.G. Hobbs, L. Cpl LRRC

H. Holdaway, AB RN

C. Horne, L. Cpl. 21st Lond. Wounded.

G. Horne, Gnr RFA

P. Horne, Pte OBLI. Wounded.

S. Horne, Cpl Royal Berks

W. Horne, Pte Royal Berks. Assumed killed.

W.J. Horne, Pte MGC. Wounded.

G. Hutt, Sgt MM Royal Berks. Wounded.

G. Imms, Pte RAF

E. Jones, Pte Glos. Reg.

J. Jones, Spr RE

J. Jones, Pte S. Staffs

W. Keene, Pte RASC

A. Kimbrey, Pte Warwicks

A. Kinchin, Dvr RFA

A. Lindsey, Gnr RGA

H. Lindsey, Pte OBLI

R.C. Lucas, Pte RAMC

M. Margetts, Tpr QOOH
A. Messenger, Stkr RN
F. Messenger, Pte RASC
W. Messenger, Pte Wilts Reg. Killed in action.
J. Monk, Pte OBLI. Wounded.
C. Neville, Sgt Royal Berks. Wounded.
F. Neville, MM QSF RGA
W. Neville, L. Cpl AIF. Killed in action.
J. Neville, Pte OBLI. Prisoner of War.
A. Parrott, Cpl RAMC
F. Parrott, Sgt Royal Berks. Wounded.
F. Parrott, Drv RGA
G. Parrott, Gnr RFA. Injured on service.
J. Parrott, Pte Glos. Reg. Wounded.
R. Parrott, Serg. RGA. Wounded.
S. Parrott, Cpl RASC
T. Parrott, Drv RFA
W. Parrott, L. Cpl. RASC MT
W.G. Pemble, Gnr RFA
J. Poole, Serg. 10th Hussars
H. Pudwell, AB RN
W.G. Radbourne, Pte Royal Berks. Killed in action.
H. Rose, Bdr RGA
H.W. Russell, Pte KOYLI. Killed in action.
A. Savage, Pte RASC MT
G. Savage, Pte RB. Died of Wounds.
F.C. Shepherd, Drv. RFA
J. Sparrowhawk, Pte Devonshires
F. Temple, Pte Glos. Reg.
G. Temple, Pte Lab. Corps. Died on active service.
H. Temple, Pte OBLI
J.J. Temple, Pte OBLI
John Temple, Pte OBLI
W.C. Temple, Pte RASC
E. Thorne, Pte OBLI
A. Townsend, Pte OBLI. Prisoner of War.
G. Townsend, Pte Royal Berks. Wounded.
W. Twelftree, Pte Gren. Guards
F. Wakefield, Pte OBLI. Killed in action.
O. Wakefield, Pte.
F.H.S. Walker, Pte Hants Reg.
R. W. Walker, Pte.

E. Watts, Tpr QOOH
A. Wenman, Pte OBLI
D.J. Wheeler, MGC, Pte
H. Wheeler, Cpl OBLI. Wounded.
A.E. Whipp, AB RN. Killed in action.
H. Whipp, Wilts Reg. Wounded.
J. Widdowson, Sgt RAF
W. Widdowson, Gnr RGA
H. Williams, Pte RASC
H. Wilkins, Gnr RFA
W. Winfield, Tpr Life Guards
E. Yeatman, Pte Devons.

The Peace was fully signed in July 1919, and when the village heard late on the Saturday afternoon, flags were put up and the bells rung.

The soldiers began to come back during January 1919 — including Private A. Townsend, who had been a prisoner of war, and Allen Parrot, who had meant so much to Clanfield because of his music in the band and at the Wesleyan chapel. Unfortunately, he was to die the following October, due to a perforated ulcer.

The village itself was beginning a gradual change. Its steam was beginning to run out. The men who had suffered so much had, for the first time, seen a much wider world. Although the churches were full for a while, the next generation was to forsake them almost totally.

In 1919 the villagers met to consider what they should do as a memorial to those who served during the war. Four suggestions were made: a clock in the Institute and a brass plate with the names on it, or a similar thing in the church. It was also proposed to put a memorial in the churchyard or on the Green. After much discussion they came down in favour of a 12ft granite cross at the bottom of the garden of The Plough, with the names of the dead on it. A wet hole was duly filled, and there it was put, at a cost of £110. A framed list of all those who served was also put in the church and chapel.

Peace celebrations were held on a Saturday in July, but rain spoiled the day. After 2.30pm it cleared somewhat, and the servicemen paraded to the field and barn lent by Mr Wallis. Rain came down again in torrents, and Mr T. Kinchin arranged a concert in the barn. The children's sports were put off until the following Monday, but late at night the bonfire was lit and the Kaiser duly burnt. The cost of the tea and sports was £36.5s.2½d. A 'Welcome Home' supper was arranged in the Masons Arms, with a concert, in October. A 'Comrades of the War Association' was formed (later called the British Legion) in December, when it was hoped that at least 50 men would join.

On Saturday June 17, 1920, the war memorial was dedicated. A procession of ex-servicemen, children and adults formed at the school, and marched up for a service at

2pm, led by the village band. There was a very large crowd. The service was begun by the Rev. E. Green, the Methodist minister of Witney, who gave a 'very good address' and the cross was blessed by the Vicar, the Rev. W. Bryant. Mr G. Hutt led the band in place of Mr Allen Parrot, and it played the Dead March, after which he and Mr Timms played the Last Post. Teachers and pupils placed wreaths, and a muffled peal of bells was rung.

This service is still held each year on the Sunday nearest to November 11. No longer does the whole land stop as it did for two minutes at 11 o'clock in the eleventh month of the year, because after the Second World War it did not carry the same significance. For many years the bugle was blown by Mr Fred 'Poot' Parrot. He used to take his instrument down to the meadows, where he was working, and during dinner time the meadows were filled with the strains of the Last Post as he prepared for Armistice Day!

Between the two wars Clanfield, like all villages, was losing out because events and facilities outside the village grew in importance. The trains and charabancs took people on holiday and to special occasions. The Plough ran a service to Alvescot station. Mr Jack Widdowson, back from the RAF, began a garage in 1921 at Bushey Farm, where his father lived, before moving to the 'Ram Jam' garage in the late twenties.

The Regatta at Radcot started, and was the centre of attention each year, when the banks were filled with people watching the races, and the swimmers chasing after ducks. The British Legion held a yearly football tournament during the Easter Holiday in Mr Secker's field.

A new telephone exchange was put in during 1924. Mr Willmer, of Friars Court, who ran a hay business there, had to find eight more people who were prepared to have a telephone, before it could be installed.

The wireless was now coming into people's homes. At first the old crystal set was used. People had to put on headphones and a hair-like wire had to be fed into the right spot in order to pick up broadcasts. Aerials had to be at the top of a very high pole.

On April 2, 1924, Mr Robinson of Bampton picked up an emergency call appealing for Mr Barnett of the council house, Clanfield, to say that his mother, Mrs K. Barnett, was seriously ill in London. Thanks to the message passed on by Mr Robinson, Mr Barnett managed to reach his mother's house in time.

After the war, six council houses were built in Mill Lane on the north side. These were needed because so many other houses were disappearing. At Queens Close, seven thatched houses were pulled down and replaced. At the Laurels, about half-a-dozen cottages were replaced by just one new one.

The school, which had previously been available to all ages, became Juniors-only in 1929. all those over the age of 11 had to go to Bampton, and were given free bikes to make the journey. Those who went to Burford Grammar School went by Barnetts coach, which operated from the Plough. This, for a few years, was a most successful business, taking the Sunday Schools to the seaside, running to Aldershot and Tidworth Army tattoos, and to Witney Feast. In the end, the larger companies squeezed them out.

The village celebrated the jubilee of King George V in 1935. The children had a meal, and commemorative mugs were distributed, and afterwards games were held. Two years later the Coronation of George VI was celebrated, and, again, it was an occasion for children.

It was during this era that cars began to appear. In the 1920s only about six to ten cars were in the village, but in the 1930s more and more came on to the scene. Clanfield had been, until that time, a village with lots of ducks. Everyone had ducks. But the cars soon disposed of most of them as they crossed from the stream.

The depression of the 1930s, whilst not so bad as it was in the north, did affect some who were not working on the land. Knapps went through a very bad patch. Some, including Mr W. Cross, cycled to work each day to the east side of Oxford where a lot of new houses were being built. The congregations at the churches now consisted mostly of the middle-aged. There was a revival during the years of the Second World War, but they continued to fall again afterwards.

In 1939 war came again, as Germany tried to regain what she had lost in the Great War. Not so many went to war from the village this time. Cyril and Jack Marchant, the two sons of Will Marchant at The Bell, went. The former went into a submarine, the latter was a rear machine gunner.

The village was blacked out — and as a consequence everyone found out how much warmer their home became. Cars and bicycles had special hoods over their lights. The chapel was blacked out and had evening sermons, but the church did not. No bells were rung — only in the event of an invasion were they to be rung. Air raid shelters were made in gardens. The following is an extract of something written by Bernadette Lyons at the school, dated January 25, 1980:

When the war broke out, children and mothers were evacuated from London down to Clanfield. People in the village took them into their homes. All evacuees' children who were old enough for school had to go to the Institute, as they held their school there with their own teachers.

When the evacuees went back to London, the Army moved into Clanfield. They were the 46th Suffolk Hussars, and were billeted in the (old) Methodist Chapel, the old Primitive Chapel and in barns around the village belonging to farmers. They had their canteen in the Institute, and local women served them

Outing to the British Empire Exhibition, 1924

Main Street near Mill Lane – with Mr Yeatman and his cart

Mr Troy Horne, his mother & sisters at Vicarage Cottages (since burned down)

Schooldays: the author, Ernest Pocock (middle row, far left), in 1927

meals. Their lorries were kept in Wicks Close. Their cookhouse was just past the Post Office in a big garage (The Manor).

They used to have a film show every week. The village people also went to see the films. It was rather difficult getting about, as there were no lights because of the black-out.

The soldiers moved out (to North Africa) and American soldiers moved in. They occupied the same places and during their stay, whilst some of the soldiers were upstairs, another was downstairs cleaning his rifle when it accidentally went off. The shot penetrated through the ceiling, and shot and killed one of the sleeping soldiers.

The people were on ration books for everything. When they wanted a cake they had to go to Bampton and queue up for hours at the bakery there. Sometimes they were lucky, sometimes not.

Mr Skuse ran a bakery at Clanfield during the war. They had to black out their windows so the Germans coming over would not see a light. The Home Guard used to patrol Clanfield every night. There were two guards altogether, and they worked four hours on and four hours off. If they were suspicious of anyone they challenged them with their rifles.

Whilst the Americans were here, there was some feeling between them and Americans in other villages, but we did not see much of it. They behaved themselves well. The Army provided them with protection against illegitimate births. These they used, so few American children were born. This was the first time such contraceptives were in general use in the villages.

I remember that we entertained a soldier from the Mid-West. He had little to say, but on his family farm they apparently used a Knapps drill!

A build-up of ammunition took place along the roadsides. From Langley Corner to Lechlade there were piles, every few yards, of bombs and shells without their fuses. From the 'T' junction at the bottom of Lew Hill to Curbridge the road was blocked with lorries side by side.

Brize Norton airport was used only in the day. By night they trained at an airfield at Kelmscot, and above Kencot by Bradwell Grove. Parachutists trained at Kelmscot. Some fell amongst the farms at Grafton, and one lad was killed in mid-air when a container hit him.

Glider training was at Kencot, and they went from there to Arnhem. The aerodrome was bombed on one occasion, and much damage was done in a hangar. Orders had not been given to fire, but one man did: he was court martialled, but later commended.

Some in Clanfield saw the planes go over. They had followed the Thames and crossed over between our village and Bampton. Those working in the fields saw them fly over. My wife was staying with her auntie at Haddon Farm, adjacent to the aerodrome. They had to rush into the shelter as they heard the bombs starting to fall.

Owing to the many towns in Belgium being over-run by motor cyclists, orders went out that every village here had to have a tree trunk that could be wheeled across the road. We had one at each entrance to the village. On one end it was pivoted to a post, on the other end was a waggon wheel. In an emergency these were supposed to be wheeled across, and the Home Guard had to take up some position whereby they could cover this spot. One position was dug behind the trees against the top pond.

To stop gliders landing, all the large fields had posts stuck up about five chains apart. Tarny and West Field had these. Trip wires were put all along the new bypass to Eynsham. to stop them using the wide road as an airstrip. All signposts were taken down, and all names of the villages and the yellow AA discs showing how many miles to London — anything that would tell German parachutists where they were.

All along the Thames concrete fortifications were built. One is in Burroway, and another at Radcot — so strong they defy time. They were built to take a certain type of anti-tank gun. Beside these, sandbagged trenches were also dug. There was one in Burroway about 200 yards west of the fort. At one time a searchlight was stationed in the Moor field, beside Radcot Road.

A local Air Raid Warden group was formed, whose chief activity was to make sure all windows were blacked out. Fortunately, no bombs fell on the village, but everyone had a shelter in their garden or somewhere close.

It was said that one farmer at Kelmscot went out with a hurricane lamp to inspect something or other, and there were planes going over at the time to Coventry and the Midlands. A stick of bombs was dropped, which luckily straddled him!

A Home Guard unit was formed which met on Sunday mornings, and took turns in guarding the village. They had a chicken house to sleep in on the top green, and were later moved to Radcot to guard the bridge. I quote from my book, *Radcot and Its Bridge (Ref: Pocock EA. Radcot and its Bridge, 1966):*

Many tales were told which, like the fish, grew with telling. One such was the time two service girls decided to go out in a boat at night. Having misjudged something or other they finished up with nothing dry. The Home Guard had to turn out of their quarters. The rest of the night was spent with two very dejected girls inside, a strong guard outside, and the rest of the guards sleeping under the wall — while the bridge had to look after itself.

There were plenty more tales which have now faded with time.

One night the church bells were rung. These were only to be rung if there was an invasion. The Home Guard immediately took action, and rang ours. The sergeant came out in such a hurry that he forgot his false teeth. The warden cursed the Home Guard for using a light to help load their guns. One gun went off in the direction of the moon. The whole village was standing at their doors. Someone, somewhere had made a mistake, but one thing was sure, the whole area was awake and ready!

Many efforts were made to raise money for various causes, including in 1941 War Weapons Week, 1942 Warship Week, 1943 Wings for Victory, and 1944 Salute the Soldier.

When the invasion of Europe was about to happen, the Americans were busy making high exhausts for their lorries. From all around the noise of bombs filled the night skies. The Americans moved off. More and more of the bombs went beside the road. After the invasion, all the gliders from Bradwell Grove went to Arnhem. Of course, we did not know anything about it until after a few days when some came back to tell what had happened.

In May 1945 the war ended and peace was celebrated. Men gradually came back. Shortages did not end at once. In fact some things which had never been rationed, like bread, became short as Europe had to be fed, but little by little things did become more available with the passing of each year. In the end, children could buy sweets once more, and bananas, which the younger ones had never seen, appeared again.

In 1947, the names of those who died were added to the Memorial.

★ ★ ★

Chapter 14

The Village of Memory

The following accounts of events which took place in the memories of Clanfield people give an idea of the changes which have taken place in modern times.

Mrs Wilkins

The Cheap Jack was on the village green with the paraffin flare lamps, lighting up the crockery and tin ware which were displayed on the grass. The hurdygurdy man was complete with monkey or lovebirds and a little German band came to the village once or twice a year.

Once a year we had a Sunday service on the lower village green. There was a camp meeting with a farm waggon for the preachers to speak from. The singing was very hearty and loud and people came from the villages and towns, so that it was quite a big affair.

Clanfield Club was very looked forward to. There would be a dinner in the Mason's Arms club room for all club members, and the band came in the morning and played round the village and in the evening they played for dancing on the green. Altogether it was a very lively day.

A very old Clanfield character was Alfred Radburn. He used to go from village to village collecting rabbit skins, rags and bones and old iron, which he would exchange for a few coppers or sweets, or perhaps some oddments of crockery and wooden dolls which the children called 'peggy dolls'. He would travel around in an old black covered cart drawn by a very favourite old horse.

At Christmas time the Clanfield mummers would entertain, if one permitted them to come into the house. Also, the handbell ringers would play round the village.

We had a shoemaker and mender who also sold coal at 10d per hundredweight. The older people would take their trucks and collect the coal and faggots of wood which cost about 2¹/₂d each. The children could buy a farthing's worth of sweets. Once a week the old people would assemble at one of the cottages to receive a large loaf of bread and 1s.6d, which was known as Parish Relief.

The old women would always wear a white slouch bonnet made in the village by a woman named Mary Ann Clack. On Sundays they wore a small black bonnet, trimmed with lace and beads and tied under the chin with a big bow of ribbon. Capes were also worn trimmed with lace. The women often worked all day in the fields at harvest and haymaking time as there were not enough machines, just horses and waggons. After the harvest was finished there would be a harvest home, usually in a barn with plenty of food and home brewed beer.

The roads and paths were very muddy and soft, with cart tracks in the road, so that stout boots and shoes were needed. The working men wore nailed boots and gaiters and smocks made from coarse hessian.

There were about twenty thatched cottages in the village. They usually had one living room and pantry and two bedrooms, and water was drawn from wells with buckets and long handled hooks, kept for that purpose. Some of the cottages had no ovens to bake in, so dinners were often sent to the bakehouse to be cooked for one penny.

I think Mrs. Walter Clare was the first lady in the village to ride a bicycle. Dr. Parker from Faringdon drove the first motor car, and then Mr. R.L. Knapp senior. I remember the big traction engines drawing the threshing machines from place to place with a man walking in front with a red flag.

Mark Kelly was the postman. He walked from Bampton to Faringdon to collect the letters and delivered in Clanfield in the afternoons.

Mr. T. Kinchin

Billy William was a roadman (two others worked on the roads of the parish). Stones came by rail, then brought by dung cart and put in a pile by the roadside. It was the roadman's job to dig holes out and refill with these stones.

The clothes of the time were rags around the feet instead of socks, boots not done up to the top, no collar and tie, but a blue neckerchief.

A black felt hat called a 'Billy cock hat' was worn. If anyone wore a collar and tie to chapel they would be thought to be the Lord of the manor.

Thomas Collett (who said he would never come back to Clanfield) was coming back in Charles Horne's pony and trap, and when he was about five chains from

Marsh Lane he fell off the seat onto the shafts and broke his neck. Walter Horne was driving. A cross was put into the side of the road and was there for a long time. He was put onto a gate and brought to 'Skittle Alley' in the Mason's Arms club room. Walter Clack laid him out. He was coming back to Yew Tree house.

Miss Kinchin

Mrs Carter provided games and a reading room for men of the village, at first in the day school after school hours and then in two rooms in Windmill House. Harry Parrot was the caretaker. Mrs Carter provided papers and games. She also gave three parties a year, one for men one for women and one for the children. The men's was a smoking party, the women's was a concert party from Bampton, and the children's was for presents of clothing.

Mr. Eustace was a leading member of the chapel. His cottage was pulled down to clear a site for the chapel. Mr. Clack used to ask for pew rents as Quarterage was now due at the chapel. The bells were taken in 1905 to Taylor's of Loughborough to be recast.

Mrs. Baston

After the relief of Mafeking in 1901 there was an after-dark torchlight procession which started at Windmill and went to the top green where there was a bonfire, dancing and singing. Mr. Walker was chased by a gypsy lady through the fire. *(Note: This was an old Celtic custom, did they but know it.* Author.*)*

After the Boer War, Bert Blunsden and George Holloway were brought down from the station in Barnett's landau. Flags were out and a banner was across the road by Eeles shop welcoming them home. They were rushed home for the Coronation, but then Edward had appendicitis.

In My Own Memory

In the village of my memory, stretching back to the mid–20s, there were but few thatched houses. The last one was by Mr Macdonald's house.

The children made their own fun. The abundant withy trees up the causeway provided them one game called 'Pussy, come pussy'. In this game each child stood by a tree and one stood in the middle. Children called an opposite one and in the scramble to change trees the middle one tried to claim one, leaving someone else in the middle. Hopscotch was another game in which children hopped on one foot and kicked a

Bampton Rd – with the Primitive Methodist chapel converted to a private house

The War Memorial, photographed before it was railed off

Pond House,Bampton Rd, home of Mr Clack the horse collar maker. Mr and Mrs Clack were the grandparents of Fred and George Farmer, still living in the village.

Mr Ernie Yeatman, the coalman, with 'Trishy'

The Forge, with George Hutt, aged 6

block of wood around eight squares drawn as a rectangle. The stream was also a source of fun for us. Through the regular cleaning it had become too wide to jump, but it could be vaulted. So, in season, out came the poles and boys vaulted all down it. Occasionally there was a splash.

At the time the school put your name up if you found the first flower of any species. Birdnesting was a boy's pleasure. Few reached rooks' nests, but crows and pigeons were always a challenge. Grants Hay always had an owl's nest in a stump topped tree. Sometimes a sparrowhawk's nest could be found. Like the pigeon it laid two eggs. If you took both it deserted the nest, if you took one it always laid another. I remember one boy so proudly went into Mr. Skuse's, the baker, with an egg under his hat. Mr. Skuse knowingly patted him on the head to say how pleased he was to see him. The boy was not so pleased, as egg streamed all down his face!

Fishing was another sport. Always there were tiddlers in the stream, sometimes sticklebacks. Opposite the vicarage there were crayfish among the stones. The road was a lovely playground as few cars and carts used it. Hoops could be run down it and tops spun along it.

The pond was another source of fun when it was frozen over. With candles around or on a moonlit night all those children allowed out had a wonderful time. Mr. Neville always trimmed the pond side of his hedge when the ice carried his weight.

The picture house took more and more people out of the village. The boys going to the pictures in Faringdon went around Coach Lane past the Police Station because the policeman was always in the square.

Sometimes the policeman would go and wait by Radcot Bridge to catch the lads without lights, for lights and batteries were expensive. Once they were over the bridge into Oxfordshire they were safe.

In those days the village was kept tidy by a roadman. For years it was Mr. Perce Betterton. He had his length from Radcot through the village and down Marsh Lane. Always a roadman was ready for a chat. If the hounds were around he was always working at the most likely spot to see the fun.

Mr. Betterton loved scything. Every spring and early summer he cut all the banks from Radcot through the village and down the lane. Some achievement! Before hay-making he always borrowed a ladder and went down the lane cutting off the branches so that the waggons would not lose their loads. Just out of my memory it was said that the old meadow lanes were so bad that four or five Oxfordshire waggons full of hay could be seen on their sides in a wet time, the ruts were so deep. Butlers from Burford had meadows there and came in the morning and returned to Burford at night with their loads.

When the roads were tarmaced the roadman had to work with the gang on his length.

The tar was heated up by fire, three or four men had the brooms through which the hot tar came and spread it on the road. Others barrowed and spread by hand the gravel and the steam roller followed to tread it flat.

Before the war there were only one or two tractors in the village, all the work being done by horses. On the large farms men still worked with the custom of 1,000 years behind them. Early to feed the horses, out to plough at 7.00 a.m., all fed in the fields, back at 3.00 pm to feed horses and men and then back in the stable to clear up. Only gradually did the working day of 7.00am to 5.00pm come in. For a long time it was six days a week, and little by little the Saturday became a half day. Summer Time was ignored for a long time by Mr. Bowden at North Court — It was "all wrong".

The corn was cut and tied by the binder. Often women stooked the corn and when the corn was drawn home, boys brought the waggons into the field. The horses drove themselves between stooks and two men pitched, another loaded and boys took them back to the rickyard. In the rickyard, they were pitched by hand with two on the rick and when the roof went on another was in the pitch hole. Later an elevator was introduced. The elevator was horse driven and the sheaves fell into the centre of the rick. Loading and rick building was an art. Mr. Drinkwater was very skilled at North Court between the wars. His ricks, his thatching and his hedgelaying were a joy to see.

The village was served by buses, the best service being to Swindon. Late at night the last bus coming to Radcot would go no further unless there were about six passengers. If not, they were turned out, irrespective of the weather.

Mr. Caddy, returning from Canada, took over Windmill Farm for his father in the 1930s. He had been a lumberjack and came home with advanced ideas. He came to Alvescot station on the late train, walked through the village and got into a pile of straw in the cowshed to spend the night. The cowman had a lad who got up early to get the cows ready. The boy came down, lit the lantern, whereupon a body appeared out of the straw. He fled. Mr. Caddy introduced the idea of rubber wheeled trolleys pulled by two trotting horses in place of the old slow Oxford waggons. These new trolleys could turn full circle whilst the old Oxford waggons only had a quarterlock. When he told his men to load two sacks on one side without having a loader and then turn the waggon round the other way to load the other side they obviously turned too sharply on purpose and spilled the lot. But they came round to it in the end.

At this time milk from the large farms was taken by train to London. The train went from Alvescot at about 7.00 am. The cows had to be milked, the milk cooled and put into the churns, placed in a trap and galloped up the road 1 1/2 miles to catch the train. Sometimes they waited patiently. Other milk was sold around the village and the rest was made into butter, a not very economical method. The skim and buttermilk was fed to the pigs.

Knapps were employing quite a few men, although, like many others, they had a bad time in the late 1930s. The bell rang to call them to work at 6.55am and 12.55 a.m. The men always assembled against the wall opposite and for years we expected to see them waiting there to go in.

Many expected a slump to soon come after the war as it had after the First World War, but it did not come for 30 years. In 1948 two council houses were built for agricultural workers up Mill Lane on a site commandeered from Mr. Seoker, High House Farm. Gradually these were added to until, as we noted in the 1970s, the whole area was built over.

Now things have changed. New people came into the village, bringing new blood and new ideas. In many ways the village life is much happier than it used to be. In earlier times, with so little from the outside to occupy people's minds, old scores built up and remained. Village feuds lasted through the years. Except for a nasty bout of factory politics which was brought into the village in the 1970s, a much better spirit prevails. People feel more free. Money is more to hand, but still tight as there is much more to spend it on. Homes are better and clothing is better. Accident and ill health or tragedy are not things to be so feared as in the past. With smaller families, children are much better cared for.

The present day problems of drink and broken homes, whilst existing, are not so bad as in the towns. "To be known" is a great deterrent, especially to young people. Transport becomes a problem as more people have cars, because fewer buses run and that leaves those without their own transport having great difficulty in getting anywhere. Television is the major entertainment. With most people working outside the village and the consequent later evening meals, it means that little goes on in the evenings.

So we come to the end of our story. A village that has grown larger, has changed much but still, in many ways, is alive. A village that, over the years, had never suffered under a dominant lord, but in which its people have always been free and independent.

★ ★ ★

Index

ABBOTS Fee 114
Abell (Mr) 102
Abingdon 75,76,116
Abraham, John 44
Abrahams, Mr 158
Acker, Mr 151
Adam's Yard 6, 113
Adams (family) 113, 124, 134
Adams Farm 135
Adams, George 158, 164
Adams, Henry 73
Adams, Henry 87
Adams, James 148
Adams, John 101, 102, 105, 141
Adams, Phoebe 120
Adams, Richard 172
Adams, Robert 86, 87, 101, 105
Adams, Thomas 73, 91, 104, 113,
115, 148
Adams, Will 104,148
Agnes of Clanfield 30
Akers, Mr 132
Alchurch, John 43
Aldworth, William (Will) 111,133
Alice Hay 141
Alif, Will 52
Alloes heye 102
Allworth, Margaret 125
Alvescot 16, 24, 27, 29, 30,
39, 58, 59, 74, 75, 83, 87, 88, 92, 94, 101,
106, 109, 124, 125, 133, 134, 136, 138, 142,
149, 153, 165, 171, 179, 188
Andrew, Will 52, 60
Arch, Joseph 131, 155
Ardeyne, Richard 69
Arkell, Lt Col 175
Arnold, John 70, 73, 86
Arnold, Solomon 73
Ashcomb, Lady 75
Ashen Bridge, 51, 139
Ashton Pill Bridge 158, 171
Ashurst, R 136
Ashwood, Dorothy 112
Asthall 32, 58, 74, 92

Asthall Leigh 92
Aston 37, 39, 59, 74, 92,
133, 155, 157
Aston Manor 159
Athote, John 43
Atkins, Elizabeth 86
Attmore, John 48
Attwood 142
Attwood, Francis 136
Austin, AB E.W. 175
Austin, Ernest 174
Austin, T 172
Aylif, Will 47
Aytwood, Capt 79

BABEL, Will 28
Bablockhythe 42
Baden Berks School, Bampton 122
Bakehouse Barn 120
Baker, Will 52
Balden, Peter 36
Baldons 83
Bampton 1, 5, 6, 9, 10, 11,
15, 16, 18, 19, 23, 24, 26, 30, 31, 32, 33, 37,
40, 42, 43, 44, 45, 49, 58, 74, 77, 83, 85, 87,
91, 92, 94, 101,103, 117, 121, 122,125, 126,
132, 133, 134, 137, 148, 150, 152, 153, 154,
155, 156, 160, 165, 179, 181, 185, 186
Bampton Castle 34
Bampton Fair 116
Bampton Hundred 114
Banbury 65
Band of Hope 172
Banting, Thomas 118
Barcote 83
Barfield, F.H. 154
Barfield, Mary 86
Barlow, Thomas 60
Barnard, Thomas 111
Barnes, Thomas 73,92
Barnet family 165
Barnett 172,179
Barnett's Coach 179,186
Barnett, Mrs K 179

Barnett, Pte T. 175
Barrow 7
Barrowfield (Barrow Field)
23, 31, 32, 68, 101, 102, 120, 137, 142
Barrowhays 85, 86
Baston, MrBatayle (Phillip) 30
Baston, Mrs 186
Baston, Pte E. 175
Batesland (Bates Lane) 7, 24, 29, 31, 67, 87
Baynel (William) 30
Beadsman (Derby winner) 112
Beard, Mr 161
Beckinsale, Thos 140, 141, 157
Beechy, Agnes 171
Belbam Hays Close 102
Belcher, Mr 132
Belham Hays Billy's 58
Bell, the 180
Beney 49
Bennett, John 69
Bennett, Thomas 69, 111, 117
Bennett, Walter 72
Benny 35
Benson, John 47
Berry ('Goodwife') 102
Besell, Will 47
Bethell, Major 78
Betterton, Cpl P. 175
Betterton, Dvr E. 175
Betterton, Gnr R. 175
Betterton, Perce 187
Bezell, Will 52
Billings 102
Birnis 52
Bishey, Henry 140, 141
Black Bourton (Bourton) 2, 15, 20, 31, 32, 50,
67, 74, 92, 94, 106, 108, 109, 114, 116, 120,
124, 126, 132, 136, 137, 138, 140, 141, 148,
151, 154, 157, 158
Blackfriars 33
Blagrove (Blagrove's) Mill 125, 140, 141, 157
Blagrove (family) 103, 120, 124
Blagrove (Jane) 31
Blagrove, Joan 106
Blagrove, John 120
Blagrove, Simon 120
Blagrove, Thomas 72, 73, 106
Blagrove, William 73
Blake 93
Blake, J.E. 175

Blake, Jack) 3
Blenheim 117, 133
Bletchingdon 76
Blunsden 186
Blunsdon, Bert 165
Blunsdon, Dvr G. 175
Boambridge 102
Booth, John 73
Booth, Thomas 73
Borough Way 109
Bottom Bridge (Closes) 101, 158
Boucher (family) 113
Boulter, Pte F.
Bourton (Black) Marsh 78, 86, 116
Bourton Mill 138
Bowden 188
Bowden, F. 165
Bowden, Mr 143, 165
Bowles, Dan 156
Bownbidge's Coppice 125
Boyd, Hugh 39, 92
Bradshaw, Edward 112
Bradshaw, Mary 112
Bradshaw, Mr 131
Bradwell 26, 59, 92
Bradwell Grove 181, 183
Breadston, Elizabeth 134
Breakspear (family) 124
Breakspear, Elizabeth 120
Breakspear, James 105
Breakspear, Robert 121
Breakspear, William 120
Bridgewell, Ralph 36
Brighthampton 59, 74, 92, 151,
157
Brighttendon 58
British Legion 179
Brize Norton 15, 30, 32, 59, 74,
92, 93, 94, 109, 116, 133, 138, 140, 141, 57
Brize Norton airport 181
Broadwell 74, 94, 117, 123
Broke Meadow 101
Brook Furlong 136
Brook, R. 152
Brooks Farm 113
Brother Andrew (Prior) 29
Broughton 48, 58, 74
Broughton Poggs 92
Browning, Mrs 168
Bryant, John 155

Bryant, Rev W. 178
Buckerel (Matilda) 30
Bucket, John 48, 73
Buckland 35, 76, 132,1 71
Buckland, Thomas 114
Buckrill ('Widow') 102
Bull, the 86, 109, 155
Burford 26, 32, 41, 59, 74,
75, 76, 81, 83, 115, 126, 146, 151, 156, 157,
173, 187
Burford Grammar School 179
Burri, William 85
Burroway 31, 119, 138, 148,
182
Burroway Bank 5
Burroway Ford 81
Burrowfield 32
Burton 57,58,59
Busby (Mr) 102
Busby Close 165, 166
Busby's 84
Busby's Field 125
Buscot 117
Bush 101
Bush, Ann 66
Bushey Close 67, 101
Bushey Farm 172
Butler, Frank 174
Butler, G.H. 151
Butler, Richard 140
Buttes Close 102
Butts 113
Bygg, Will 57

CADDY, Mr 188
Calcroft (Cowcroft, Calcroft Lane)
8, 24, 35, 109, 124,
126, 151, 152
Camp, Stephen 43
Cane, Pte P. 175
Canon, Capt 78
Capell, George 140, 141
Carpenter, Nicholas 73
Carpenter, Solomon 73
Carpenter, Thomas 73
Carswell 59, 66, 114
Carter, John 52, 62
Carter, Mrs 166, 171, 186
Carter, Robert 43, 60
Carter, Walter 103

Carter, Will 43, 53, 62
Carterton 157
Casswell (Nr Astrop) 140, 141
Castle (Mr) 102
Castle Eaton 117
Castle, Elizabeth 94
Castle, John 83, 112
Castle, Tom 98
Castle, Will 98
Castle, William 83, 91, 92, 94, 98,
104, 112
Causeway, the 140
Cavendish, Will 56
Chadlington 93
Chalkley, Thomas 45
Challow 130,146
Chambed, Matilda 52
Chambers, John 48, 52
Chambers, Matilda 48
Champe, Jacob 140
Chapman, Elizabeth 112
Chapman, Hiddesey 91
Chapman, John 72, 87, 98, 101,
112
Chapman, Joseph 73
Chapman, Katherine 112
Chapman, Robert 98
Charlbury 93
Charney (Sharney) Brook 7, 142
Charney Meadow 17, 117
Charny (Charney, Charney Hurst)
51, 67, 101, 109,
139
Chasterlon (Hugh) 29
Chasterlon (Richard) 29, 31
Chasterton, Elizabeth 43
Chasterton, Hugh 43
Cheap Jack, the 184
Cheney (Alistair) 28
Cherurgion, John
Chesney (Alice) 29
Chesney (Ralph de) 29, 31, 83
Chessus,Richard 114
Chestlion (Chestlyon, Chestlyons)
1, 7, 16, 28, 29,
31, 36, 43, 47, 51, 52, 59, 69, 66, 70, 85, 86,
92, 93, 97, 103, 106, 111, 119, 124, 134,
137, 142, 152, 165, 166, 171
Chestlion family 43
Chestlion, Richard 36

Child, John 39
Chimney 37, 39, 59, 74, 92
Chipping Norton 65, 115, 154
Christ Church 109, 111, 134, 136,
   143, 165
Christ Church Cottage 102
Church Army 174
Church Close 48
Cinch, Simon 73
Cirencester 43, 44, 75
Clack, Alban 174
Clack, Cpl A. 175
Clack, Edward 121
Clack, Gnr C.A. 175
Clack, James 115
Clack, Mary Ann 185
Clack, Pte N. 175
Clack, Pte W. 175
Clack, Sgt H. 175
Clack, T. 164
Clack, Walter 186
Clack, William 137
Clampe, James 141
Clanfield Club 184
Clanfield Cross 126, 151, 156
Clanfield Friendly Society 151
Clanfield Manor 7
Clanfield Manor Farm 113
Clanfield Mummers 184
Clanfield School 154
Clanfield Tavern 1
Clare's Stores 165, 166
Clare, Fred 171
Clare, L Cpl W.T. 175
Clare, Mr 166
Clare, Mrs Walter 185
Clare, T. 158
Clare, Tpr F.W. 175
Clare, Troilys 158
Clare, W. 166
Clare, Will 158
Clare, William Tuckwell 173
Clark 114
Clark, Alice 69, 133
Clark, Andrew 68, 69
Clark, Ann 135
Clark, Catherine 86
Clark, Cpl G. 175
Clark, Drogo 85
Clark, James 119, 135, 148, 153,

   156, 166
Clark, John 50, 51, 52, 53, 60,
   68, 86, 102, 112, 113, 116, 119, 135, 139,
   154
Clark, Mr 147
Clark, Priscilla 113, 135
Clark, Richard 57, 68, 69, 86,
   124, 133, 140, 141
Clark, Robert 114
Clark, Solomon 57, 72, 73
Clark, William 68, 73, 112, 119,
   133
Clarke, John 141
Clarke, Mrs 117
Clarke, Richard 73, 114
Clements, Robert 93
Clerk, John Pope 49
Clerkeson, John 52
Clifton 83
Clinch, C.H. 152
Clinch, Mr 152
Clinch, W. 152
Clohen, Pte A.R. 175
Clunch and Garnes, Messrs 171
Clyffe, Martha 98
Cockhill, P 124
Codon, Will 39
Cogges 93
Cohen quads 174
Cohen, Alfred 174
Cohen, Alfred 174
Cohen, Gwen 174
Cohen, Katherine 174
Cohen, Mildred 174
Cohen, Vera 174
Cokethorpe 32, 59
Cokke, John 69
Coles, John 86
Coles, the 86
Coles, Thomas 73
Coleshill 114, 169
Collett (family) 113
Collett, Allys 60
Collett, Henry 136, 145, 148, 150
Collett, John 60
Collett, Lance 156
Collett, T. 152
Collett, Thomas 185
Collett, William 112, 124, 125
Collier, W.G. 134

Collins, Charles 111
Collinson (family) 113
Collinson, the Rev 122, 123
Colston 113
Comley Pte J.G. 175
Comley, Amelia 172
Comley, Amos 167
Comley, Henry 157
Comley, Jesse 174
Comley, Pte A. 175
Comley, Pte J. 175
Connoway 94
Cooper's Close 86
Cooper's Stile 109
Cooper, Nick 109
Cooper, Richard 86
Copse Crabtree Ground 102
Cornish 94
Cote 49, 69, 74
Cotmore, Henry 53
Cotmore, John 53
Cotmore, Will 53
Cotta, John 60
Cottman, Richard 48
Cottman, Thomas 48
Coventry (Field) 5
Coventry (Mr) 102, 113
Coventry Farm (Lower Green) 113
Cowlease 102, 106
Cowleaze Corner 117
Cowper, Will (Cobby) 57
Cox (family) 113
Cox, Mr 116
Cox, William 154
Coxter, Richard 114
Crass, Roger 73
Crass, Solomon 72
Crawley 92
Cridland, Cath 156
Cridland, John Davis 156
Crofts Close
Cromwell 77, 78, 81
Cross, Bdr H. 176
Cross, Dvr G. 176
Cross, Pte W. 176
Cross, Richard 43
Cross, Robert 147
Cross, W. 180
Cruckfield, Richard 94
Cullis, Wilf 75

Culvery Furlong 102, 125
Cummings (family) 113, 159
Curbridge 92, 116, 132, 181
Curtis, Thomas 73, 86

D'IVRY 15, 16, 18, 114,
137
d'Woodcut 36
Davis, Ann 106
Davis, T. 117
Dawes, Robert 69
Dawes, William 111
Dawson, Rev 152
Day, Lady 114
Dayer, Robert 69
de Karr 34
de Putre 34
de Vere, Robert 41, 42
Deddington 38, 65
Denton, Phatmell (Rev) 72, 73, 85, 93
Denton, Simon 141
Denton, Sims 140
Denton, Thomas 136
Diaper 141
Dier, Simon 73
Dillon, Robert 36
Dimmocks (Dimmock, Dimock), Rev John
117, 125
Dior, Simon 101
Dix, Richard 121
Dod94
Dodwell, John 111
Dokaland, John 43
Dow, John 140
Draper, Rich 48
Dring, Francis 93
Drinkwater, Mr 188
Drying, Will 58
Duber, Edward 73
Duber, Thomas 73
Duckleton 88
Ducklington 29, 59, 74, 92,
132, 153
Dudds Plain, Wychwood 132
Dudgrove 111
Duffin, Humphry 93
Duret, John 52
Duxford 169

EACHEATER, John Silvin 43

Eagle, James	174	Farmer, F.W.	166, 172
Eagle, Jesse	174	Farmer, Gnr G.	176
Eagles, Sgt E.	176	Farmer, John	117, 119
Early, Edward (Early's Mill)	131	Farmer, Lt W.H.	175
East Field	137	Farmer, Mr	171
Eaton Hastings	98	Farmer, Richard	49
Eckland, Dan	116	Farmer, Spr F.W.	176
Edgerly (Edgerley)	7, 113, 119, 174	Farmer, Spr W.	176
Edgerly (Edgerley) Farm	67	Fauckner (William)	102
Edgerly, Robert	60	Faulkner, Mr	118
Edmonds (daughters)	111	Faulkner, William (Will)	140, 141
Edmonds (family)	55, 56, 57, 67, 97,	Faulks, Mr (Postmaster)	159
135		Fawlkner	91
Edmonds, Agnes	98	Fereman (family)	165
Edmonds, Dan	113	Fereman, James	135
Edmonds, Elizabeth	98, 105	Fettiplace, Jaccatis	53
Edmonds, John	98	Fettiplace, John	53
Edmonds, Marie	98	Fettiplace, Thomas	53, 68
Edmonds, Mary	98	Fiennes, John (Col)	76
Edmunds, Elizabeth	88	Filkins (Fylkins)	5, 6, 26, 34, 59,
Edmunds, John	88	74, 91, 92, 115, 147, 153, 155	
Edney, James	60	Firs, the	120
Edwards, Francis	140	Fisher, John	43
Edwards, Mark	62	Fitzherbert, Humphrey	66, 69
Edwards, Thomas	102	Fitzherbert, John	66
Edy, John	156	Folly Hill	168
Eeales Shop	186	Folly, The	77
Eeales, Cook's Mate S.	176	Football (Line) Field	136
Elliott	113,125,164	Football Club	172
Elliott, Captain	152	Forbes, Lt Col Arthur	165
Elliott, G.H.	117, 145	Fore Meadow (Four Meadow, Foremead)	
Elliott, John	36		17, 102, 120
Elscott	116	Foundry House	142
Elstow, Abbey of	55	Fox and Hounds	138, 153, 157
Enslow Bridge	65	Fox Meadow	58
Eustace, Mr	186	Franchner, William	103
Ewelme	89,114	Francis, Richard	73
Expedition, The	86	Franklin, Roland	72
Eynsham	40, 42, 182	Fretwell (Richard de)	32
		Frewin, Dr Richard	111
FAIRFAX, Sir Thomas	78, 81	Frewin, Elizabeth	112
Fairford	127,153	Frewin, John	111, 112
Faringdon	18, 19, 20, 25, 34,	Frewin, Salena	112
41, 42, 43, 76, 78, 79, 80, 115, 116, 117, 118,		Freyeshuyde	31
119, 126, 131, 132, 133, 134, 136, 143, 149,		Friars Court	1, 3, 7, 16, 23, 28,
151, 154, 155, 156, 164, 166, 168, 169, 171,		29, 31, 47, 50, 57, 67, 83, 85, 89, 92, 98, 101,	
185, 187		103, 105, 112, 113, 125, 133, 135, 137, 138,	
Faringdon House	77	139, 142, 153, 157, 158, 165, 171, 173, 179	
Farmer family	85	Friars Court Cottages	114
Farmer, Dame Emote	49	Frilford	133

Fryam Court	57	Grey, Thomas	124
Furze, John	114	Gunn	113
		Gunn (Gun), John	88, 101, 106
GABLES, The	124	Gunn, Julienne	88
Galley Hill	151, 156	Guy, Thomas	145
Gardener, Dvr J.	176	Gypsy Lane	138
Gardener, Dvr W.	176		
Gardener, John	114	**HADDE, John**	60
Gardener, Pte C.	176	Hadden	58
Gardener, Will	164	Haddon Farm	181
Garford Coppice	125	Hailey	92, 158
Garlords Coppice	102	Haines, James	136
Garmon, Will	43	Haines, Robert	140
Gaunt House		Hamand, Richard	73
Gee, Capt A.	175	Hambridge, John	121
Geremer, John	43	Hampton	111
Gernan, Will	47, 48	Hanks, Richard	117
Gilbert (Mr)	101, 102	Harang (Ralph)	23, 28
Giles, Dr	132	Hardwick	26, 74
Gillam, John	69, 86	Harris, John	73
Gilpin, James	111, 112	Harris, Mr	155
Goddard, Mrs	173	Harrison, Gnr C.	176
Goff, Richard	73	Hart, the	87
Golden Ball (The)	104	Hartmann, Mr	108
Gomes, the	137	Haryng	42
Goodaway,E.C.	174	Hatton, Bdr A.	176
Goodenough, John	73	Hawley	113
Goodenough, Mary	119, 137	Hawley, Henry	112
Goodenough, Thos	140	Hawley, James	111, 112
Goodway, Sgt C.	176	Hawley, Sir Joseph	112
Gould, Capt H.R.	175	Hay, Alice	125
Gould, Lt W.J.	175	Haywards Ham	142
Gould, Will	173	Heath, Robert	87
Gower, John	106	Hedges	105
Grafton	2, 24, 30, 43, 50,	Hedges, Adam	87
57, 67, 74, 92, 121, 148, 154, 181		Helforde	59
Grafton Green	7, 17, 24, 102, 140,	Henley	83
141, 142		Herbert (Peter)	102
Graham, Mr	124	Heyes	101
Grange, The	109, 173	Heyes, Adam	73
Grant's (Close)	101, 102, 187	Hicks, Robert	140
Great House	106	Hicks, Will	52
Great Milton	136	Higgins (family)	113
Green Benny	3, 31, 143	Higgins, John	125
Green Close	17, 138, 142, 158	Higgons, John	148, 149, 150
Green, Rev E.	178	High Bridge	157
Green, Will	148	High House	159
Greenaway (Mr)	102	High House Farm	113, 189
Greford, Richard	52	Highworth	116, 117
Grey, Sarah	112	Hill, Bdr G.	176

Hill, James	73, 103	**ILLOT, Thos**	156
Hill, Sgt R.	176	Ilot, Will	115
Hill, Sir Thomas	47	Imms, Pte G.	176
Hobbs, L Cpl W.G.	176	Ingram, Richard	58, 67
Hobbs, William	73	Institute, the	151, 174
Hogeson	70	Institute, the	173, 180
Hogg, Alex	111		
Holcombe	113	**JACKSON, Col**	114
Holdaway, AB H.	176	James, Mr	116
Holley, John	43	Janner, J.H.	157
Hollies, the158		Janver	53
Holloway, George	165, 186	Janver, Henry	50, 52
Holmes, Ann	84	Janver, Will	48
Holmes, Christopher	84	Janyor, Henry	47
Holmes, Margaret	84	Janyor, Will	47
Holmes, Thomas		Johnson, Samuel (Bampton)	115
Holwell	74,92	Johnson, the Rev G.	123, 125
Home, Charles	172	Jones, Jesse	166
Home, George	172	Jones, Pte E.	176
Home, Walter	186	Jones, Pte S.	176
Homstall	125	Jones, Spr J.	176
Hore, Thomas	102	Joy (s) Emma	148
Horne, Bill	173	Joy, James	147
Horne, Charles	185	Joy, Richard	39
Horne, Cpl S.	176	Jureshead (La)	26
Horne, Cpl W.	176	Jyde, James (Gent)	76
Horne, Gnr G.	176		
Horne, L Cpl C.	176	**KEENE, Pte W.**	176
Horne, Pte P.	176	Kelly, Mark	185
Horne, Pte W.J.	176	Kelmscott	32, 59, 74, 92,
Horns Cottage	160	112, 168,1 81	
Horns Cottage	87	Kelmscott Airfield	181
Horse and Jockey, the	116	Kemble, Gnr W.G.	177
Hospitalers	16, 31	Kempsford, Christopher	69
House Behind the Plough	114	Kempster's	93
House, John	73	Kencot	58, 92, 94, 109,
Hower (family)	113	116, 123, 138, 168,1 81	
Howes	113	Kendall, Tim	87
Howes, John	112	Kent, Countess of	89
Hules, Nicholas	73	Kilkenny	5, 6
Humphrey, John	50	Killing(s)worth	8, 151
Humphrey, Will	50	Kimbrey, Pte A.	176
Hunt, Richard	125	Kinch, Mr	152
Huntley, Rev J.W.	124, 145	Kinche B.	102
Hurt, Simon	39	Kinchin, Dvr A.	176
Hutchings, Charles	166	Kinchin, Miss	186
Hutt, G.	178	Kinchin, T.	178, 185
Hutt, Sgt G.	176	King, John	48,53
Hyde, Mr	84	King, Philip	48
Hyde, William	84		

King, Robert	48	Lays, the	136
King, Will	48,53	Leafield	5,131,164
King, William	48	Lechlade	48, 79, 115, 117,
Kingston Bagpuize	18	133, 148, 168, 181	
Knapp family	103, 105, 154	Lee, Charles	75
Knapp, G.	150	Lee, Postman	156
Knapp, George	154	Legg, Eadrigg	48
Knapp, J.T.	168	Letcombe Regis	116
Knapp, John Thomas	154	Lew	59, 74, 92, 132
Knapp, L.R.	158	Lew Hill	181
Knapp, Leonard	154	Lewtis	69, 85, 86
Knapp, Mrs	166	Lindsey, Gnr A.	176
Knapp, R.L.	185	Lindsey, Pte H.	176
Knapp, Richard	114, 120, 124	Line (Football) Field	137
Knapps (Tincknells)	1, 165, 166, 172,	Linsey, John	73
180, 181, 189		Linton (Lintern) Field, Furlong	
Knights Hospitalers	30		102, 120, 125,
		137, 142	
LA DISPENSER, Constance	44	Linzy (Linzey), John	91, 103
la Palmer, Simon	39	Lisle, Col George	76
Laffer, John	73, 103	Little Clanfield	7, 8, 113, 125,
Laffer, Robert	73	137, 138, 142, 159	
Laffer, Thomas	60	Little Clanfield (Railway)	119
Laffin, Richard	73	Little Clanfield Mill	114, 157
Laffter, Adam	85	Little Coxwell	152
Lake, Thomas	73	Little Green	102
Lamboard, John	52	Lococke	51
Lamsden, Mrs	79	Lococke, John	139
Lanarkshire (Lankashire), Robert	140, 141	Loder (Mr)	102, 103
Lander family	168	Loder (Mrs)	
Langford	24, 26, 32, 74, 119,	Long Ground	140
121, 123, 152, 156, 167		Long Lands	8
Langley (Langly) Lane, Meadow	17, 94, 126, 138,	Lord, Chris	140
142, 151, 152		Lowberry	5,9
Langley Brook	141	Lower Farm	113, 143, 157, 172
Langley Corner	181	Lower Green	31, 142, 158
Langlies (The)	3	Lucas, Mr (Headmaster)	174
Langton, Mr	84	Lucas, Pte R.C.	176
Lappers Field	151	Lucket, Thomas	73
Latham, Charles	66	Luckock, John	60
Latham, Elizabeth	47, 59	Lyons, Bernadette	180
Latham, Ralph	47, 59		
Latham, Thomas	52	**MACDONALD, Mr**	186
Latters (Aliz)		Maisey, Simon	101
Lauder, Robert	73	Manor Farm	8, 114
Laugher, Henry	148	Manor, the	180
Laugher, John	148	Marchant, Cyril	180
Laurels, the	179	Marchant, Jack	180
Lay, Arthur	114	Marchant, Reginald	171
Lay, R.	150	Marchant, Will	180

Margetts, Tpr M.	176	Mill, The	102
Marl (Maw) Brook	24, 137	Milnersacre	31
Marlborough, Duke of	117	Milton	155
Marsh Brook	24	Milton-under-Wychwood	93
Marsh Close	102, 124	Minster (Lovell)	32, 132
Marsh Lane	109, 116, 137, 138,	Mobey, David	148
145, 151, 166, 186, 187		Monk, Gen	81
Marshes	138	Monk, Pte J.	177
Marston, Edward	60	Monkeyshide	31
Martin, Christian	59	Moor (Bottom) Bridge	142
Martin, Edward	59	Moor (More), the	32, 102
Martin, Ellen	60	Moor Close	53
Martin, John	59	Moor Field	182
Martin, John	60	Moor Lake	141
Martin, Thomas	59	Moor Lane	138
Martin, Toby	59	Moor Mead	125
Mason's Arms	1, 104, 114, 119,	Moore, Agnes	111
120, 135, 137, 142, 148, 150, 152, 156, 157,		Moore, Henry	73
171, 171, 178, 184, 186		Moore, Rev James	112
Matthew, Elizabeth	86	Moore, Rev John Frewin	112
Maw (Marl) Brook	24, 137	Moors (Moor) Bridge	126, 140, 141
May, Alex	73, 91, 104	Moors (The)	17
May, Anthony	141	More Mead	102
May, Arthur	140	More, Francis	72, 83, 97
May, John	73	More, John	73, 91, 92, 98
May, Joseph	119	Morse, Thomas	154
May, Richard	119	Muachet, Robert	52
May, Richard	72, 103, 140, 141	Mulchet, Dominus Robert	47
May, Thomas	141	Mulchet, Richard	47
May, William	73, 154	Munster, Count	165
Mayes	102	Muschet, John	43
Mayfield, John	141		
Maysey, John	102, 103	NEVILLE, L Cpl W.	177
Mead, the	139	Neville, MM F.	177
Meisey, Isaac	91	Neville, Mr	145
Merett, Robert	60	Neville, Mr	187
Messenger, Pte F.	176	Neville, Pte J.	177
Messenger, Pte W.	176	Neville, Sgt C.	177
Messenger, Stkr A.	176	Neville, Will	174
Messenger, Will	173	New Brook	138, 142
Methodist Chapel (old)	180	Newbridge	32, 41, 81
Meysey, Isaac	85	Newbury	78
Meysey, Richard	140, 141	Newman, Alice	135
Middleton, Rev	111, 116	Newman, Ann	159
Middleton, Thomas	121, 122	Newman, Henry	135, 149, 154,
Miles, John	120	157, 159	
Miles, Richard	115	Newman, Miss	150
Mill Brook	139, 140, 142	Newman, Priscilla	135
Mill Lane	1, 143, 152, 171,	Newman, W&H	150
179, 189		Newman, W.	152

Newman, William (Will) 112, 133, 135, 136, 142, 148, 153
Niceturned, Nicholas 30
Nicholas, James 117
Nicholls 114
Nine Page Butts 125
Nippenham 17, 30, 138, 148
Nisternon 31
Norden (family) 113
Norden, John 119
North Court 7, 16, 28, 29, 68, 133, 137, 165, 166, 188
North Leigh 93
Northern, John 124
Northleach 75
Norton Bruern 114
Norton's Foundry 154
Norton, Will 57
Nuneham Courtenay 83

OLD BAKERY 1
Old Chapel 114
Old Man's Bridge 153
Old Mill 1
Old Nan's Bridge 153
Osmond, Thomas 47
Osney 92, 113, 136, 137, 143
Oxford 111, 115, 132, 133, 155

PALMER, Col. 80
Palmer, Rev W. 152
Palmore, John 91
Palseke, Richard 60
Parish Relief 185
Parker, Dr 185
Parrot, Allen 172, 173, 177, 178, 179
Parrot, Cpl A. 177
Parrot, Cpl S. 177
Parrot, Drv T. 177
Parrot, Dvr F. 177
Parrot, Fred 'Poot' 179
Parrot, Gnr G. 177
Parrot, Harry 186
Parrot, J. 158
Parrot, Pte J. 177
Parrot, Sgt F. 177
Parrot, Sgt R. 177

Parsonage 101
Parsons, Roger 91
Pauling, Anthony 72, 73
Pauling, John 73
Pauling, Simon 73
Pauling, Syman 72, 73
Pauling, William 72
Pawling ('Widow') 102
Pawling (Pallying), Will 52, 58, 59, 60, 62
Pawling, Andrew 60
Pawling, Anthony 87
Pawling, Christine 68
Pawling, John 67, 68, 69, 103, 113, 125
Pawling, Thomas 67, 69
Pawling, William 91, 92
Pawlings Close 102
Payne (John) 31
Pearson ('Widdow') 102
Pearson (family) 113, 124
Pearson, John 72, 105
Pearson, Roger 105
Pearson, Thomas 105
Peason, Richard 140, 141
Pencot, Richard 73
Penfold, Joseph 156
Penson, Rev J.P. 148, 152
Personeyeshyde 31
Pettifer, Ellen 86
Philips, Lt W.H. 175
Phillip de Clanfield 28
Pidnell (Pidnal, Pidnall) Bridge 21, 116, 126
Pigeon House 113
Piggott, Rev R. 152
Pill, MrPimnock, William 84
Pinnock, Francis 72
Pinnock, Thomas 72
Pittslands (Pittlands) 24, 30, 101
Plough Inn (Hotel) 48, 67, 103, 117, 152, 165, 167, 171, 172, 178, 179
Ponter, William 73
Poole, Sgt J. 177
Pope, Thomas 113
Poplars, the 120
Post Office and Garage 113
Post Office, the 159, 168, 180
Potters (Lower Green) 66
Pound Lane 113, 158, 165, 171
Powell, Walter 106, 124

Preferthendels 31
Primitive Chapel 148, 180
Primitives 172
Prince, Thomas 84
Prior, Richard 103
Prospect House 119
Puckety Farm 155
Pudwell, AB H. 177
Pursey, William 43
Putts 16, 24, 28,2 9, 30,
114
Pye, Sir Robert 80
Pye, Will 60
Pyp, John 60
Pyper, James 48
Pyper, William 48

QUEEN'S CLOSE 179
Quenham Meadow 30
Quenington 119

RADBOURNE, W.G. 174
Radbourne, W.G. 177
Radburn, Alf 161, 184
Radcot 2, 5, 10, 11, 18, 19,
21, 23, 24, 25, 26, 30, 31, 34, 36, 41, 43, 47,
49, 68, 74, 79, 80, 85, 91, 92, 93, 103, 106,
114, 115, 117, 118, 126, 133, 149, 151, 154,
155, 158, 160, 166, 169, 173, 182, 187, 188
Radcot Bridge 36, 41, 42, 77, 78,
156, 168, 169, 187
Radcot Farm 165
Radcot House 19, 78, 126
Radcot Lock 171
Radcot Regatta 179
Radcot Road 138, 182
Radhourn, James 117
Rainey, Mrs 167
Ram Jam Garage 1, 179
Rand, Mr (Headmaster) 160
Reading 116
Reason, J. 158
Reason, Mr 159, 166
Rectory Farm 113
Red Cross, the 173
Red Lion, the 116, 153
Redlands 8
Regers, John 98
Reynolds, Alex 60, 69
Reynolds, John 47, 60

Reynolds, Richard 67
Reynolds, Robert 52, 85
Reynolds, the Rev 122
Reynolds, Will 58, 67
Rhymes, Mr 158
Richard de Hallingworth 28
Richmanneyeshyde 31
Ringwood (Abrahams) 133
Robert of Hicks 26
Robinson, Mr 179
Rocce, John 43
Rochester, Lord 114
Rock Farm 157
Rogers, Herme 60
Rogers, John 60, 76
Rogers, Julia 85, 106
Rogers, Marie 84, 106, 111
Rolff, Will 37
Rookshill 67
Room, Francis 88
Rose, Bdr H. 177
Rouse, Robert 44
Royer, Andrew 75
Rushey Lock 158
Russell, Pte H.W. 177
Ruxhill (Rookshill) 24, 29, 31, 87
Rye (Meadow, Ryemead, Bridge)
17, 102, 120, 138,
153

SALOW, Thomas 60
Samuel, Nicholas 62
Sanderson, Col 80
Savage, George 174
Savage, James 28, 29, 31
Savage, Pte A. 177
Savage, Pte G. 177
Savage, Walter 69, 98
Savage, William 31
Saviles, Sir George 89
Sayer, John 87
Seacole, Robert 93
Secker, Mr 179, 189
Seiger, Will 114
Seymour, John 69, 85
Shaylor, Amos 148
Shaylor166
Sheapherd, John 73
Sheephouse Close 102
Shepherd, Drv F.C. 177

Shepherd, Henry	121, 122	St Leonard's	23, 51, 139
Sherbourne	146	St Vallery	28, 29, 92
Shifford	11, 26, 59, 74, 92,	Standlake	26, 32, 59, 74, 88
122		Stanford in the Vale	103
Shillbrook36		Stanton Harcourt	89, 117
Shilton	9, 10, 32, 124, 148	Stephen, Thomas	117
Shilton, Ann	85	Stephens, Anthony	120
Shilton, Frances	85	Stephens, James	120
Shilton, Robert	85	Stephens, John	140, 141
Shiltons	102	Stephens, Mary	120
Shipton Downs	115	Stephens, Robert	36
Shipton-under-Wychwood	168	Stevens (family)	113
Shrivenham	111	Stevens (Farmer)	133
Sighnett	58	Stevens Farm	134
Simons, Ralph	73	Stevens, Anthony	73,114
Skuse	181,187	Stevens, Charles	171
Smith (Mrs)	102	Stevens, Edward	86
Smith (Widow)		Stevens, John	73, 87, 91, 102,
Smith, Anne	98	104, 140, 141	
Smith, Ben	165	Stevens, Margaret	114
Smith, Benny	173	Stevens, Robert	101, 102
Smith, Gladys	174	Stevens, Thomas	73, 86, 101
Smith, Henry	86	Stevens, William	73
Smith, John	98, 106, 111, 120	Steward, Mrs	150
Smith, Katherine	97, 106, 111	Stock (Richard de)	31
Smith, Leonard	72, 83, 86, 97, 103	Stocks Close (Lane)	31, 142
Smith, Martha	86, 111	Stocks Lane	31, 68, 142
Smith, Mary	97, 111	Stone, Mr	151
Smith, Richard	98	Stow on the Wold	41, 75
Smith, Samuel (Rev)	93	Stych, Will	39
Smith, Stephen	43	Sullebury	48
Smith, Thomas	91, 97, 103, 133	Swan, the	169, 171
Smithier, Thos	140	Swinford, George	147
Smyth, Samuel	91	Symonds, John	43
Smytheshyde	31	Symonds, Richard	76, 83
Southrop	119		
Southwick	7, 8, 16, 24, 29, 31,	**TADPOLE**	168
48, 53, 57, 67, 83, 92, 98, 104, 112, 113, 114,		Tailor, John	72,73
133, 137, 165		Talbot family	35
Sparrowhawk, Pte J.	177	Talbot, Richard	35
Sperrinck, Benjamin	120, 140, 141	Tarny (Tarney)	5, 7, 8, 24, 68,
Sperrinck, Mary	120	101, 120, 127, 137, 138, 142, 182	
Sperrinke (Mr)	102	Tawney	126
Sperrinke, John	69, 72, 73, 103	Taylor (family)	135
Sperrinke, Thomas	69	Taylor, John	86, 105
Sperrinke, Will	70, 105	Taylor, Marguerita	84
Sperrinke, William	85, 86, 91, 103	Taylor, Marie	88
Sprinke	91	Taylor, Mary	68
Spurgeon (Preacher)	133	Taylor, Richard	68
St John's Order	173	Taylor, Robert	88

Taylor, Thomas	93	Turner, Thomas	67, 87, 98
Taylor, William	84, 140	Twelftree, Pte W.	177
Taynton	21, 32, 93	Twilford, Ursula	66
Temple, Pte F.	177	Twiss, Thomas	84
Temple, Pte G.	177	Tyler, Edward	94
Temple, Pte H.	177	Tyler, Rev Edward	116, 121
Temple, Pte J.J.	177		
Temple, Pte John	177	**UMFREY, John**	47
Temple, Pte W.C.	177	Underhill, R	124
Temple, Thomas	73	Upper Green	142
Thames Meadows, the	116	Upton	58
Thames, the	132, 133, 181, 182		
Thames-Severn Canal	160	**VAFREY, John**	47
Thickette, Richard	87	Valance, Aymer	33, 35
Thomas, Hugh	55	Vase Butts	102
Thorne, Pte E.	177	Vaughan, Sir Richard	77
Thorold, J. (Curate)	123	Vesey, Richard	73
Tilby, Trooper Fred		Vicarage, The	87, 113, 114, 152
Timms, Mr	179	Virarey, Simon	60
Tirer (Mr)	101		
Tomes, 'Widow'	91	**WADLEY**	164
Toms, Arthur	140	Waine (family)	113
Top Green	158	Waine, John	73
Torchard, Richard	39	Waine, Mary	135
Townsend, Mr	156	Waine, William	73
Townsend, Pte A.	177, 178	Wakefield, Agnes	52
Townsend, Pte G.	177	Wakefield, Pte F.	177
Trapdoro House	48	Wakefield, Robert	52
Troughton	94	Walker, Mr	171, 186
Tuckers (Faringdon)	167	Walker, Pte F.H.S.	177
Tuckewell	113	Wallis, Mr	171
Tuckwell, William	125	Wantage	43,132
Tufrey (Tuffrey), Katherine	98, 105	Warbilton, Marjorie	45
Tull, John	72, 87	Warbilton, William	45
Turfrey (Turfry	51, 135	Warbulton, William	48
Turfrey, Francis	112	Ward, Mr	136
Turfrey, John	112, 139	Ward, William	114
Turfrey, Sarah	112	Warren	102
Turnbull, Prof	165	Warren, John	98, 103
Turner's Gate	109	Watkins, John	149, 150
Turner, 'Widow'		Watter, John	43
Turner, Adam	67, 73	Watts, Tpr E.	177
Turner, Amy	87	Wayman, Richard	66
Turner, Bartholomew	84	Wayne, Andrew	86
Turner, Drew	67, 68, 83, 98	Wayne, John	87
Turner, John	84	Wayne, Leonard	87
Turner, Robert	67, 68, 72, 73,	Wayne, Marjory	87
102, 103		Wayne, Richard	87
Turner, Robert	119	Wayne, Thomas	87
Turner, Thomas	119	Wayne, William	87

Weald	16, 17, 23, 30, 48,	White, E.	166
67, 74, 137, 154		White, Ernest	134, 165
Weaver, Richard	133	White, Ferdinando	98, 105, 111, 112,
Webb, Mr (Headmaster)	157	120	
Webb, Simon	43	White, John	58, 72, 158
Weder, Henry	53	White, Joseph	73
Wedger, William	48	White, Mrs	157
Weeks Piece	125	White, Thos	149
Weir Bridge	142, 159	White, William	159
Weir, the, Burroway	119	Whitehorn, Sarah	114
Welcome (Welton) Way	117	Whitehorn, Thos	60, 69
Welde	57	Whitehorne, Alice	103
Wells, Flora	106	Whithorn, John	73
Wells, George	114	Whithorne, Francis	73, 102
Wells, John	106	Whiting, Adelm	52
Wells, John	149	Whiting, Elizabeth	52
Wenman (Winman) Grounds	125	Whittaker	131
Wenman family	49, 66, 85	Whydan Meadow	47
Wenman, Anne	59, 66	Whytes, Adeln	47
Wenman, John	51, 52, 59, 66, 70,	Wicks	172
861		Wicks Close	180
Wenman, Pte A.	177	Wicks Estate	113
Wenman, Richard	52, 59, 66	Wicks, John	68
Wenman, Thomas	59, 66	Widdowson (Jack)	1, 179
Wesleyan Chapel	172	Widdowson (Walter)	6
West Field	24, 125, 137, 182	Widdowson, Gnr W.	178
Westbrook	80	Widdowson, Sgt J.	178
Westbury (family)	29	Wilkins, Gnr H.	178
Westbury (Walter)	29	Wilkins, Mrs	184
Westbury (Will)	23	Wilkinson, William	117
Westerne	31	Willen, The	87
Westfield	5, 7, 8, 20, 127	William, Billy	185
Westweld	49	Williams, Pte H.	178
Westwell	30, 32, 50, 59	Willmer, John	165
Wetherham, Henry	48	Willmer, Mr	179
Wheeler, Cpl H.	177	Willmer, R.W.	165
Wheeler, Edward	114	Wilmot, Catherine	84
Wheeler, John	48	Wilmot, Leonard	66, 76, 83
Wheeler, Pte D.J.	177	Wilmot, Leonard	86
Whelford	113	Wilmot, William	83, 84
Whipp, AB A.E.	178	Wilson, G.	155
Whipp, Albert	173	Wilson, Will	148
Whipp, H.	178	Winchcome, Richard	73
White	140, 142, 150	Winchcome, Thomas	73
White Horse Hill	133, 157, 158, 164,	Windmill (Farm, House)	1, 5, 6, 67, 113,
167		116, 136, 143, 158, 186, 188	
White, Adelm	52	Winfield, Tpr W.	178
White, Amy	111, 114	Winnetts (Coopers)	101
White, C.	150	Winstone, Glos	112
White, Charles	135, 165	Wise, Dorothy	5

Wise, Edward)   93
Withers   113
Withy Beds   138, 158, 164
Witman, John   69
Witney   26, 32, 40, 41, 42,
   49, 58, 65, 74, 75, 83, 85, 89, 92, 98, 106,
   112, 119 126, 131, 132, 133, 134, 153, 156,
   161, 164 172, 174, 178, 180
Women's Institute   174
Women's Land Army   174
Wood, William   72
Woodstock   65
Worth (Manor of)   18
Wotherham, Henry   48
Wright, John   154
Wright, Nathan   112
Wrothesley   58
Wychwood   131
Wyck Farm   84
Wyman's Place   43, 47
Wymans   52
Wymonds   138

YAPMAN, Richard   48
Yate, William   103
Yateman   119
Yateman's Bridge   141
Yateman, Mary   120
Yateman, Nicholas   119, 124
Yateman, Richard   105
Yateman, Robert   120
Yateman, William   120
Yateman, Winifred   120
Yatt in Weald   117
Yeate, Sir Edward   87
Yeatman (Yateman)   48, 114
Yeatman (Yateman), Nicholas
                             86, 101
Yeatman (Yateman), Richard
                             68, 101
Yeatman (Yateman), Solomon
                             73, 105
Yeatman, John   73
Yeatman, Jonathan   101, 102, 103, 140,
   141
Yeatman, Mary   86
Yeatman, Nicholas Jnr   73
Yeatman, Nicholas Snr   73
Yeatman, Pte E.   178
Yeaton, William   73

Yelford   49, 74
Yells (family)   113
Yew Tree House   113
York, Rev   153